Suffering and Persecution

Suffering and Persecution

Rethinking Church in the 21st Century

General Editors
Riad Kassis and Mark Labberton

Volume Editor
Myrto Theocharous

Series Editor
Joshua Barron

© 2024 Myrto Theocharous

Published 2024 by Langham Global Library
An imprint of Langham Publishing
www.langhampublishing.org

Langham Publishing and its imprints are a ministry of Langham Partnership

Langham Partnership
PO Box 296, Carlisle, Cumbria, CA3 9WZ, UK
www.langham.org

ISBNs:
978-1-78641-034-4 Print
978-1-78641-078-8 ePub
978-1-78641-079-5 PDF

Myrto Theocharous hereby asserts her moral right to be identified as the Author of the General Editor's part in the Work in accordance with sections 77 and 78 of the Copyright, Designs and Patents Act 1988.

All rights reserved. No part of this publication may be reproduced, stored in a retrieval system or transmitted, in any form or by any means, electronic, mechanical, photocopying, recording or otherwise, without the prior written permission of the publisher or the Copyright Licensing Agency.

Requests to reuse content from Langham Publishing are processed through PLSclear. Please visit www.plsclear.com to complete your request.

Scripture taken from the New Revised Standard Version Bible, copyright © 1989 National Council of the Churches of Christ in the United States of America. Used by permission. All rights reserved.

Scriptures taken from the Holy Bible, New International Version®, NIV®. Copyright © 1973, 1978, 1984, 2011 by Biblica, Inc.™ Used by permission of Zondervan.

British Library Cataloguing-in-Publication Data
A catalogue record for this book is available from the British Library

ISBN: 978-1-78641-034-4

Cover & Book Design: projectluz.com

Langham Partnership actively supports theological dialogue and an author's right to publish but does not necessarily endorse the views and opinions set forth here or in works referenced within this publication, nor can we guarantee technical and grammatical correctness. Langham Partnership does not accept any responsibility or liability to persons or property as a consequence of the reading, use or interpretation of its published content.

Contents

Series Introduction ix
Volume Introduction xii

Africa

Nigeria: *No More Cheeks to Turn?* 1
    Contributed by Alfred Sebahene (Tanzania)

South Africa (and Germany): *Suffering, Persecution and Martyrdom: Theological Reflections* 7
    Contributed by Brent Hamoud (USA/Lebanon)

Uganda: *The Sacrifice of Africa: A Political Theology for Africa* 15
    Contributed by Muhindo Malunga (Democratic Republic of Congo)

Asia

China: *The Chinese Epaphras* 23
    Contributed by Xiaxia Xue (Hong Kong)

China: *The Carving of God: The Biography of the Lord's Servant – Simon Zhao* 27
    Contributed by Alansoe Yan (China)

Hong Kong: *Chan Kin-Man's Prison Writings* 31
    Contributed by Kam Yuen-Shan (Hong Kong)

Hong Kong: *Authentic Forgiveness: A Biblical Approach* 37
    Contributed by Loreen Maseno (Kenya)

Hong Kong: *The Courage to Live: Reimagining the Gospel for Our Times* . . 41
    Contributed by Barry Cheung (Hong Kong)

India: "The Problem of Suffering: A Theological Analysis" 45
    Contributed by Lanuwabang Jamir (India)

India: "Lessons from Orissa: Peacemaking in the Face of Anti-Christian Violence" 51
    Contributed by Lanuwabang Jamir (India)

India: "A Christian Response to Hindutva" 57
    Contributed by Lanuwabang Jamir (India)

India: *When Time Stood Still: A True Life Answer to the Question –
    Where Is God When it Hurts?* 63
    Contributed by Riad Kassis (Lebanon)

Japan: *Theology of the Pain of God: The First Original Theology
    from Japan* 67
    Contributed by Alfred Sebahene (Tanzania)

Japan: *Silence* 73
    Contributed by Dimitrios G. Oulis (Greece)

Japan: *Silence and Beauty: Hidden Faith Born of Suffering* 79
    Contributed by Myrto Theocharous (Cyprus)

Pakistan: *Suffering for Christ* 85
    Contributed by Riad Kassis (Lebanon)

Philippines: *How Long, O Lord?: The Challenge and Promise of
    Reconciliation and Peace* 89
    Contributed by Adrian Paul P. Morales (Philippines)

Philippines: *Why, O God? Disaster, Resiliency, and the People of God* 95
    Contributed by Adrian Paul P. Morales (Philippines)

Philippines: *It's OK to Be Not OK: Preaching the Lament Psalms* 101
    Contributed by Myrto Theocharous (Cyprus)

Singapore: *Hope for the World: The Christian Vision* 107
    Contributed by Adrian Paul P. Morales (Philippines)

Singapore: *When Christians Face Persecution:
    Theological Perspectives from the New Testament* 113
    Contributed by Chee-Chiew Lee and her student, T. Lee (East Asia)

Sri Lanka: *Sarah's Laughter: Doubt, Tears, and Christian Hope* 119
    Contributed by Nathanael M. Somanathan (Sri Lanka)

Sri Lanka: *The Call to Joy and Pain: Embracing Suffering in Your Ministry* .. 125
    Contributed by Nathanael M. Somanathan (Sri Lanka)

Thailand: *A Christian Theology of Suffering in the Context of Theravada
    Buddhism in Thailand* 131
    Contributed by Nathanael M. Somanathan (Sri Lanka)

Central and South America

Bolivia: *A Nazarene Church: Theology from the Insignificant* 139
    Contributed by Riad Ghobrial (Egypt)

El Salvador: *Witnesses to the Kingdom: The Martyrs of El Salvador and
the Crucified Peoples* 145
    Contributed by Riad Ghobrial (Egypt)

Europe

Germany: *Christian Persecution in Antiquity* 153
    Contributed by Brent Hamoud (USA/Lebanon)

Germany: *The 21: A Journey into the Land of Coptic Martyrs*.......... 161
    Contributed by Brent Hamoud (USA/Lebanon)

Greece: *My Sister* 169
    Contributed by Myrto Theocharous (Cyprus)

Greece: *The Enigma of Evil*.. 175
    Contributed by Olga Politi (Greece)

United Kingdom: *A Theology of Suffering* 181
    Contributed by Angukali Rotokha (India)

United Kingdom: *Faith That Endures: The Essential Guide to the
Persecuted Church*... 187
    Contributed by Angukali Rotokha (India)

Middle East

Egypt: *Martyrdom and Martyrs: A Spiritual Study*................... 197
    Contributed by Riad Ghobrial (Egypt)

Lebanon: *Following Jesus in Turbulent Times: Disciple-Making in the
Arab World*... 203
    Contributed by Angukali Rotokha (India)

Palestine: *The Politics of Persecution: Middle Eastern Christians in an
Age of Empires* 209
    Contributed by Brent Hamoud (USA/Lebanon)

Syria: *Called for Martyrdom, Called for Victory* 217
    Contributed by Riad Kassis (Lebanon)

North America

Canada: *Prison Power: How God Uses Imprisonment to Enlarge His Kingdom*... 225
    Contributed by Ashkenaz Asif Khan (Pakistan)

The United States of America and the United Kingdom: *Creating Shared Resilience: The Role of the Church in a Hopeful Future*...... 231
    Contributed by Loreen Maseno (Kenya)

The United States of America: *Finding Hagar: God's Pursuit of a Runaway*.. 235
    Contributed by Loreen Maseno (Kenya)

The United States of America: *What Can We Expect from God Now: Seven Spiritual Truths for Trusting God in Troubled Times*......... 241
    Contributed by Loreen Maseno (Kenya)

The United States of America: *Forgiveness and Justice: A Christian Approach*.. 245
    Contributed by Ruth Barron and Joshua Robert Barron (Kenya)

Series Introduction

God's love in Jesus Christ for the salvation and recreation of all things is still the hope of the world. This Christian affirmation is the reality that "holds all things" and "holds all things together." Over the millennia of the biblical narrative, the God revealed in Scripture is present and active to a world in all its glories and agonies, in both personal and collective stories. In seasons when the people of God have flourished in God's faithfulness or doubted, even fought, God's intentions and desires, still God is faithful. The church belongs to its loving, healing, and renewing Saviour and Lord, Jesus Christ. Nothing will separate us from the love of God and even the gates of hell will not prevail against the church.

And yet, the church is always a very mixed picture. Great reasons exist for the vitality, truthfulness, and love of Christian communities. Right alongside are all the doubts and insults hurled against God because of the church – from inside and outside – which have been and are profuse. Generation by generation, the church has struggled to discern and practice its spiritual and theological identity in real time and in real places. As we look at the church around the globe today, we give thanks for faithful Christians, often in extreme conditions of poverty, war, violence, and more, who live each day dependent on God, who alone keeps and preserves them. Holding faithful in the midst of authoritarian states, with persecution and suffering constantly at hand, the church faces enormous pressures to surrender its identity, to compromise in the face of such trials, and to neglect or distort its mission. The ever-present danger of the church being hypocritical towards God, towards itself, and towards the world is unavoidable. The church's inclination to teach and preach a gospel it fails to practice, especially in relationship to the poor and the marginalized, adds still more to the list of dangers and challenges faced by the church.

In this increasingly globalized world, it is not difficult to understand why the church is in pain and declining in its Christian and moral influence. No one is surprised in 2024 that many so-called Gen Zers and millennials, for example, have no time for the church or Christianity. We can find this pattern around the world, but especially in urban centres. The reasons are many, but "church" and "Christianity" are assumed to be irrelevant, problematic, or probably worse. This is not just a pattern for youth and younger adults, but people in their middle and older years too. For devout people of Christian faith, such condemning conclusions can seem simplistic and unfair; but for oceans others, these disaffected opinions are justified and self-evident conclusions. We might even say they are convictions reached by doing what seems to come naturally in this era and in places across the globe.

Every pastor and church leader who may be reading this knows many faces in this sea of disregard and disaffection. Hopefully, we are highly attentive in our roles, listening as carefully and deeply as we can to what this phenomenon is telling us. If we are tending flocks that are dissipating, we need to ask why it is happening, and how we pursue the sheep that are not just lost by circumstances, but by deliberate choice.

Rethinking Church in the 21st Century is an effort that began in 2021 to gather Christian leaders from a range of backgrounds and nationalities online in order to listen to what gratitude and concerns we had about the state of the church as seen from many different angles. We were all Protestants, broadly evangelical, deeply committed to the holistic gospel of Jesus Christ, in varying roles of theological, pastoral, organizational, and congregational responsibility. We came together for an initial six months and our work has gone on for an additional two and a half years. These three books are the product of the international members (and others) of the group, and the the leaders from the USA have produced a podcast series. All of us have tried, within the bounds of our many other responsibilities, to contribute to our common cause. The community God has built among us during these years through hours and hours of online video conversations and through our writing collaboration has been a gift beyond what we could initially have imagined, forming and strengthening enduring friendship in Christ.

The three volumes in this series are responses to the top three concerns identified: *Suffering and Persecution*, led by Dr. Myrto Theocharous of Cyprus; *Metaphors the Church Lives By*, led by Dr. Elizabeth Sendek of Colombia; and *Faith and Public Life*, led by Dr. Alfred Sebahene of Tanzania. The general editors are Dr. Riad Kassis and Dr. Mark Labberton. We are very grateful for the contributions of all of our writers in each volume. These three volumes are briefly summarized here by the respective volume editors:

In this volume a variety of scholars and church leaders from or in the Majority World interact with writings, mostly from non-Western contexts, on topics such as violence, natural disasters, and ancient and modern persecution, and present their own reflections on these writings. The hope is that this volume will make available a variety of perspectives on suffering and persecution,

and invite personal or communal contemplation on these universal themes.
—**Myrto Theocharous**

We explore seven biblical metaphors that are foundational for our understanding of the church in the twenty-first century. They transcend historical and sociopolitical categories. Three come from the gospels: yeast, salt, light; four come from the Pauline epistles: people, temple, body, and ambassadors. The aim is to engage readers with the conceptual content of the metaphors and how they intended to shape experience and attitudes, so that we can live them out today. —**Elizabeth Sendek**

Times have changed. The global public space is filled with a myriad of challenges. We live in an era that allows new contradictions and opportunities to emerge. But the love of God and the gospel of Christ never changes. How then should the church be engaged in the public space of the twenty-first century? This book seeks to answer this pertinent question by inviting Christians to respond with vigour to Christ's call to follow him in whole-life discipleship in this century and beyond. Throughout the pages of this book, Christians from diverse walks of life have given Bible-based testimonies about life in the public square, one of the arenas in which believers' love of God and love of neighbours must be exhibited. The book calls the church and Christian believers to constantly review how to proclaim and serve in the world, while appreciating evident signs and wonders witnessing to the nature and character of God, especially his grace. —**Alfred Sebahene**

In these volumes, each author speaks for themselves only, and not as a representative of any organization or institution. We offer our great thanks for individuals whose generous financial contributions made this effort possible. They are people with hearts full of the grace of God and love for the church.

Our hope is that these books will prompt pastors and thoughtful Christian leaders to be stimulated by these reflections and admonitions during such a dynamic, vulnerable, and hopeful time as the twenty-first century is presenting. We believe that "God is the same yesterday, today, and forever," and that the church is alive in settings that are constantly changing. This is the intersection we take with great faith and seriousness as we trust the Lord Jesus Christ who reigns in love, justice, and mercy.

To God's glory and honour, and for the welfare of God's church around the globe, we dedicate these books.

Riad Kassis and Mark Labberton

General Editors:	Riad Kassis (Lebanon), Mark Labberton (USA)
Series Editor:	Joshua Barron (Kenya)
Volume Editors:	Alfred Sebahene (Tanzania)
	Myrto Theocharous (Cyprus)
	Elizabeth Sendek (Colombia)
Meditations Editor:	Milton Acosta (Colombia)
Dialogue Participants:	Wojciech Szczerba (Poland), Antonio Barro (Brazil), David Tarus (Kenya), Jonathan Kavusa (Democratic Republic of Congo), Sergiy Tymchenko (Ukraine), Alejandra Ortiz (Mexico), Antonina Szczerba (Poland)
Illustrations:	Antonina Szczerba (Poland)
Administration:	Stefanii Morton, Mandy Macintosh

Volume Introduction

After the COVID-19 global crisis – a pandemic that left countless grieving families, people without jobs, and numerous populations on the brink of starvation – we found ourselves in a disoriented world. It was a challenge to find comfort. All of us were experiencing increasing polarization in our countries, in our churches, and in our own families. All over social media, we were witnessing apathy and cynicism at the rising hostilities, attacks, and full-blown wars around the globe; many times, Christians were the primary participants and/or supporters. An example is Patriarch Kyrill of Moscow blessing the Russian troops for engaging in a "holy war," as he has called it,[1] or the Christian Zionist support for the destruction of Gaza.[2] But we have also felt despair and helplessness in seeing the persecution of Christians spreading almost exclusively in many corners of the Global South.

Then, in the midst of 2021, the idea was born that various theologians, biblical scholars, pastors, and ministry leaders from around the world must gather, collect our voices, share our experiences, thoughts, agonies, and dreams with each other, and, above all, pray together that the Spirit might lead us to rethink, reimagine, and relove the church of the twenty-first century. We craved a renewed hope for God's people. At the invitation of Mark Labberton, then president of Fuller Theological Seminary, and with the masterful coordination of Stefanii Morton, individuals from around the world gathered together and committed to meeting regularly online. As difficult as that was with time differences, packed schedules, challenging internet connections, and especially with some of us fleeing war zones, we did manage to meet and bond into our colourful little online community.

Out of these meetings the project *Rethinking Church in the 21st Century* was born. Together, we came to realize that suffering and persecution is a major topic that needs addressing by and for the global church. Rev. Dr. Riad

---

1. Katarzyna Chawryło, "A holy war. The Russian Orthodox Church blesses the war against the West," OSW Center for Eastern Studies, 12 April 2024, online: https://www.osw.waw.pl/en/publikacje/osw-commentary/2024-04-12/a-holy-war-russian-orthodox-church-blesses-war-against-west.

2. Jean-Pierre Filiu, "American Christian Zionists crusade against Palestinian 'evil,'" Le Monde, 29 January 2024, online: https://www.lemonde.fr/en/international/article/2024/01/29/american-christian-zionists-crusade-against-palestinian-evil_6476239_4.html.

Kassis (Lebanon–Syria), Dr. Kivatsi Jonathan Kavusa (Democratic Republic of Congo), and myself (Cyprus) decided to take this on together. Joshua Robert Barron (USA–Kenya), sharing our vision, was later invited to join us and serve us with his editing skills and valuable input. Luke Lewis and Mark Arnold, on behalf of Langham Publishing, enthusiastically agreed to assist us in publishing this volume, and generous donors funded this endeavour. We have nothing but gratitude!

We did not want to add more words to this topic; we wanted to listen. Our goal was to gather the flowers that had already blossomed in a variety of fields, gifts offered by the global church that were not known by all of us. We wanted to collect those blooms and let their aroma spread to those of us not acquainted with them. Or to use another analogy, we wanted to create a table of ethnically diverse flavours and taste a sample of what sisters and brothers from around the world have already written on the topic of suffering and persecution. There is so much wisdom out there and we were hungry for it. So we asked friends who are connected to the Global South to serve these dishes to us.

We asked these friends to read authors who have written on the topics of suffering and persecution, examine them through the lenses of their own contextual experience, and then share their readings with us. Each reviewer presents a work, offers their reflections, and closes with an artistic expression in the form of a picture, poem, prayer, or quotation that captures the sentiment of the work reviewed. As these contributions are written from global Christian perspectives, those who reviewed books from different contexts to their own often found fruitful applications for their contexts. We decided not to interfere with the presentation and language register of the contributors, so you will find a variety of writings here – from highly academic and philosophical language to a very direct and approachable style. The final product is a nourishing and enjoyable feast that we hope you will enjoy as much as we did!

This book may be read by you as an individual reader or, ideally, as part of a small group so that it can be discussed contextually, and the thoughts offered in each review may be considered and enriched by the group as a whole. Finally, we hope that the artistic pieces may inspire you, stir your affective side, and lead to prayer.

* * *

While the book could have been laid out based on where the contributors are from, we decided to organize the chapters based on the location of the authors or editors of the reviewed books. The final grouping has the following order alphabetically: Africa, Asia, Central and South America, Europe, Middle East, and North America.

From *Nigeria*, we receive an agonizing pastoral word from and to the persecuted church, suffering daily violence with the exhortation to reject retaliation and follow Jesus's teaching to "turn the other cheek."

From *South Africa*, we are offered perspectives on how persecution can be missionally positive in advancing the kingdom of God on the one hand, and how, on the other hand, it should be seen as something demonic and antagonistic to Christ and his reign.

From *Uganda,* we hear deep reflections about the need to reimagine Africa's future through different narratives that embrace the inherent value of Africa and its people. This involves us discarding the inherited colonial models that African countries tend to perpetuate.

From *China*, we see the attitude of Chinese believers, such as Wu Weizun (Epaphras), who exemplify a Christian life similar to the ascetic figures of the Egyptian desert with their relentless rejection of material things that could "possess" their souls. Suffering is "a way to be worthy of God." We are also shown Simon Zhao's life of intense suffering, with harsh conditions of imprisonment, yet an unbroken determination to be available to God, and to be "carved" in his hands.

From *Hong Kong,* we hear voices from prison on how one may suffer faithfully under authoritarian regimes, how the church should connect with and commit to common people, and how we can live in truth outside its protective walls. We are shown how the gospel, understood alongside capitalism and devoid of a theology of suffering, has become distorted and detrimental to the Christian vision. We also learn how a submissive hierarchical culture may redefine forgiveness for the purpose of avoiding conflict or may focus solely on western understandings of self-healing, thus hindering restoration in the community.

From *India,* we hear of the need to understand suffering beyond the classic understanding of it being a consequence of sin, to find its meaningfulness, and to thus empower suffering believers. We are shown how religious ideology merged with nationalism in Hindu fundamentalism led to waves of Christian persecution in Orissa (a state in eastern India), and Christians are shown that it is still possible to love even the neighbour who acts as our enemy. We also hear stories of personal loss and how one deals theologically with intense pain.

From *Japan*, we are taught that suffering originates within God himself, from the tension between wrath and love, and was eventually manifested on the cross of Christ. We see how authors like Endō, who wrestles with the challenges of mission and the recontextualization of the Christian message, explore the martyrological anthropology of the church. We also learn how Japanese culture has adopted Christianity and how indigenous understandings of pain and suffering have given Japanese Christianity its own flavour, one that may often be incomprehensible to the West.

From *Pakistan*, we receive the challenge to prepare our churches for the realities of persecution, even going as far as praying for and attempting to understand our persecutors.

From the *Philippines*, we learn about the pain of trauma and unresolved conflict, and we receive inspiration from biblical narratives of reconciliation. We delve deeply into the necessary work that needs to be done by both the perpetrator and the victim in order to reach repentance, receive forgiveness, and break the cycle of violence. Through a theology of creation and theological reflection on natural disasters, we revisit the role of the church in lament, suffering with those who suffer, and at the same time participating in the work of community transformation.

From *Singapore*, we dive deep into the New Testament world to understand persecution in the Greco–Roman world, to see the variety of attitudes among New Testament authors and learn how we can appreciate different stances on persecution today. We hear about the concept of hope, which is not blind optimism but a power that embraces the world in its suffering while imagining new possibilities.

From *Sri Lanka*, we see the political dimensions of lament, and how ecclesiastical suppression of lament is connected to the suppression of protest and resistance that ends up favouring and preserving the status quo. Moreover, we see what we know as "natural evil" questioned and interpreted as God's way of bringing about "ecological changes and biodiversity on the planet." We are also introduced to the concept of the Christian call as a call to both joy and suffering, with both elements being inseparable aspects of participation in the life of Christ.

From *Thailand*, we see how contextual theological engagement with Theravada Buddhism may inform the way we think about and respond to suffering, away from the dominant western models of theodicy.

From *Bolivia*, we hear about the significance of the Nazarene identity of Jesus, and how that signifies his solidarity with those from whom "nothing good can come out of." The Nazarenes are the oppressed throughout time and space but, at the same time, are the ones who teach the church and call her to "come and see."

From *El Salvador,* we hear that remembering the martyrs is one way of believing in the resurrection. Those who argue that martyrdom is a masochistic glorification of suffering come from places where the reality of martyrdom is absent. The killing of thousands of innocent lives in El Salvador has generated the need to reflect on another type of martyrdom, the *non-voluntary* one, which in turn calls for the *voluntary* martyrdom of the church in the form of solidarity with the oppressed.

From *Germany,* we are cautioned as we read accounts of Christian persecution in antiquity, and we are called to acknowledge how records of such persecutions may often be inflated for one reason or another. We are also called to see the ugly side of history where the ones who were once persecuted end up persecuting other Christian groups once they rise to power. We are also given a tribute to each of the twenty-one martyrs of Libya whose broadcasted martyrdom shook the world; through them, a window into the Coptic outlook on martyrdom is opened.

From *Greece,* we hear hard questions asked about suffering when illness hits our loved ones and is felt as divine harshness. We are also shown deep philosophical reflections on the origins of evil understood as humanity severed from its dependence on God and striving to "become like God" (*theosis*) on its own, apart from God.

From the *UK,* we read insights on global persecution and delve into examinations of different types of persecution as well as causes such as nationalism and totalitarian insecurity operating in a variety of contexts. We are also invited into the difficult concepts of God's own suffering and how these relate to his impassibility or immutability. St. Paul's suffering is also examined as a way of sharing in Christ's suffering, of authenticating his ministry, and of opening him up to further revelation.

From *Egypt,* we are invited to reflect on the role of the Holy Spirit in the path to martyrdom and how conquering the fear of death is not humanly possible, but divinely granted.

From *Lebanon,* we learn how ministry among Muslim refugees who have experienced the severe trauma of war and displacement calls local churches to reconsider their leadership structure and practices. Models such as the host becoming the hosted are extremely empowering to new believers and serve as great equalizers in the community of faith.

From *Palestine,* we hear thundering prophetic voices about how persecution is not primarily due to Islamic intolerance but to Western oppression.

From *Syria,* we read about the need to understand the identity of the martyr, not only from the historical perspective, but as the church's missiological identity.

From *Canada,* we read reflections on particular experiences of imprisonment, inspired from Old Testament and New Testament examples as well as by modern day heroes.

From the *USA,* we learn about the preparation of local faith communities for disaster and relief, and models of resilience are proposed at both social and the spiritual levels. We are also exposed to the figure of biblical Hagar as an exercise in empathizing with the oppressed, especially the African single mother. Moreover, we delve into the pain of multiple personal losses and consider how one may reconcile faithful service to God through Job-like suffering. Finally, we are taught how to develop a robust understanding of forgiveness by avoiding the cheap forgiveness that risks blurring the lines between good and evil.

Myrto Theocharous
Greek Bible College, Athens, Greece

Africa

Nigeria

No More Cheeks to Turn?[1]
Sunday Bobai Agang

Contributed by Alfred Sebahene (Tanzania)

Summary

No More Cheeks to Turn? presents a detailed account of Pastor Sunday Bobai Agang's personal testimony about how the power of God can transform an angry, arrogant, and self-pitying person into a faithful peacemaker. Agang regards himself as a person who met the God of the universe and received an answer regarding his suffering. Throughout the book Agang's testimony is distinguished by its vivid biblical faithfulness, fascinating style, and an experiential authenticity.

No More Cheeks to Turn? shines light on the problem of suffering and persecution and explores a biblical solution. It begins with the question asked in the title, which is a humble reaction and response to Jesus's words, "You have heard that it was said, 'Eye for eye, and tooth for tooth.' But I tell you, do not resist an evil person. If anyone slaps you on the right cheek, turn to them the other cheek also" (Matt 5:38–39). Whereas in the twenty-first century world in which we live many expect that punishment or sentencing should always equally match the crime, Jesus, speaking the wisdom of God, condemns the practice of such retaliation in the Sermon on the Mount.

Although Sunday wrote specifically to the Nigerian church, his message applies to Christians everywhere; it is relevant outsdide Nigeria to all of Africa and beyond. This book offers a biblical and practical answer for those facing day-to-day violence and persecution at different magnitudes and of different types – not only to ordained pastors and lay church leaders, but also to ordinary church members.

Each of the sixteen chapters in this book ends with a few study questions that challenge the reader to reflect on the chapter's teachings and also warn

---

1. Bukuru, Nigeria: Hippo Books, 2016.

readers to revisit their attitudes towards violence. For Agang, the outcome of this reflection is a shift from fears and frustrations, anger and disillusionment, to an experience of the sense of God's overwhelming peace.

The author is clear on his own experience of the peace he received from God. It is this experience which led him to become a peacemaker (after being taught about it). For him, he was and still is motivated by profound peace, unshakeable joy, and life-changing faith. He thanks God for his amazing grace.

The materials to which he points readers in the footnotes, together with the "Further Reading" list at the end, are practical and helpful features of the book. Most of the highlighted resources have to do with the persecution of the Nigerian church and include works on non-violence. Another key feature of the book includes the author's use of the Bible, directly quoting or alluding to biblical texts related to key topics:

- Encouragement for the persecuted church in Nigeria

    Job 13:15; Matthew 5:10–12; Mark 13:13; Luke 6:22–23, Romans 8:35–37, 1 Corinthians 12:26–27, 2 Corinthians 4:8–12; Hebrews 12:1–3; 1 Peter 3:14–17, 4:12–19; and Revelation 2:10

- Selected teachings on violence, suffering and persecution

    Matthew 5:44; John 15:18–25; Romans 12:17–21; 1 Corinthians 4:12; 2 Timothy 3:12; and Hebrews 13:3

- Stories of persecution

    Acts 5:17–21; 2 Corinthians 12:10; Philippians 1:12–14; 1 Thessalonians 3:4; and Revelation 7:13–17.

Response
On the Summary

The teachings of *No More Cheeks to Turn?* resonate with the context of twenty-first century Nigeria, where decades of violence continue to test the faith of Nigerian Christians. Nigeria began the twenty-first century with the slaughter of thousands in Kaduna in northern Nigeria over the introduction of Shari'ah law in 2000. Following this came church and mosque burnings in Jos, also in northern Nigeria, following disputed local elections. This triggered clashes between Muslim and Christian youth in Jos and the surrounding region. Today Boko Haram militants continue to urge Christians to leave the north.

Throughout *No More Cheeks to Turn?*, and in the context of the circumstances described, the author maintains that the church still has the potential to restore distorted community. Nigerians may believe that violence is more redemptive than non-violence and therefore resort to human efforts in the form of traditional retaliation as they seek justice. Sunday believes that the church can correct that common but mistaken view. It is good that Sunday has repeatedly spoken of violence as a moral problem which, for him and for the church in Nigeria, should challenge the core of the nature, presence, and power of the gospel in the country.

In My Context

In my context as a Christian living and serving in Africa, Sunday's Nigerian (African) past feelings and experience – of fear, frustration, bitterness and being angry at God – provide unmistakable evidence of spiritual deficiency and poverty in African contexts. This reminds me of the other type of poverty, material poverty, which is often linked with injustice and is both a spiritual and moral crisis on the continent of Africa. The appendices in Sunday's book help to locate its message within its African context – where communities continue to suffer as individuals are exposed to prolonged grief and suffering, with no or limited sign of human flourishing, of freedom from oppression, or of the renewal of all creation. On a positive note, the book *No More Cheeks to Turn?* reminds the people of Africa of God's sovereignty: when life is full of pain, it is important to know that sometimes God extraordinarily delivers us, making all things new and bringing forth beauty from ashes. Likewise, sometimes God is not yet delivering us, but we can still be assured of true contentment in our circumstances. When this is granted, the world can enjoy peace and satisfaction – values which led Agang to become a peacemaker. It is also important for Africa and other parts of the world to know that, at times, God leaves us with pain, so that we can be reminded that this world is not our home. We are mere strangers passing through. It is therefore important, in this context, to listen to Sunday's call to follow the costly way of Christ. Instead of adding to the existing pain by revenge and violence, amidst suffering and persecution ours should be a noble ministry of serving the poor, the powerless, and the oppressed.

Questions for Further Discussion and Reflection

1. A Christian's response to evil finds its foundation in the Bible. Give an example to support this idea.

   The Bible tells us that we are expected by God to be our brother's (or sister's) keeper, to not repay evil with evil. We should not resist an evil person but turn the other cheek and go the extra mile. The Bible also reminds us to forgive those who persecute us and, instead of vengeance, we are to pray for them, be perfect as our Father in heaven is perfect, love our enemies, and not be overcome by evil, instead overcoming evil by good.

2. How can reading the Bible help your community to engage in peacebuilding and transformation?

   A good starting point is remembering that Jesus calls us all to be peacemakers and to love one another, including our enemies (Matthew 5). Then it is important to know that peacemakers, like Jesus, are concerned about division, suspicion, and hatred. In other words, peacemaking is not something Jesus calls us just to do, but what he calls us to be (Matthew 5:9). It should be our lifestyle. As we read the Bible, we will discover that true peace is not simply about stopping violence. Instead, it is shalom which means restoration and reconciling of each one of us in relationship with God, with those around us, and with all of creation.

3. Take a critical look at your country and community. Describe the influence of violence and persecution. Discuss this with others. What stands out?

   Generally speaking, in most communities of the twenty-first century there are so many things from which people need liberation. In *No More Cheeks to Turn?* the author challenges us to rethink liberation in order to have a vibrant life of true humanity to which God has called us. Although there are many types of liberation, in this case it is violence and persecution that we should be liberated from. What stands out today is the manifestation of violence and suffering in the form of colonization, discrimination, ecological and religious abuse, dishonesty, immorality, disregard for human life, materialistic greed, along with religious fundamentalisms and religious violence and extremism.

Reflection

An Ecumenical Approach – Discipleship, Violence and What the Bible Teaches on Oppression, Suffering, and Forgiveness

Church Leaders' Meetings on Discipleship and Peace Building, 5–6 June 2023[2]

In both Sunday Agang's Nigeria and in my Nigeria, the ecumenical nature of churches' engagement in addressing persecution is both apparent and necessary. Committed to walk with their communities, church leaders have committed to various peace building and conflict resolution ventures. Though the church continues to experience violence and some degree of persecution, the church has long played central roles in peoples' lives and continues to do so. Here, in Tanzania, the church often provides basic services. In line with Agang's narrative in *No More Cheeks to Turn?*, the Tanzanian ecumenical approach applies to local experiences of violence the Bible's teachings on oppression, suffering, and forgiveness.

Prayer

My Lord and my God, I thank you so much that my country, Tanzania, continues to be a shining example of peaceful coexistence in Africa. Lord, I thank you for making this happen. It is you, Lord, who is doing this because, despite having more than 123 different ethnic groups and all major faiths present, Tanzanians have managed to live peacefully. I pray that your people will discover and understand that the church still has the potential to

---

2. Source: Christian Council of Tanzania. Photo available at https://cct.or.tz/hm_hab?slide_id=1&&page=index.php.

restore any distorted community and that I will continue to work for love and peaceful coexistence among all people to ensure that there shall be no more cheeks to turn. In your name, Amen.

South Africa (and Germany)

Suffering, Persecution and Martyrdom: Theological Reflections[1]
Christof Sauer and Richard Howell (editors)

Contributed by Brent Hamoud (USA/Lebanon)

Summary

Suffering, Persecution and Martyrdom: Theological Reflections is a 2010 text edited by Christof Sauer and Richard Howell as the second volume in the Religious Freedom Series; the first volume was *Re-Examining Religious Persecution* (2008). The book stems from a global initiative facilitated by the World Evangelical Alliance that gathered church leaders in Bad Urach, Germany, during September 2009 for a theological consultation about suffering, persecution, and martyrdom. The gathering produced a comprehensive document, *The Bad Urach Statement*, which has been summarized for this text as *The Bad Urach Call*. Following a summary report, the document has twelve chapters of contributions by global theological thinkers who expand the discussion through a diverse set of voices. The book serves its purpose well by bringing a prominent issue to the table for high-level theoretical engagement; it presents suffering, persecution, and martyrdom as an urgent issue in need of critical theological understanding and sets out a range of reflections to address the heavy and complex topic from different perspectives. For readers interested in developing a strong foundation for the discourse, *Suffering, Persecution and Martyrdom: Theological Reflections* is a helpful introductory resource that sets a pragmatic framework for the discussion and provides core ideas to build upon in further examinations.

A key purpose of this text rests in furthering the broad ideas of *The Bad Urach Call*. The document is presented at the front of the book with the subsequent chapters serving as companion pieces to further disseminate prevailing ideas and offering more pointed (and debatable) notions. The

---
1. Religious Freedom Series 2. Parow, South Africa: AcadSA Publishing, 2010/Bonn, Germany: Verlag für Kultur und Wissenschaft, 2011.

statement itself is a meaningful accomplishment, successfully bringing together what was surely a comprehensive (and perhaps contentious) set of meetings to a thorough document that offers something of substance while also proving widely acceptable to members of the global Christian body.

As the leading feature of the book, *The Bad Urach Call* stands as a type of manifesto that sets pragmatic parameters for addressing the topic and articulating the deep spiritual convictions necessary to drive a productive discourse. It defines the terms "suffering," "persecution," and "martyrdom" by anchoring their notions in a broad reading of Scripture and a framework for missions. A strength of the statement is that it aims to be corrective by dispelling misconceptions, correcting harmful claims, and identifying areas of disagreement – building a dialogical character to the document which increases its credibility. Though primarily concerned with the way we hold the topic theoretically, the practical is not neglected, and applicative considerations are offered at various levels. The *Bad Urach Call* is not contextual nor particularly analytical, but this is not surprising for a general document attempting to be highly function and widely accepted. Overall, it is an achievement in establishing grounds for approaching the challenges (and opportunities) of suffering, persecution, and martyrdom in a way that is productive, faithful, and relevant to a diverse Christian community.

Following on from the *Bad Urach Call*, the subsequent chapters offer varying levels of insight about topics related to suffering, persecution, and martyrdom. The chapters comprise a collection of voices speaking from various contexts, and the results vary piece by piece. The chapters are not designed to carry a cohesive argument, nor do they interact with one another, but there is a coherence to the ordering – the earlier chapters examine broader questions of theodicy, and the latter chapters consider more grounded, practical questions. That said, readers will find that the pieces exist independently from one another and even from the *Bad Urach Call*.

There is certainly a strong element of biblical studies in the book (which is not unexpected given that contributors are theologians and Christian scholars). The biblical bases for suffering, persecution and martyrdom are covered comprehensively. Nearly all relevant Scriptures are addressed (it appears), and some are commented on numerous times by different writers to the degree that the point almost becomes redundant. Nonetheless, the truth is effectively conveyed that suffering, persecution, and martyrdom are thoroughly biblical realities demonstrated most profoundly in the person of Jesus Christ. There are many mentions of the early church period as well (contemporary examples are rarely included). From this biblical and historical basis proceeds a core premise of the book: suffering, persecution, and martyrdom are very real, necessary, and mysteriously productive in manifesting the mission of the church. Writers say in many ways that this element of the Christian faith and life should not be shunned or despaired of but embraced as evidence of faithfulness to Christ and a means to demonstrate life-giving, faith-refining, gospel-advancing witness. In fact, the validation of suffering, persecution, and martyrdom is so strongly implored that one walks away from the book almost despairing the extent to which much of the church *is not* subject to hardships. That is not, of course, a point the book intends to make but rather an impression gathered when considering its overall message.

Each of the twelve chapters contributes to the conversation on suffering, persecution, and martyrdom in separate ways, and a few stand out as especially helpful. Three chapters to note are those by Isaiah Majok Dau ("Facing Human Suffering"), Thomas Wespetal ("Martyrdom and the Furtherance of God's Plan"), and Reg Reimer ("Persecution, Advocacy and Mission at the Beginning of the 21st Century"). Dau, a South Sudanese bishop, speaks much on the topic of character formation and the merit of suffering to grow and develop character (and character as a means to measure the value of suffering). It is a crucial concept and I wonder why other authors mentioned do not highlight character formation in their discussions. Wespetal argues unapologetically that martyrdom advances God's plan but is mindful to include points at which different perspectives have different positions on the topic. Reimer makes an effective discussion about the topic by *not* drawing extensively from Scripture (this is not an oversight since numerous other writers do so to great extent). Instead, he offers some consideration of real-life contexts while making sure to make an important point that threatens to be overlooked in other chapters: persecution is not good! Additionally, he offers one of the rare cases from the book where advocacy for the persecuted is proposed as a vital cause. Other articles have much to offer as well, but these three chapters are particularly helpful in thinking through the book's questions.

Suffering, Persecution and Martyrdom positions its topic squarely as a spiritual matter. Christocentric qualities and eschatological hope for suffering underpin the entire discussion to frame how all that happens here in this world is tightly bound to the spiritual realms and the coming reality of God. The demonic and Satanic forces driving suffering, persecution, and martyrdom are given hearty attention in ways that may not be expected of a mainline Evangelical book. For example, the chapter "Suffering and Martyrdom" (Josef Ton) casts the entire issue cosmologically as a showdown between two leaders, Jesus and Satan, while the chapter "The Church of Christ Under the Shadow of

Antichrist" (Peter P. J. Beyerhaus) takes the discussion to highly contested areas of Bible interpretation and Christian thought (though the chapter presents its ideas as if they are standard theological positions). These chapters indicate that the writers are not presenting a unified argument on suffering, persecution, and martyrdom; rather, the book is a series of reflections from a diverse set of theologians, many of whom have personal encounters with intense forms of suffering and persecution.

Unsurprisingly, the book provides varying types of reflections that will resonate with readers to different extents. Some will prove more informative than others depending on who is engaging the text and why. That said, a regrettable weakness of this resource is the lack of female voices. Of the twelve chapters, only one is written by a woman. This male-heavy lineup is regrettable given the nature of the topic and the unique ways women encounter religious persecution. Also, a wide range of geographic and cultural contexts are represented in the book but the lack of contributions from the Middle Eastern and North African or Indian subcontinent regions is unfortunate since the topic is pressing to Christians in these places.

Suffering, Persecution and Martyrdom provides an ample first foray into oppressive situations confronting the global church. Understanding that this book serves as a companion for the *Bad Urach Statement* helps to set right expectations and grasp its intent to galvanize church communities towards greater unity on an important ecclesial and human matter. It serves the purpose well, but greater critical analysis on suffering, persecution, and martyrdom from weightier texts is needed to build necessary knowledge and understanding for Christians and churches.

Response
On the Summary

Suffering, Persecution and Martyrdom makes a strong case for the importance of thinking seriously about the challenging realities embedded in the Christian faith experience. Any tendency to respond to religious mistreatment with defeatism or despair is corrected by the Scripture's assurance of hope in the face of trials – and this is a sorely needed message. However, the book's collection of reflections can at times anchor so deeply in the ultimate hopefulness of Scripture that it fails to properly account for how horrible persecution can be when manifested against its victims. Much of the discussion seems to think about individuals' experiences, but what of families' (and children's) and community's experiences as well? I would have appreciated holding the two hands of hopefulness and despair a little closer when addressing the tensions of suffering, persecution, and martyrdom.

The book's arguments are highly theoretical, deriving from philosophical, theological, and historical perspectives, but they can feel rather detached from human realities and experiences. There is little in the way of empirical research to ground the issues of suffering, persecution and martyrdom in lived experiences; we can easily identify what we are talking about but who we are talking about remains abstract throughout. This does not emerge from a lack of knowledge or concern about real people and their situations – many of the writers themselves have personal encounters with extreme forms of suffering – but it does limit the book's capacity for engaging in the topic multidimensionally. Having many good points with so few stories is a missed opportunity, although I understand if the text is intentional about being primarily ideas-based.

The book is helpful in setting parameters of suffering, persecution, and martyrdom to clarify what it is and (just as important) what it is not. This is a needed reminder for Christians who tend to move away from original meanings of terms and adapt concepts to their own purposes and inclinations. The text is aware of this and sets out to correct the misappropriation of language used within our conversations. However, it could do more to expand our concern beyond the Christian community towards other forms of religious suffering. Mention is made that this is an interreligious problem but attempts to build solidarity across persecuted religious groups is passed over by the primary focus on theological explanations, and I believe this is, again, a missed opportunity to add nuance to our thinking. Likewise, too little attention is brought to the need for activism and advocacy on behalf of victims of persecution. In many cases the source of the problem is systems, and these need systematic engagement across various levels of cultures and societies.

In My Context (The Middle East)

The arguments of the book are highly relevant to Christians in the Middle East where church communities contend with forces hindering faith and witness. In some contexts, Christ-following communities here are abjectly oppressed institutionally and, in too many other cases, there are instances of individual persecution. The way this text offers clarity and a practical framework for the discussion, particularly in the *Bad Urach Call*, is very useful and should be used to communicate what is being experienced in the region. That said, it is unfortunate that greater relevance to the Middle Eastern context is lost because of the lack of discussion on Islam and abusive political systems. Both factors can be serious forces contending against churches and Christ-followers in the region, but the attention given to these matters in the book is thin. Islam is mentioned very briefly, and the arguments are so poorly researched and presented that it would have been better to not mention Islam at all. Likewise, the failure of theology to consider structural socio-political problems in the region (or elsewhere) is apparent. Though mentioned occasionally as a problem, there is little discussion as to how political dimensions can be understood and engaged. In the Middle East where sectarianism, violent occupation, authoritarianism, and religious domination cause serious harm to people of Christian faith, the need to think critically about these is imperative. That this book does not move beyond the traditional theological discourse to address socio-political topics is a reminder that theology needs to become more robustly engaged with studies of the social sciences.

Our Commitment

Though confronting a layered issue with an array of situational and contextual dimensions, this book sets clear grounded truths that should shape the way we understand suffering, persecution, and martyrdom. Its prevailing point is profound: Jesus is Lord over all hardships and his hand is never absent from those oppressed for their faith; God works through persecution for the glory of the gospel. This is a radical understanding of suffering that undermines worldly conventions by shaping a Christocentric outlook centred on the cross as a model and source of meaning. Considering this, our entire attitude about suffering, persecution, and martyrdom, whether done to us personally or to others, should conform to Christ and see hopefulness through the pain. This is not as easy to attain as *Suffering, Persecution and Martyrdom* may imply, but it makes clear that faithful devotion to scriptural truths turn despair into deep peace and anticipation for the good things of God.

Our commitment should then be to:

- Care deeply for the suffering, persecution, and martyrdom endured by brothers and sisters across the church.
- Have faith in the goodness and providence of God through suffering, persecution, and martyrdom and to take joy in the great hope of heaven's promises that all things will be made right.

- Utilize suffering, persecution, and martyrdom to grow spiritually, witness courageously, and look expectantly to what God will do to reveal his glory.

Reflection

These biblical claims help shift the orientation on suffering, persecution, and martyrdom from something of despair to something with great spiritual value and purpose. As Margaretha N. Adiwardana states so eloquently in *Suffering, Persecution and Martyrdom: Theological Reflections*:

> Many tribulations sadden the believers, but their faith is proved to be more precious than gold which perishes. The aim of suffering is to redound to the praise, glory and honour when Jesus Christ will be revealed. (184)

Uganda

The Sacrifice of Africa: A Political Theology for Africa[1]
Emmanuel Katongole

Contributed by Muhindo Malunga (Democratic Republic of Congo)

Summary

Originally written under the title *Church and State in Africa: Toward a Constructive Social Imagination*, in *The Sacrifice of Africa* distinguished author Emmanuel Katongole has put together a groundbreaking reflection with remarkable simplicity and clarity that qualifies as a guide to all who are and have been concerned by the many contradictions and paradoxes of the state of the church and the nation-state in Africa. What might a constructive social re-imagination of Africa look like? Could we put forward a compelling argument for a fresh, concrete and doable social alternative for Africa that will not only remain a theoretical possibility?

Africa needs saving! This salvation is long overdue. It is not (only) salvation in a spiritual sense, but salvation from a ghost that the author, borrowing from Adam Hoschschild's eponymous title, calls "King Leopold's Ghost." This salvation is needed as the lack of it explains why all efforts and strategies for improving and managing failing institutions in Africa have had little success.

Emmanuel is convinced that all politics are about stories and imagination. Stories not only shape how we view reality but also how we respond to and interpret life, thus defining the sort of persons we become. In other words, we are how we imagine ourselves to be and how others imagine us. Who we are and what we are capable of becoming depends very much on the stories we tell, the stories we listen to, and the stories we live and accept. Stories not only share our values, aims, and goals; they also define the range of what is desirable and what is possible.

That is why a notion like "Africa" names not so much a place, but a story – or a set of stories – about how people of the continent called Africa are located

---

1. Eerdmans Ekklesia Series. Grand Rapids, Michigan: Eerdmans, 2010.

in the narrative that constitutes the modern world. Stories are the predictors of performances within the script of life. The author asks: What underlying stories produce corruption, murder, selfishness and other social ills with Mobutu, Bokassa, Idi Amin, and Mugabe (with the politics of greed and plunder) as radical examples of their manifestation? And what differences does or could Christianity make in Africa?

The book guides us to detect, deconstruct, and understand the operative assumptions of the nation-state in Africa. The social history of Africa sufficiently shows that the post-independence African leaders were colonial "types," that is, mimetic reproductions of the colonial actors. Africa needs to address the ways in which the colonial imagination continues to live in the present, even while these ways include seemingly noble ideals of "civilization, humanitarian and concern for the poor" – all of which have led in many cases to deception or perpetuation of the colonial system. In short, the actors have changed but the script has remained unchanged.

Part of the manifestation of King Leopold's Ghost is that in the minds of all – African and non-African – the waste of African lives seemed to have reached a certain degree of acceptability as part of the way of life. Once this dispensability of African lives had been both accepted and expected as part of the official "normal" way of nation-state politics, postcolonial successors to the colonial project have had no problem perpetuating the same shameful sacrificing of lives in pursuit of their political ambitions and greed. This mentality, this story, needs to be vehemently confronted in all spheres of life in Africa. Christianity itself will have to find a way of overcoming its Western heritage.

Emmanuel's central argument is that there is a "Big Lie" at the heart of Africa's inception into modernity. Modernity claims to bring salvation to Africa, yet the founding story of the institutions of modern Africa rejects Africa itself. This story has shaped colonial Africa and continues to drive its successor institutions, the nation-states. Historically, the story translated into myriad forms of use and abuse, sacrificing African lives and, ultimately, Africa itself. This is why a new future in Africa requires much more than strategies and skills to solve the problems of nation-state politics. It requires a different story that assumes the sacred value and dignity of Africa and Africans and can thus shape practices and policies, or new forms of politics, which reflect this sacredness and dignity. (*Sacra* + *fecere* means to make sacred therefore *The Sacrifice of Africa* could be read, *Making Africa Sacred*).

"We must dare to invent the future."
– Thomas Sankara, 1985[2]

Chapter 4 of *The Sacrifice of Africa* is titled "Daring to Invent the Future: The Madness of Thomas Sankara." Sankara (1947–1987) was a Burkinabé revolutionary, Pan-Africanist, and military officer. He was appointed prime minister in 1983, and shortly thereafter made a political prisoner by the government of President Jean-Baptiste Philippe Ouédraogo. Sankara's supporters launched a successful coup d'état, released him from prison, and appointed him as the new president of Burkino Faso, a position which he held until his assassination in 1987. His brief but impressive revolutionary leadership in Burkina Faso gives a good example of the type of social re-imagination that is needed for a new future to take shape in Africa:

- Intellectual clarity – Sankara clearly understood the foundation of Burkina Faso, tracing neocolonial exploitation and the story of plunder being hardwired into African modernity and making Africa a "paradise for some and a hell for others."
- Revolutionary madness – for Sankara the whole project of seeking to "invent the future" was a form of madness. For instead of shaping the future according to predictable patterns of the past and realities of the present (the rational thing to do), inventing the future required reshaping the present according to a vision of a future yet to come. The task of inventing the future is essentially one of imagination.
- Commitment and sacrifice – By launching immediate and far-reaching reforms and projects, Sankara's revolution reveals the importance of courage, urgency, passion, and relentless commitment and sacrifice for facing the challenges of Africa.

With all their shortcomings, how are leaders like Sankara formed? What drives them? Where do they find their energy and focus? And how is the clarity of vision, courage, and madness essential to the task of inventing the future cultivated? How can such commitment and sacrifice be nurtured and sustained over time?

Katongole points to the futility of trying to invent the future without the necessary elements of *memory*, *community*, and *story*.

- Memory – inventing the future requires more than catching the vision. It requires a sustained practice of memory that includes but

---

2. Katongole uses this well-known quote from Sankara as the first of two epigraphs for chapter 4 of *The Sacrifce of Africa;* the second epigraph is Joel 2:28.

is not limited to telling stories like Sankara's and other trailblazers (Bishop Paride Taban, Angelina Atyam, Maggy Barankitse, etc).
- Community – there is need for communities that reflect the message of the revolution. Each such community must be a community of convinced people, not conquered people.
- Story – behind Sankara's use of quasi-religious language and metaphors one can detect a desperate search for a vision, a story, and language with which to shape and communicate his revolutionary ideals, although he never found one.

A story is needed, but story to what end? A new social imagination. A new story of "in the beginning." Church is not only well suited for this task, it is uniquely gifted for it and called to it. For the Church's very mission and identity is to be a community of conversion, a community that is constantly gathered not only to lament the social, cultural, economic, and political disintegration of Africa, but to remember, and celebrate the story of creation, God's constant journey with his people, and God's self-giving through his Son.

Response
On the Summary

As an African from the Democratic Republic of Congo (DRC) with a passion to see change in my country and in Africa, I have taken time to think about the source of our ills. My conclusion is that Christians and people with good morality have to be involved in politics in order to improve the nation-state (in essence, by finding ways for the current political institutions to work better).

In *The Sacrifice of Africa*, the author shows that this approach is not enough as it is trying to improve institutions that are inherently deficient. The author instead calls readers to think deeper about the heritage of violence and seek solutions from that new understanding. This is really interesting as it explains most of the reasons for the vicious circles of violence, plunder and greed in Africa.

While the main argument is coherent, there are no grand scale examples in the book of how such ideas can be implemented in a world that is not ready to stop and go for a retreat to rethink its way of life. Furthermore, while the book provides some stories of hope, initiated by individuals in response to the worst of atrocities, it is yet to be seen how the main argument of the book would fair in a complex political situation where self-interest is the order of the day. However, the author, in my opinion, has succeeded in depicting the kind of church and leaders who will bring about change.

In My Context

It is widely known that the DRC has had long protracted wars for over a century. The first chapter of the book *King Leopold's Ghost* is actually based on the story of the DRC. So, if there is any place where a reflection on a new way of life in Africa should start, it has to be the DRC – the country radically exemplifies all the ills of Africa on a grand scale.

Furthermore, the DRC is said to be more than eighty percent Christian. How do you explain that an overwhelming proportion of the population identifies itself with Christianity and yet the nation produces some of the worst leaders in the world? On top of having numerous church congregations, the majority of schools, hospitals, and most social services have been taken over by Christian denominations because of the failing political institutions. The church is, therefore, well-placed to reflect and initiate change with far-reaching impact.

Our Commitment

I have made a personal commitment to work towards crafting a new story for my country, the DRC, and the Africa region. A story that is grounded in love and the abundance of God's creation. A story of communities living together in fellowship. A story of shared prosperity.

20 Suffering and Persecution

Reflection

The Lord's Supper[3]

---

3. Editor's picture of Tanzanian cloth painting, original artist unknown.

Asia

China

The Chinese Epaphras[1]
Wu Weizun

Contributed by Xiaxia Xue (Hong Kong)

Summary

The Chinese Epaphras is an autobiography of Wu Weizun (1926–2002), whose pseudonym is Epaphras. Epaphras experienced the vicissitudes of time, from the pre-liberation of modern China (before 1949) through the period of the Great Leap forward (1957–1960) and throughout the Cultural Revolution (1966–1976). In that particular time, he greatly suffered and was persecuted because of his Christian faith – he was starved, beaten for no given reason, and imprisoned.

But Epaphras was a warrior, equipped with the word of God in the face of all his hardships. He emerged from his valley of death and announced to the world, "I have fought the good fight." How was it possible for him to faithfully endure such immense suffering for his devotion to Christ? The autobiography describes at least three key stages of his life which illustrate his devoted love toward the Lord.

First, beginning in his teenage years Epaphras was committed to obey the word of God. His regular prayer was, "Lord, whatever you ask for me, I obey." In the face of poverty as a high school student (1942–1945), he insisted on telling the truth. One winter, when the snow was a foot and a half thick, Epaphras was still wearing straw shoes because he could not afford better ones. He was advised to go to the association of townsmen to appeal for financial support, even though he was from the neighbouring town and would not qualify for aid. Though in desperate need of funds, he refused to lie and followed the command in Ephesians, "putting away falsehood, let all of us speak the truth to our neighbours" (Eph 4:25). When his church got some relief supplies and clothing from USA in 1946, Epaphras was given an army wool skirt and asked

---
1. Taipei: CMI Publishing, 2002.

a tailor to make it into short pants for him. But then he became afraid that the pants would become his idol, weakening his affection for the Lord. After keen praying, he was reminded by Matthew 5:29, "If your right eye causes you to sin, tear it out and throw it away." So, he decided to give up the pants. Out of his love for the Lord, Epaphras was willing to give up everything.

Second, Epaphras regarded suffering as a way to be worthy of God. From 1949 to 1957, he taught physics in a high school. After the communist party came to power in China in 1949, an ideological reform movement began. All teachers were required to be Marxist, which meant being atheist. Epaphras loved his teaching job, but he knew he couldn't be a Marxist. But what could he do? Finding any job was difficult. If he lost his teaching job, he could lose everything and become a beggar. But he knew he couldn't be a beggar, because 2 Thessalonians 3:10 warns, "Anyone who does not work shall not eat." Worried and desperate, he heard a voice saying, "It is okay to starve to death." Finally finding peace, he told his school leader that he is a Christian, not a Marxist. As a result, he finally lost his teaching job and was sent to labour in the rural area.

Epaphras continued to suffer even as he sought to follow the leading of God's Spirit. He insisted that "God created the world," not "labour created the world," as the Communist Party said. As a result, he was cut off by his peers and sent to heavy labour in a poor region, in an effort to purge him of his Christian world view. Because the Communist Party was afraid he would preach the gospel and poison the minds of others, he was asked to give a detailed report about what he did, what he said to others, and how others responded to him. In his prayers, Epaphras recalled how Jesus had offered no word of response to the accusations of the chief priests and Pilate. So Epaphras likewise did not give any response to the questions asked of him. As a result, he was separated from other people and was required to do the most difficult and tiring work. But, in his mind Epaphras was at peace for he regarded all these trials as worthy sufferings for God.

Third, we can describe Epaphras' life in terms of spiritual warfare. He sought to distinguish between holy and secular paths and remained committed to God's way in all the circumstances he found himself in because of his faith in the Lord. For his refusal to forsake his Christian faith, he was put into jail in 1964. For more than ten years, he had no Bible to read, and was not allowed to pray aloud or say grace before meals. When he did pray, he was beaten and was refused food. Epaphras realized that he needed to do something to confirm his belonging to the Lord. In his silent prayers, he realized the battlefield the Lord gave him was to give thanks before meals. But since prayer was not allowed, Epaphras decided to fast. At the brink of death, he was forced to take milk through his nose. Even into the 1980s, he was kept in prison because he would not confess his offence of being a Christian and would not answer any questions his accusers posed. When he was released in 1987, he was the last prisoner to be released from that prison.

Response
On the Summary
In sum, the life of Epaphras was full of hardship and spiritual warfare. He seems to have had a tendency toward asceticism, but his commitment to Christ shone through the darkness and brought blessings to people around him.

In My Context
Epaphras dedicated his whole life to the Lord and to obedience to God's word. He endeavoured to distinguish what is holy from what belongs to the world. His faithfulness and obedience enabled him to walk through his many dark times. Such exemplary faithfulness is needed in the current Chinese context. Although China has experienced huge changes since Epaphras' time, Christians still face pressures from the government. The political persecution of Christians is not like before. We are not being put into jail just because we are Christians or give thanks before meals. However, that does not mean we can spread our faith and live it out freely. For example, many Christians struggle whether to publicly acknowledge their Christian identities. If they do, they may not be able to get their ideal jobs. Also, they may lose their path to promotion. On the other hand, the way Epaphras distinguished between the holy and the secular may not work in the same way for today's Christians, since the mission of the church is to enter into society so that God's kingdom may be built up in this world. As Christians, we have our responsibilities to participate in establishing God's kingdom in the world. That means all the work we do is holy when it is done out of faithfulness.

Our Commitment
Epaphras's life is a good example for Christians, particularly in how he listened to the Spirit and the Word of God. He counsels us to:
- Have a pure heart toward God by listening to his voice via the Scriptures and prayers.

- Devote our life to God's calling.
- Imitate Christ, contribute to others, and create a true community of Christ.

Reflection

We lift the cup of life, to affirm our life together and celebrate it as a gift from God. When each of us can hold firm our own cup, with its many sorrows and joys, claiming it as our unique life, then too, can we lift it up for others to see and encourage them to lift up their lives as well. Thus, as we lift up our cup in a fearless gesture, proclaiming that we will support each other in our common journey, we create community.

– Henri Nouwen, *Can You Drink the Cup?* [2]

---

2. Henri Nouwen, *Can You Drink the Cup?*, Tenth Anniversary Edition (Notre Dame, Indiana: Ave Maria Press, 2006), 62.

China

The Carving of God: The Biography of the Lord's Servant – Simon Zhao[1]
Chuansheng Fu

Contributed by Alansoe Yan (China)

Summary

After the Qing dynasty ended in 1912, China was involved in years of continuous warfare. In 1931, Japan initiated the incident of 18 September which led to the occupation of Northeast China. The 1937–1945 war against Japan was followed by the Chinese civil war between the Nationalist Party and the Communist Party, which lasted for four years. Finally in 1949, the Communist Party emerged victorious; the People's Republic of China was established in mainland China whereas the Republic of China continued to exist only in Taiwan. During the following years, China underwent various political movements which led to religious persecution, particularly towards the Chinese churches. Simon Zhao, who was born in 1918, grew up in war time and faithfully served the Lord under the "red regime," was destined to spend his life in suffering, turmoil and hardship. But more importantly, by God's amazing grace, Simon also experienced God's wonderful guidance, timely provision, powerful protection, and deep spiritual formation.

Simon Zhao's Life Is Like a Legend

In 1946, he received a calling from God to go to Xinjiang to preach the gospel. Despite the ongoing civil war, Simon began three years of theological and pastoral training and embarked on a perilous journey from Nanjing to Xinjiang in 1949. Since all transportation from Nanjing to Xinjiang was interrupted, Simon had to travel on foot. It took him three and a half months to travel ten thousand miles across five provinces (Jiangsu, Anhui, Henan, Shaanxi and

---

1. Hong Kong: Way Publishing, 2016.

Gansu) and to cross three major rivers: the Yangtze, the Yellow and the Wei, finally entering Xinjiang, an area three times the size of France. In addition to the distance which he had to travel, he also needed to pass through numerous checkpoints, war zones, and was even arrested three times as an alleged military spy. However, God kept Simon and guided him to overcome all the obstacles along the way, so he finally arrived in Xinjiang.

After two years of ministry in Xinjiang, Simon was persecuted by the government for his faith. He was sentenced as a counter-revolutionary leader and put into prison in Kashgar for twenty years. In prison, he went through inhuman torture designed to make him recant his faith, yet he remained faithful. He was subjected to heavy physical labour that nearly killed him and forced to live with heavy shackles for five long years. He endured interrogation and trial without food, drink, or even sleep for seven days and nights. He was also forced to stand naked on the ice overnight at thirty degrees below zero (-30°C / -22°F) and kept in a dark room for two and a half years (in such conditions, people normally cannot survive more than six months). Despite these unimaginable conditions, God kept Simon alive and led him peacefully through the valley of death.

Simon Zhao's Life Is Like a Poem

Before he was called to be a preacher, Simon was a literary man. He had a passion for literature, drama, and poetry, and he had a desire to use his writing to purify the people's hearts and then change the sinful world. However, after he was called by God, Simon realized there is salvation in no one else but Jesus. From then on, he surrendered all he had to God and served him wholeheartedly. He no longer saw literature as a way to salvation, but as a sacrifice offered to God for his use. Simon wrote many poems to express his faithfulness to God, spiritual enlightenment, and pain and hope in suffering while in jail. Like the Old Testament prophet, Jeremiah, most of Simon's poems are laments written in his blood and tears. In each lament, we not only hear the deep cry of suffering in his body and soul but also the voice of his faith and hope in God. After his calling to preach, most of his poems were composed as church hymns; these have been a great contribution to Chinese Christian spirituality. Looking back on Simon's life, it is clear that God is the greatest poet of all. Simon became the pen in God's hand, and his life is a magnificent poem written by God. Through Simon's life, God proclaims his mighty power, unfailing love, great faithfulness, and wonderful salvation to the world. Simon's life is a testament to the power of God's love, which sustained Simon through the trials and tribulations he faced. His story serves as an inspiration to us all, reminding us of the importance of faith and perseverance in the face of adversity.

Simon Zhao's Life Is Like a Sculpture

After having been imprisoned for twenty years and released in 1971, Simon lived another twenty years under government restrictions until an official reassessment and vindication in 1991. Simon then left Xinjiang with the guidance of God. He spent his last eight years spiritually training church coworkers all around China. You may ask, "Why did God put Simon through forty years of imprisonment and suffering and just use his last eight years serving the church? What a waste of life!" We may find the answer in the name of this book. The reason the book is titled *The Carving of God* is because when he was young, Simon not only liked painting and calligraphy but also loved craft carving, always carrying a small sharp carving knife with him. This love for carving was a prelude to his long-suffering experience. Simon became a hard piece of wood in the hands of God, and God was the master carver. God used every experience in Simon's life like the small carving knife, carving him deeply and carefully from top to bottom, from the inside to the outside, until he became a fit vessel and a masterpiece carved through blood and tears for the glory of God. Though Simon has passed away, his testimony is still surrounding us as clouds, touching our hearts, and inspiring us to follow his footsteps. Actually, God is more glorified by Simon's being than by his doing.

Simon's life was and is not wasted. He is a God-given spiritual treasure to the Chinese church. As Simon wrote in the preface of this book, to be a Christian one must be spiritually reborn and have a good testimony for the glory of God. Simon not only said this, but he also lived it. And may his poems be more widely heard, his life story be better known, and his footstep be more deeply followed so that the testimony of God is spread over all the earth.

Response
On the Summary

What is the deepest impact of Simon Zhao's testimony on me?

Live for God alone. Simon could have pursued his personal passion for literature or prioritized his family's happiness. He could have settled for a comfortable pastoral position within a local church. Instead, he embarked on a journey to Xinjiang to be a witness for God in a 'wilderness' lacking the gospel.

He left behind his hometown, lost the support of his family, and even lost his beloved wife, who was martyred in Xinjiang. For forty years, he endured a life of bitterness and suffering, like a sour fruit soaked in bitter water. All of this was for one purpose: to testify God. Simon's life was a testament to his unwavering dedication to God and his desire to fulfil God's calling, no matter the cost.

In My Context

What does it mean to me that we have to be carved by God before we can testify him?

Living for God is more than just a mindset or a feeling, it involves a transformation of one's life. This requires a change in direction and manner of living, which can only be accomplished through God's work in our lives. Similar to Simon, God may use hardships and challenges to shape us into vessels that reveal his glory. These experiences can be like carving knives in God's hands, moulding us to live out his image. Therefore, it is important for us to embrace difficulties and allow God to work in us, so that we may become better reflections of him in our daily lives.

Our Commitment

What adjustments will you make to let yourself be better used by God? In this biography on Simon, there is an emphasis that for a worker to be better used by the Lord, he or she must be clear about four things: 1) one's rebirth in Christ; 2) God's calling 3) one's life offering; and 4) God's mission. I take these lessons and apply them to my own spiritual life by:

- Cutting myself off from sin and pursuing a holy life.
- Spending more time to seek the deeper purpose of God for my life.
- Tithing and offering and training myself to rely more on God.

Reflection

Pray This Verse with Me

For we are his workmanship, created in Christ Jesus for good works, which God prepared beforehand, that we should walk in them (Eph 2:10).

Hong Kong

Chan Kin-Man's Prison Writings[1]
Kin-Man Chan

Contributed by Kam Yuen-Shan (Hong Kong)

Summary

Chan taught sociology at the Chinese University of Hong Kong and was one of the co-founders of Hong Kong's pro-democracy Occupy movement which led to the 2014 "umbrella movement." He was jailed for sixteen months as a result. As the title reflects, the book is a collection of his forty-three prison letters, dated April 2019–March 2020, and framed by an introduction and an appendix which comprises of reminiscences from his best friends and a list of books he read while in jail. The book aims at a wider readership in the public arena. Yet the spirit of it betrays his reflection following the Christian tradition of works by authors like Dietrich Bonhoeffer, Václav Havel, and Kim Dae-jung. After all, though he refused to be identified as a member of the mainstream churches, he remains a Christian intellectual who embraces Christian values.

The letters are his observations, feelings, and reflections behind bars. Though living in a poor environment and separated from his wife and daughter, he gets a sense of serenity and clear conscience as he reflects on his insistence in refusing to accept falsehood. What he shares in the letters is somewhat diverse. It is comprised of stories of other people, daily routines in prison, and visits from his family and friends. However the majority of his sharing relates to the situation of Hong Kong at that time. To illustrate some of his sharing, he tells us the unfortunate stories of other prisoners whose lives had been trapped at the bottom of society. They remind us of the basic need for sustainable living as well as the need to pursue simplicity in a greedy and never-satisfying city. Chan also observes the absence of clocks in jail. Through this, he learned the significance of not being rushed, enjoying each "here-and-now" moment. As the political crisis due to the government's extradition bill fermented in 2019, from time to

---

1. Hong Kong: Chan Kin-Man, 2021. [Chinese]

time he shared Bible passages (along with various books) that had given him wisdom and which show how ridiculous the ruling regime was. Chan shared his reflections on his reading inside the prison while contrasting that with what was happening outside, as he understood it through the limited news he saw on the TV or heard on the radio. When reading through the history of Taiwan's fight for democracy, he learned how the churches in Taiwan stood for moral conscience as well as the Christian faith.[2] At that time, it really comforted him as he knew the Hong Kong churches were willing to step forward to uphold the moral baseline regarding the political crisis. Yet Chan reminds readers that all these stances have a cost to bear. As the experience of people in nearby Asian countries testifies, sacrifices cannot be avoided. Nevertheless, intellectuals, being Hong Kong citizens, ought to pursue what is right with vigour and enthusiasm, to take up their responsibility to help build a civil society. In doing so, Chan champions non-violent civil resistance throughout the struggle, standing on the shoulders of Mahatma Gandhi, Martin Luther King Jr., Nelson Mandela, and Kim Dae-jung.[3]

Chan was not afraid to expose the lies of pro-government leaders and the lies of the government's propaganda, such as "one country, two systems," "Hong Kong people ruling Hong Kong," "high degree of autonomy," "principal officials accountability system," and even the complaint handling systems inherited from the colonial past (particularly, for those behind bars, the Justices of the Peace visits and, for those outside, the Independent Police Complaints Council).[4] The payoff from these liars' efforts is a growing number of unashamed lackeys among the ruling class. Yet, for all these Orwellian lies, he believes that the common people, through their actual experiences in their everyday lives, are capable of eventually recognizing them for what they are. (Chan here adopted the Yale anthropologist James Scott's perspective on hegemony.[5])

---

2. 11 June 2019, see pages 59–61.

3. Chan, *Chan Kin-Man's Prison Writings*, 92–94.

4. Chan, *Chan Kin-Man's Prison Writings*, 77–80, 97–100.

5. Editors' note: James C. Scott argued that oppression and resistance are not primarily manifested in historic events such as rebellions and collective revolutions, which are rather uncommon, but they are more subtle than that. Scott focuses on "every day resistance" which takes different cultural forms of non-cooperation with the dominant system. Examples are foot-dragging, false compliance, sabotage, slander, etc., but also contesting "public transcripts," i.e. prescribed roles and language, through the use of rumour, linguistic tricks, folktales and euphemism. His influential books are *Weapons of the Weak: Everyday Forms of Resistance* (New Haven and London: Yale University Press, 1985) and *Domination and the Arts of Resistance: Hidden Transcripts* (New Haven and London: Yale University Press, 1992).

As the political crisis went up and down in the society, he often offered his own comments on them. He talked about whether the youth should stay behind or leave Hong Kong (emigration). Behind bars, his analysis of the political turmoil was often apt and penetrating, even when read years later. If prison is a form of "total institution" and prisoners are undergoing "re-socialization," controlled and remoulded in every aspect as he used to teach in university, he rightly posits that Hong Kong is, in this sense, a "big prison" after all these years and in many aspects. Despite his imprisonment due to his political stance, his will remained strong and as inspired by Bonhoeffer's words, he is determined to simply suffer ". . . – that is what will be needed then – not parries, blows or thrusts such as may still be possible or admissible in the preliminary fight, the real struggle that perhaps lies ahead must simply be to suffer faithfully."[6] Such wisdom of Bonhoeffer is still fitting now.

Response
On the Summary

Although the world has been disrupted by COVID-19 since 2020, the book is focused on the author's imprisonment due to the 2014 Umbrella Movement. Initially, this may give readers an impression which is a little bit distanced. This is because many things have happened, and we feel that events have been going very fast. The social unrest in Hong Kong was hit by the COVID-19 pandemic in late 2019. The National Security Law was imposed on 30 June 2020. Protesters, politicians, news reporters, and media tycoons have been arrested, detained, and imprisoned. Whether with or without COVID vaccines, elderly people were infected, and many died. Families and friends left this place for the West. In light of the rapidity of events, Chan's suffering in 2019–20 seems long, long ago. Yet we are truly grateful for what Chan and others have sacrificed. What they have done has "awakened" Hongkongers from our materialistic and self-centred dreams. And those awakened will not fall asleep again, whether we stay or leave.

---

6. Dietrich Bonhoeffer, Letter 28 April 1934, *Dietrich Bonhoeffer Works*, vol. 13: *London: 1933–1935*, ed. Keith Clements, trans. Isabel Best (Minneapolis, Minnesota: Fortress Press, 2007), 135. Quoted in Chan, *Chan Kin-Man's Prison Writings*, 223.

In My Context

Nowadays, fighting for democracy can be something on the verge of breaking laws. Yet the core of the pursuit is about defending what was originally promised by the central government to the citizens. At the core of the Hong Kong protests lie the demands which are in line with the principles our Creator has laid out in the Bible. To name a few key ones: the freedom to express oneself, being treated with fairness (disregarding one's social status and political stance), effective checks and balances for the government administration, requiring those who have authority and power to be held accountable to the society, and more basically, the right of the people to choose their own leaders. Chan's thoughts, along the teachings of Dietrich Bonhoeffer and Martin Luther King Jr., are very relevant to the real needs of Hong Kong. As Christians, we ought to connect with the common people through our walk with them in real terms, not within the walls of churches. Chan is one who is doing this.

Our Commitment

Truly, Hongkongers are living in a big city-prison, especially for those who are unable to leave. Reading Chan's letters was like reading a friend's sharing, sent to someone who is in prison. The resonances, though seemly "far away" as mentioned, are clear and strong. Václav Havel's idea of living in truth is a good reminder for those who need to face various kinds of falsehood and hypocrisy under authoritarian regimes. Chan's encouragement and testimony to "suffer faithfully" has demonstrated his commitment to truth, his God and this place. Even though readers are in various situations, we need to renew our commitment to God for living in truth, for speaking truthfully in our own particular situations. We pray that, on every Sunday, the sermons that are delivered and heard in the churches here will shine forth as God's words of truth, such that people's hearts are warmed, enlightened, and strengthened to bear the darkness and coldness of this sinful world.

Reflection

A Prayer

Lord of Hong Kong,
Have mercy on us while we suffer, no matter it is we ourselves
or our neighbours, youngsters or professors, poor or rich.

Walk with us while we go through a dark
tunnel with no end in sight.
Sigh with us when the ridiculous news comes every day. They
simply do not know what they are doing, the significance of
destroying this city's system of fairness and righteousness.
Judge us when we ignore your truth, when we
pretend to be asleep and not see the needs of
others and the hypocrisies in the society.
God on high, hear our prayers for Hongkongers –
Bring them peace, bring them joy, bring
them justice and, above all,
bring them home, to your presence wherever they may be.

Hong Kong

Authentic Forgiveness: A Biblical Approach[1]
John C. W. Tran

Contributed by Loreen Maseno (Kenya)

Summary

In this book, John Tran considers the parameters of forgiveness in Chinese and Western contexts. According to Tran, forgiving is difficult – so much so that we all end up creating a wide variety of homemade solutions. Further, forgiveness has a variety of meanings and expressions within different cultures. These solutions are temporal and are designed only to save face. Not all of these solutions and practices are biblically based, nor are they life-affirming.

Forgiveness is not forgetting the past nor maintaining harmony at all costs; rather, it is a social transaction that comprises genuine repentance by the offender, the offer of forgiveness by the victim to the offender, and the restoration of a broken relationship by the parties involved. But how should the offender repent? Genuine repentance should consist of remorse, restitution, and renewal. Forgiveness should align with what Jesus taught his disciples, in which case complete healing can happen and genuine communion can be restored.

Tran posits that there are important influences from our contexts that distort the practice of forgiveness within churches. These distortions arise mainly due to our understandings of forgiveness being rooted in cultural contexts. This is often exemplified when people "forgive" by forgetting the past – passively accepting it – in order to avoid conflict and maintain outward harmony or to achieve self-healing, but without dealing with the damaged relationship. Still others "forgive" by simply pretending that all is well.

Tran suggests that Christians in Hong Kong, where he is a minister, are deeply rooted in Confucianism, with its elements of respect, hierarchy, connectedness in community, social harmony, submissiveness, public

---

1. Carlisle, UK: Langham Global Library, 2020.

conformity, and inexpressiveness. Western culture brought to Hong Kong certain influences such as individualism, human self-worth, and personal dignity. In Western cultures, unilateral forgiveness is the norm for the purpose of self-love and private intrapsychic release. This is catastrophic for the Christian community because there is no sense of reconciliation of broken relationships or restoration of communion. A unilateral act from an individual trivializes forgiveness by making it therapeutically easy so victims feel better (though perhaps only superficially so) by simply letting go. Since Christianity is not a solitary endeavour, Tran argues that the Christian community should not be directed by individualism.

He takes readers to another level when he notes that conflict and brokenness are inevitable on the journey of life. Accordingly, unless we altogether refuse to enter into relationships, conflict and hurt are inevitable. However, he notes that it is possible to transform hurt from being life-destructive to being life-constructive by way of forgiveness. Both parties need to strive for reconciliation of the broken relationship.

Tran maps out seven voices from seven select books which touch on the themes of conflict, sin, hurt, and forgiveness. These books in sum point to the inevitability of sin, conflict, and daily hurt. Tran describes seven steps of sin, beginning from innocence and proceeding to maximum profanity – worship of the devil. He further shows that conflict and hurt are inevitable, but these also provide opportunities for a person to be strengthened. However, strengthening only occurs only if hurting people: choose carefully which pain and hurt to respond to and how to respond to them; listen to critics; do a self-examination; get good advice; be honest and kind; forgive and reconcile; and allow God to access one's heart. From an eighth book, Tran summarizes that hurt has three dimensions – personal pain, unfair pain, and deep pain.

Tran borrows from L. Gregory Jones in addressing the meaning of authentic forgiveness.[2] He notes that forgiveness involves accountability and that one cannot separate forgiveness from justice. Forgiveness without repentance invites continuity of sin, while repentance without forgiveness can lead to despair. The importance of authentic forgiveness in practice is seen in the act of taking the risk of reopening the relationship and allowing trust to regerminate. Forgiveness recognizes the complexity of reopening the future in risk, restoring relationships in trust, and recreating the nature of that alliance. Authentic forgiveness is a risky affair but one which can reconcile us

---

2. Tran, *Authentic Forgiveness*, 40. See also L. Gregory Jones, *Embodying Forgiveness: A Theological Analysis*, (Grand Rapids, Michigan: Wm. B. Eerdmans Publishing Co., 1995).

to ourselves, to God, and to each other. True forgiveness leads to embrace as opposed to exclusion. To move from exclusion to embrace, there is need for repentance, forgiveness, and making space in oneself for the other and for the healing of memory. As such, forgiveness is not a quick fix but a long, deep, difficult, and painful process of wrestling with the injury and risking a return to conversation and a resumption of relationship.

Tran takes the readers to what he calls the foundations of authentic forgiveness, for which the Bible is the standard. Here we take the love and mercy of Jesus seriously and act according to God's mandate. While forgiveness is desirable, oftentimes it ends up being hypocritical and self-seeking. Tran urges believers to practice biblical forgiveness, something he considers a better path than what we have been accustomed to. For Tran, no matter the nature and extent of wrongdoing, we can and should forgive so as to cultivate an attitude of love for the offender in true reconciliation, even as one works through the anger and the pain. Tran suggests a plan of action that can be implemented in the church and offers final words for our reflection. He suggests a one-year plan which churches can follow if they really want their members to experience authentic forgiveness.

In conclusion, just as repentance is a necessary response to divine forgiveness and salvation offered by Jesus, so must perpetrators of injustice repent. Repentance has three elements from biblical foundations: remorse, restitution, and renewal. For the church which would like to practice authentic forgiveness, the following is necessary: acceptance of the inevitability of conflict, offering forgiveness, understanding authentic forgiveness, confronting trivializing cultural influences, practicing authentic forgiveness, and cultivating authentic forgiveness as a way of life. As we have been forgiven, so must we forgive through genuine repentance and reconciliation in broken relationships.

Response
On the Summary
My reaction to the thoughts of the author was an immediate identification with the Eastern culture of Hong Kong – that of hierarchy, respect, communality, and insistence on (outward) harmony around me. I saw in these cultural norms similarities with my own cultural background. The book was an eye-opener about how I have handled conflicts and situations of hurt.

The author's suggestion that one needs to choose which pain and hurt is worth responding to – and which can be ignored – was alien to me, because it was not clear what would be the criteria or threshold for that selection.

In My Context

Tran's words are relevant to my context. In the face of increasing wickedness and hurt in my country, forgiveness is central – but that must be authentic forgiveness. The biblical principles for authentic forgiveness remain relevant to any and all Christians.

I have learned that passive and individualized forgiveness is not sufficient on the journey of faith: I must include the component of reconciliation of broken relationships or restoration of communion. This changes my practice of forgiveness to seek to have a restored communion, to avoid exclusion, and to insist on embracing.

Our Commitment

This book leads me to seek reconciliation and to risk in order to have restored relationships. This will necessarily impact not only my practices of forgiveness, but also my thinking and my worship. My repentance cannot follow the so-easy exclusionary options and tendencies in the face of conflict or hurt. I am challenged to leave my gift at the altar and be reconciled with my brothers and sisters.

Reflection

A Prayer

Jesus, as you forgave so help me forgive. I want to forgive authentically and I want to be a peacemaker who thrives in reconciliation and restoration of communion. Please help me, God.

Hong Kong

The Courage to Live: Reimagining the Gospel for Our Times[1]
Tsz Fung Tin

Contributed by Barry Cheung (Hong Kong)

Summary

Tin's main task in this book is to articulate the meaning of the gospel in the present context of Hong Kong. He first describes what Hong Kong people lost in the past years. They lost their familiar social environment due to the collapse of democracy. Under the wave of emigration, they lost their close relationships with friends and relatives. While they see little hope for the future, they feel lost along the life journey ahead. In face of these threefold losses, Tin attempts to renew our understanding of the gospel, which is not only for the individual's salvation in the far future, but also addresses the current struggles of the people and cultivates the virtue of courage for them to live resiliently.

After the introduction, the book's chapters develop a way of perceiving the gospel through different theological perspectives. Tin gives an outline of how Hong Kong churches understood the gospel one-sidedly in the past, influenced by the rise of the capitalism in Hong Kong. Then he retrieves different resources from the Bible and the Reformation tradition in order to reimagine the meaning of the gospel for Hong Kong people today. For example, the author reminds us that the tradition of the lamentation in the Old Testament is very relevant to the mental conditions which Hong Kong people experience now. God's people could voice their grief and sadness in front of God, their Lord. Tin also introduces Moltmann's theology of the God who suffers to open a horizon in which to perceive God's solidarity with people in their sufferings. This emphasis on God's humanity leads us to see how God remembers his beloved people without keeping a distance.

Tin spends two chapters exploring the functions of the biblical narrative and emphasizes that readers of the Bible could get a new meaning of life

---

1. Hong Kong: FES Press, 2022. [Chinese]

through interweaving their life stories with biblical narratives. This kind of new insight could transform our vision and empower us through recharging our inner energies. For example, Tin guides us to read the story of Jesus talking with his disciples on the road to Emmaus in Luke 24. The expression, "their eyes were opened" (v. 31), should be understood as God opening their eyes to see his presence. The same word "open" is repeated in the review of the journey, "Were not our hearts burning within us while he talked with us on the road and opened the Scriptures to us?" (v. 31). "Open the Scriptures to us" means to give out the meaning of the Bible so that they could understand now. The same experience would be shared with the contemporary readers while they are eager to see any new possibility from God in their own desperate situation.

More importantly, the author encourages the readers to open their hearts and to sense the movement of the Holy Spirit. In response to turbulent times, Christians should seek their personal callings from God with the guidance of the Holy Spirit and get emotional support from the church community. It is an urgent call to restore soul care to our churches. Individuals cannot walk through the darkness by themselves, alone, but should come together to deal with the critical issues with love and encouragement in Christ. At the end, they will rebuild the church community through the revival power and the healing grace of the triune God. In this sense, we look forward to transforming the church community through engagement with challenges and crises.

Response
On the Summary

Tin's book is a valuable resource for Christians living in Hong Kong to understand their ecclesial life, mental conditions, and their social environment. Though only a brief explanation is given in each section, the overall presentation offers a helpful theological overview for handling the key issues which the church in Hong Kong cannot avoid. Depression and post-traumatic stress resulting from major social unrest in Hong Kong could not be resolved or settled quickly. The people bearing these symptoms seek mental and spiritual care with different levels of diagnosis and/or professional assistance. For Christians, the religious perspective is also a kind of belief and practice in which they are looking for comfort and peace. Tin's book would be a timely gift for those who feel confused or hopeless for the future. It would be a good starting place for them to find ways of understanding God's plan and get their own pace in their life journey. If someone looks for a deeper reflection on the struggles of the Christian life, Tin's book may not provide sufficient guidance.

It is a good introduction for various related themes but does not offer a deeper line of thought on specific topics.

My Context

After 2019, almost two million people in Hong Kong are estimated to have experienced symptoms of post-traumatic stress disorder (commonly known as PTSD) during the social unrest in the city. If you are involved in or witness a traumatic event, it is common to experience upsetting, distressing, or confusing feelings afterwards. The feelings of distress may not emerge straight away, but later you may develop emotional and physical reactions, such as feeling easily upset or not being able to sleep. Tin is fully aware of the conditions of the people's mental health and encourages readers of his book to name the emotions they bear and to retell the traumatic experience(s) they had. Wounded people have the right to cry out to God. Lament is a personal expression in a specific situation, and with this precious gift we could compose our own laments and make them our cries to God, our Lord. Tin observes that humans are by nature relational beings, with an eagerness to share with others their personal experiences. However, in reality, we see that many people do not want to open themselves to God or other people because they have experienced so much mistrust or hurt in human relations. The church should correspondingly exercise the very important task of rebuilding faithful relationships among the believers and with their neighbours.

Our Commitment

Under the wave of emigration, the churches in Hong Kong are reminded here and now of the time for renewal. We are aware that many people are trying out new pastoral models. Both pastors and believers understand that they cannot stay in the old way of thinking. The churches have embarked on the road to "recovery," not by going back to the past, but by courageously facing the truth, admitting ignorance and incompetence, seeking the liberation of humanity brought by the gospel, leaving behind the habit of hierarchical thinking, and seeking a way out from common collaboration. Only in God's mercy and grace can the churches be restored to their true self.

The Sunset at Mong Kok[2]

The Sunset at Mong Kok is a painting by two young ladies. They want to show that "this city is beautiful because the people here are beautiful." Nathan Road, the main road in Kowloon, Hong Kong, is in the middle of the painting. We see the prosperous and busy scene around this road, filled with warmth and joy radiated by the sunshine.

---

2. © all things bright and beautiful. Used with permission.

India

"The Problem of Suffering: A Theological Analysis"[1]
Christina Manohar

Contributed by Lanuwabang Jamir (India)

Summary

Suffering, persecution of the church, and the cry of the martyrs have been part of the history of the church since its beginnings. The church in India has also seen its own share of persecution for the sake of the gospel. This article was first presented in the annual Centre for Mission Studies (CMS) of Union Biblical Seminary, Pune Consultation, along with J. Edwin Davids's *Persecution and Suffering According to Peter* and Roger E. Hedlund's *Response to Persecution and Suffering in the History of Christian Mission* (chapters three and five in the book) – each highlighting the perennial issue of persecution and suffering in the history of the Indian church.

Suffering is universal. But how do Christians respond to this pertinent question of the origin and the meaning and purpose of suffering? Christina Manohar's "The Problem of Suffering" provides a thorough discussion on the different perspectives on suffering based on the work of many Christian theologians and thinkers. Among others, she explores the work of Raymond Pannikkar (1918–2010), a Roman Catholic theologian, who affirms that suffering is an integral part of creation and that there is a redemptive component in suffering. But suffering is not just a part of humanity; it is more of a divine problem. It is in pain that communion takes place between God and humans, which is stated as "the cosmo-theandric mystery of reality." The Creator God is not detached from his creation or suffering but sacrifices himself for its redemption and unity because God, the cosmos, and humanity are all integrally connected with each other. A similar view on the relationship between God, creation, and suffering is seen in the works of German philosophers

---

1. In *Persecution and Suffering: Christian Reflections and Responses*, edited by Mark T. B. Laing, 58–78. Contextual Theological Education Series 23. Delhi: ISPCK, 2002.

Schelling (1775–1854), Hegel (1770–1831), and Jewish theologian Isaak Luria (1534–1572). Manohar provides a similar viewpoint as that of Gunther Schiwy: each affirms that this perspective of God's suffering in creation gives us the motivation to pursue the same for the sake of others and, in doing so, we participate in God's suffering.

She then presents another perspective on the problem of evil and suffering by referring to Karl Barth's concept of *das Nichtige* ("the void"). Das Nichtige originated in the process of creation when God rejected what he had not willed. It stands in primary opposition to God and reveals itself in sin, pain, suffering and death. In that sense, humans are only the secondary target. Since the primary attack is on God, the battle with evil is God's own affair. Though evil has some resemblance of power now, God has ultimately destroyed it through Jesus Christ and also uses it to serve his purpose.

Manohar then presents the view of Paul Tillich (1886–1965) who sees evil and suffering as a result of the exercise of human freedom. In other words, it is sin which leads to self-centredness affecting all relationships. The essence of being a human means that sin becomes part of one's existence. Similarly, the traditional Christian view, as held by Augustine (354–430), also understood that humanity's misuse of freedom leads to sin, resulting in suffering. However, God still uses all these failures to fulfil his ultimate purpose. However, as Edgar S. Brightman (1884–1953) points out, there are problems with this understanding, namely that ultimately evil is good; one can even argue that good is, in reality, evil and thus human ethical responsibility becomes irrelevant. Finitism seems to be the right approach to navigate these issues of evil and suffering; God's intention for humanity is good, but evil and suffering occur because God is self-limited.

She also highlights Gordon H. Clark's (1902–1985) dealings with the question of "Can a good God cause suffering?" He understands God as an arbitrary ruler who can cause humans to sin, but ultimately it will result in good. She then highlights the relevance of Jesus as the liberator in a world wrought with suffering due to human greed, precisely because God identified with humans' suffering.

An important aspect of this article is that Manohar explores the Indian concept of *satyagraha*, which is a non-violent resistance to overcome evil. Satyagraha involves renouncing world pleasures, taking on hardship, including excommunication from family – undergoing suffering willingly, without resentment, to establish truth and for a good cause. Though satyagraha was practiced by many Indian heroes for a good cause, it cannot be compared with the suffering of Jesus who suffered solely for the sake of others at the cross. The issue of vicarious suffering is discussed from the viewpoint of Brahmabandhab Upadhyay (1861–1907), an important Indian theologian. Vicarious suffering is a common experience of humanity because all are interconnected and interdependent. In similar manner, blessings also come due to the good works of others. Jesus's death on the cross could be understood in the same way – the sufferings of Christ brought forgiveness and life for others. More importantly, this virtue of suffering for one another brings about love and care for one another in the community. Another important idea Manohar deals with is the law of karma – which basically means that "whatsoever a man sows he also reaps" (cf. Gal 6:7) but which does not give room for suffering on behalf of others. However, in the biblical principle, a person reaps what is sown by another (John 4:37). In that sense, suffering becomes an integral part of Christian living, through which one bears one another's burdens. Christina then concludes the issue of suffering by returning to the theme of the centrality of the cross of Christ which is the meaningful part in the whole unending discourse. By reflecting on the profound action of the self-emptying (*kenosis*) of the omnipotent God (Phil 2:6–9), we see the need and responsibility for Christians to do the same for the sake of others. Participating in the suffering of the Christ implies that we participate in the same ministry of reconciliation and alleviate human suffering by bringing a reversal in an unjust world order.

Response
On the Summary

The theological problem of evil and suffering in this world created by the all-powerful God is analyzed through the works of various theologians and thinkers. Christina Monahar reviews a comprehensive debate, referring to both eastern and western thinkers on the most difficult question as to why evil exists in this world in relation to theodicy. The variety of views on this shows that the answer remains inconclusive. Nonetheless the incarnation shows a dimension of the necessity of suffering and the involvement of the Godhead in it. In that, the positive dimension of suffering is portrayed as an essential reality; this, in turn, leads us to appreciate the other side of human existence in its eschatological culmination.

The various theological perspectives highlighted in this article help one to be aware of the spectrum wherein suffering and theodicy can be understood. The points highlighted by Panikkar, Barth and others – that God is integrally part of the suffering of humanity – gives a worldview in which the divine is part of the struggles and pain of humanity. God not only shares in the suffering with creation, but it is his own suffering manifested in creation. And this answers in part the biggest question, "Why does God allow suffering?" Further, the understanding that suffering has a purifying value gives a sense of purpose in a world which is self-centred and individualistic. It also can provide a sense of assurance and consolation to people going through difficult times that God is near to those who are suffering.

Manohar has highlighted that one's attitude towards suffering can change when it is seen against the backdrop of the suffering of Christ – a symbol of selfless service, love and offering to the world. The comparison of Christian sufferings with the Indian concept of satyagraha and the understanding of karma highlights the significance of the gospel, as well as suffering for others, and how one's life is interrelated with others.

Whether it is Panikkar or Barth, suffering is seen as something in which God is actively involved, and one can see God's greater purpose in suffering. This fits the biblical concept of God's sovereignty and purpose and helps one to see meaning, even in the midst of perverse suffering. At the same time, it also betrays the presence of the cosmic forces that are at war with God's children. As Barth has highlighted, there is a positive dimension for it is only in the context of evil and suffering that grace could exist. It reminds us of God's covenantal faithfulness and election. It shows that God is directly involved in everything that involves humanity. Barth shows the importance of the incarnation and resurrection of Christ as a victory over evil and suffering. Jesus Christ in his incarnation subjected himself to suffering, but resisted and overcame evil and suffering and this gives us hope.

Suffering is an integral part of our existence. The question about the existence of evil in relation to theodicy cannot be fully comprehended as the different views in different religious traditions show. Manohar rightly concludes that theology cannot give an absolute answer to the pertinent question. However, suffering with a greater purpose which is exemplified at the cross, and which is unique in Christian tradition, can give relevance to the church in its mission to the world.

In My Context

Suffering and persecution of the church in India is a prevalent reality. Many will grapple with the issue of suffering and its relation to belief in an omnipotent God. It is important that the Indian church is aware of the different perspectives on suffering through which a theology of suffering can be developed, also using the Indian cultural and philosophical traditions, so that the gospel becomes relevant in the Indian context. Though the idea of the origin of evil and suffering is a complicated one, a consolation to the believers in India is that God is not detached from the experiences and suffering of the church but is intimately involved and affected. This is proved when one understands the implication of him sending his own son as a sacrifice for the redemption of humanity. This is the basis of how one should perceive suffering even in present time – that it has a redemptive value not only for oneself but, in a mysterious way, for the bigger community. At the end, all evil and suffering become relative, as the cross is the place where it is negated.

The main idea contained in this article helps one to narrow down the essential points that can give meaning and significance to one's experience in the midst of suffering. In the Indian context, suffering can have a broader context, such as poverty, oppression and so on, along with the persecution for one's faith. We need to affirm the interrelatedness of one another, not only among humans but the whole universe, as seen in the work of Panikkar, for we all reflect the image of God. This is an important lesson for the Indian context where casteism is another factor in suffering that affects even the church. And we need to be respectful of the multicultural and religious traditions as well.

The connection Manohar brings between the cross and one's responsibility in society is an important one. Many Indians are from the rural context where suffering in the form of various kinds of oppression often takes place. The call for all to participate in revering the cross, which implies participation in voicing out against injustices, is an important call for the Indian church. The chapter is a good reminder that those who follow Jesus indeed will have to carry the cross as well but, in the midst of these sufferings, proper direction to the faith community based on the Scripture can help them find meaning and purpose in all their sufferings.

Our Commitment

We pray for the church that is persecuted and those in the midst of suffering who are trying to find meaning in it. We pray that the word of God will be made accessible to many who still do not have access to it, and that the Bible becomes the foundation upon which they build their faith. We pray for patience and perseverance in the midst of suffering, that God's ultimate plan will be fulfilled at the end.

Reflection

Unbroken Legacy

Exuberant rejoicing
But for a season
Heaviness overtakes you
Thought unspeakable tribulation

Dragged down, laid low
Still the undying spirit tarried on
The cross a symbolic heavenly reminder
Christ's legacy should unceasingly
Be carried on.

India

"Lessons from Orissa: Peacemaking in the Face of Anti-Christian Violence"[1]
Richard Howell

Contributed by Lanuwabang Jamir (India)

Summary

Richard Howell's chapter, "Lessons from Orissa: Peacemaking in the Face of Anti-Christian Violence," provides an excellent case study of how Christians should respond even when persecution and violence is at its worst. In 2008, the violence against Christians in Orissa[2] was one of the worst ever recorded in Indian church history: scores were killed, beaten, raped, houses burned, thousands were displaced, and forced proselytization to Hinduism took place. It was an ethnic cleansing of Christians by the militant group of the Sangh Parivar, a supremacist Hindu group. It was triggered after a political leader along with four others were killed by Maoist guerrillas, for which the Christians were blamed.

Howell traces the genesis of this communalization of Hindus against Christians and other minorities back through the long history of Hindu fundamentalism, which had its beginnings in the 1870s and 1920s. In three stages of development, Hindu fundamentalism has permeated not only the religious, but also the cultural, ethnic, and political spheres, by exploiting political and communal issues. The ideology of militancy and violence was advocated as early as the 1930s through leaders like Vir Savarkar and others. Howell shows how these leaders were able to achieve their goals by infusing their religious ideology with nationalism. In doing so they were able to infiltrate and influence every level of social and political life. Another effective method

---

1. In *Violence and Peace: Creating a Culture of Peace in the Contemporary Context of Violence, Papers from the 15th Annual CMS Consultation UBS, Pune*, edited by F. F. Fox, 49–68. Bangalore: ATC & CMS, 2010.

2. Odisha is a state in Eastern India on the coast of the Bay of Bengal; its legal name in English was changed from Orissa in 2011.

highlighted is the fear-psychosis that is created by the propaganda machinery of the movement. Their main ideology is to create an exclusive Hindu nation into which the other cultures and religions are to be assimilated and their identities destroyed. As in many similar instances, they use religious language, traditions, and rationalization to legitimize acts of violence against others.

In the next section he deals with the violence against Christians. In the midst of these stark realities, how do Christians respond to such violence? He reminds the church to respond within the framework of the command to love one's neighbour, even when they act as our enemy. This response was exemplified by Christ when he responded to the crucifixion with his offer of forgiveness to those who committed the barbaric act. Based on such a Christian principle, Howell states that justice for the perpetrators of such crimes should also include forgiveness and reconciliation. While naming, remembering, and condemning injustice is a prerequisite for reconciliation to happen, we respond to injustice not with violence and retribution, or else evil will succeed; instead, the way forward is to overcome evil with good. He also asserts that the best form of condemnation is shown in the act of forgiving the doers of such act and thus separating the perpetrators from their deeds.

Howell asserts that, instead of revenge, repentance should be part of the response to persecution, as this brings transformation and hope and empowers the victims and likewise disempowers the oppressors. For repentance brings about new creation in the midst of the old and effects transformation for the rest. This is necessary because it can be easy even for the oppressed to inherit the values of persecution and become like their oppressors. He also asserts that one should accept suffering as an integral part of our Christian identity and should be willing to suffer for the sake of true justice. Only then can we find meaning and significance in the midst of these sufferings, as well as empathizing with those who suffer. Based on the cross of Christ, Christians should live out their faith as a witnessing community so that, through their lifestyles and testimonies, they will provide an alternate way of life to those engaged in violence. This indeed was demonstrated by the believers in Orissa, who stood for the gospel, even as everything was destroyed around them.

Response
On the Summary
Howell's chapter is helpful in understanding the history and the cause of Hindu fundamentalism. The in-depth analysis of their ideology, the strategies used, and the growth of this movement is an important resource for us to understand

the root of this movement – which is necessary if we are to respond to the issue of fundamentalism in India. He presents the significant danger that this movement has for the whole nation and for the existence of other minorities. In contrast to the ideology of Hindu fundamentalism that is based on violence and retaliation, he shows the unique Christian response of non-violence and forgiveness. As he shows, violence can be immensely empowering and give potency to the masses, and this potency is exploited by the leaders. But Christians are to derive their potency in the power of forgiveness. Yet, the church needs to speak out against injustices to anyone or else history will repeat itself.

The call for peace and reconciliation in the midst of human suffering and tragedies is a radical approach which can be actualized only if one's faith and conviction is based on the suffering and forgiveness of Christ exemplified on the cross. The calls for repentance on the part of the persecuted people are a powerful message, for only when they are first transformed with kingdom values will they be able to respond to the oppressors in a manner compatible with the gospel message. Repentance is not only a response to the persecution suffered by the church but can be a catalyst to bring transformation to the society as a whole. The point that he highlights is an eye-opener – that both the oppressed and the oppressors need repentance and transformation to bring about reconciliation.

In My Context

This is an important case study of persecution of Christians in India. It is important to first understand the history of any movement and its impact, if we are to respond to it. Christian scholarship is thus necessary to make a concerted effort to deal with issues like religious fundamentalism. The church also needs to strategize very carefully and elaborately against these attacks since it is deeply rooted in every aspect of the society. Moreover, because many of the believers are first generation Christians, persecutions start within the family. Many are led to give up their faith due to external pressures and persecution.

Howell's chapter presents the danger that the Hindu fundamentalism poses for the very existence of the church, since the demand is to give up the theology and mission of the church and conform to the Hindu belief system. The Christian response Howell gives can provide further directions to the ongoing response of the persecuted church. The Bible and the cross should remain the central point of reference for any action or response on the part of the church. Another factor is the rise in false theologies like the prosperity gospel which can bring about false expectation and disillusionment in the face of suffering, so a proper and relevant theology of suffering needs to be preached.

Another helpful process of healing that he recommends is the act of remembering the atrocities by the community. This can serve as an act of justice; channelling that act in the direction of reconciliation can be an effective way of healing the community's pain through participation. The church needs to stand united and overcome the denominational differences which often cause a barrier in the fight for justice and truth. At the same time, Christian sensitivity is required in witnessing in the Indian context. Also, the church should not be focused on numerical growth, but growth based on true Christian convictions so that the church will be able to stand the test of times.

Our Commitment

- We pray for all the martyrs, that their seeds of sacrifice will bear the fruits for church growth.
- We pray for courage to be more proactive in participating and identifying with the persecuted church.
- We must focus on the centrality of the cross and the suffering Christ which provides the ultimate example and response to the issue of suffering and persecution of the Indian church and elsewhere.

Reflection

Oppression

In the dead silence of a sultry dark night
A piercing cry rips the stillness
Trampled? Ripped off? Beaten? Butchered?
Beheaded? Enslaved? Raped? Burned down?
Heartbeat racing, mind exploding
Groping for a long-lost answer

Huddled in somewhere yonder
A poverty-stricken mama breast feeding
Her newborn babe
When out of nowhere a bullet hits her
Blood spurting leaving her lifeless
While the infant babe is still suckling on
Blanketed in mama's crimson flow

A long ago ghastly event
Deeply buried lost and forgotten
But the deep etched scars and the pathetic
cries of the martyrs
In the deep abyss of my mind sets an explosion
of confusion and writhing pain
Reliving each nightmarish moment
All over again.

India

"A Christian Response to Hindutva"[1]
L. Stanislaus

Contributed by Lanuwabang Jamir (India)

Summary

In his chapter "A Christian Response to Hindutva," Stanislaus provides excellent coverage of the whole issue of Hindu fundamentalism in India in the form of the Hindutva ideology and movement and its effect upon the church in India. As the ideology creeps in and effects every aspect of Indian society, the chapter focuses on the Christian response which has to be multifaceted due to the nature of the ideology and the peculiarity of the Indian context. Stanislaus advocates Christian engagement in politics because Hindutva is political in nature and not a religious movement. It aims to achieve its mission for Hindu hegemony through the control of the state apparatus and every other means, including violence. So, he asserts that the church should not be merely confined within the church compound but must be engaged in political participation in every level of the society. Moreover, he calls for the church to cooperate with other faith communities in its stand against this threat. Women need to be further encouraged to participate, not only because they are twice affected but to be a counter voice against the female voice within the Hindutva movement. The church should be vocal in its stand against this threat by participating in a protest movement, which will also have the effect of bringing awareness to all.

Stanislaus highlights the process of cultural homogenization based on caste hierarchy being imposed by the Hindutva movement that results in the subjugation of other subaltern sections of society. This is evident in the imposition of food restrictions, demand for the Sanskrit language to be learned by all, creation of new symbols of national identity, and the acceptance of hierarchical structures. In response, the church should promote the

---

1. In *Nationalism and Hindutva: A Christian Response, Papers from the 10th CMS Consultation*, edited by Mark T. B. Laing, 177–203. Delhi: ISPCK, 2005.

multiculturalism of India, which is seen in its diverse cultures and traditions, to counteract attempts to bring about a monoculture which is against the very ethos and values of the Indian society. Since Hindutva oppresses and negates other identities (except Hindu identity), the church should act as a catalyst so that minorities can assert their own identities, which is an important part of the liberative process. Stanislaus also asserts that the church should develop and affirm the Indianness of the Christian faith, since to a larger extent the Hindutva critique of the church has to do with the colonial face of Christianity in India.

He further asserts that the church should respond to the issue of Christian conversion, which is seen by Hindutva advocates as a proselytization achieved by coercion and allurements and as anti-national. This has led to anti-conversion laws being implemented in some states giving power to the district collectors to decide whether a person can convert or not.[2] Any aberrations that come under these legislations makes such offences cognizable. At the same time, the Hindutva forces are more intimidated by liberation theology since it disrupts the social hierarchical order that helps them to maintain their dominance over people at the margins.

The strategy of violence employed by proponents of Hindutva as the means to suppress the religious minorities and the downtrodden should be responded to by the church as a whole – not through counter-violence, but by continuing with the just activities. By fighting this battle, the church should be ready even for martyrdom. Stanislaus maintains that the church's response should not be limited only to the threats by extremist movements and when Christians are directly persecuted but should always be the voice for the voiceless. It is through the active participation of the church in establishing a just society that the reign of God is actualized in and through the church. By building a just society, the church will be able to confront the main tenet of Hindutva ideology, that is, to dominate others though perpetuation of structural hierarchy.

The advocacy of religious nationalism, with Hindu identity as the only accepted national identity, is a particularly dangerous aspect of the Hindutva movement. India is a secular state which constitutionally allows for plurality of cultures and religion. But the downside of such secular pluralism, according to Stanislaus, is that it does not allow much religious engagement in society. In response to this dilemma, he proposes that the church should promote

---

2. Editors' note: In Indian local government, district collectors are the the highest-ranking officer of revenue in a district's governmental administration. These officers are political appointees of the state government.

humanistic nationalism. It entails the church focusing on nation building by ensuring that democracy is safeguarded and by upholding and safeguarding the intrinsic value and dignity of every person.

Stanislaus also recommends prophetic dialogue with proponents of Hindutva, which should be characterized by respectful openness to one another, in order to challenge and facilitate correction. However, he also raises the question whether dialogue in all its fairness will be possible with them. Persecution is carried upon false premises and propaganda based on faulty research suggesting that Hindus and others will become a minority. To counter such views the church should also respond by initiating research studies and presenting the real data and truth. The church should then engage in dissemination of correct information at both local and national levels since attacks on Christians are a result of "hate" materials and propaganda against the church. The church should also mobilize protests when its rights are violated. He concludes that the main intention of these responses is that the reign of God is made known to all, for which one should also be ready to die.

Response
On the Summary

Stanislaus provides thorough research on the way the Hindutva movement is trying to infiltrate all of Indian society in order to gain dominance. As shown in the discussion, this can happen through varied ways. The Hindutva movement tries to force people to conform to their way of thinking, speech, and behaviour; this is also a form of persecution. The ideology of violence that Hindutva propagates openly – especially against Christians – shows the seriousness of the matter at hand. In fact, the danger that it poses is not only to the church but the nation as a whole. Though his primary concern is about Christian persecution, Stanislaus looks at the bigger issue of marginalized people, their suffering, and the church's responsibility to alleviate such suffering. Thus, the church needs to stand in solidarity with awakening movements that are increasing among the subaltern groups and which are in line with Jesus's mission to liberate the marginalized.

The practical steps that Stanislaus provides to deal with persecution arising from religious fundamentalism and intolerance has relevance for believers worldwide who also find themselves in similar situations. It is relevant for minority people groups, witnessing their faith alongside other dominant and, at times, hostile majority groups. His message that the Indian church has to be proactive in engaging with the issue of persecution and beyond should find resonance with the global church. Many Christians tend to shy away from politics due to various reasons, including corruption, and this is an important aspect of his article. Christians should be encouraged to participate in the civil and political life as an expression of their faith, which is the need of the hour.

His assertion that the church should identify with the oppressed and the marginalized, since they can be persecuted even more, gets to the heart of the issue for many communities around the world. The alternative humanistic nationalism that he proposes for nation building whereby justice, equality, and fellowship of all is achieved is a challenge to the church that is currently mainly focused on charity works. At the same time, we should also respond to the issue at hand at a spiritual level for the powers behind the worldly manifestation of human forces are spiritual powers. More importantly, persecution should not deter us from being witnesses to those people who instigate violence so that their lives are also transformed.

In My Context

Stanislaus provides not only a study on why the church in India is persecuted but also an elaborate response to the issues at hand. The practical steps presented are surely relevant to the church in India to deal with this stark reality. Indian contexts are unique and multifaceted; thus, the church needs to response in a manner that is effective and multifaceted. The call for political engagement for Christians, especially the empowerment of the weaker sections of the national community, is the need of the hour. Politically engaged Christians can be involved in governmental decision making and, when policies are drawn up, can have an impact on all, especially safeguarding the rights of the minorities. As Stanislaus has rightly pointed out, the church needs to both move its activities out of the confines of its compound wall and to overcome the compartmentalization of spiritual and worldly matters.

His stand that the church should be relevant to the Indian context by incorporating its cultural traditions and transforming the Indian context in the process is truly essential. It is also a wakeup call for the church to receive and respect all cultural and religious traditions; this will foster unity and tolerance and resistance against the homogenization of culture. Since the church runs many educational institutions, these values can be inculcated upon the younger generations. More importantly, Christian intellectuals and theologians should engage fully with the ideologies behind the Hindutva movement and expose them for what they are. Christians need to be sensitive in their missional approach but, at the same time, stand for the truth and be vocal when it comes to speaking out against the oppressive systems.

Our Commitment

- We pray for those who are deprived of freedom to worship, and may we not take our liberty and freedom for granted.
- We pray against ideologies and movements that are oppressive and destructive.
- We pray for God's illumination upon the oppressors that their lives may be transformed.

Reflection

Gainful Pain

May we be granted an undaunted spirit like Paul
Amidst trial to brazenly declare
"For me to live is Christ
And to die is gain"
And may this sweet refrain
Echo down the ages
Thro' hills and vales
Touch the azure skies
Penetrate the deepest ocean
And be enshrined in the hearts of men
Perpetually, again and again.

India

When Time Stood Still: A True Life Answer to the Question – Where Is God When it Hurts?[1]
Prema Ruth Kumar

Contributed by Riad Kassis (Lebanon)

Summary

The author shares in this book her painful story and struggle as she and her family went many years grieving the tragic and sudden death of her only little son. After an introduction by her husband entitled "From Tragedy to Triumph," Prema tells their story in several brief chapters. The titles of the chapters express well the flow of the story. In "A Child's Dream," Prema reflects on her childhood upbringing and the loss of her parents at a young age which affected her sense of security. She also writes about her ultimate dream to get married and have children. In the next chapters, "In Quest of Meaning of Life" and "God Unravels His Plan," the author shares her joy as the dream became a reality – she got married and experienced motherhood when her daughter and son were born. She tells about the happy relationship between her daughter and son.

Then "Time Freezes" tells the tragic incident that led to the death of her son who was only one year and nine months old. The reader can feel the deep pain as she depicts in graphic details what took place on 27 September 1998 at 3:45 pm. The chapter asks many "Why?" questions of God. Some of the questions are, "How could this have happened to people who were living on a seminary campus fully involved in Christian ministry? Why? Why? Why?" and "What did we do to deserve this?" "Coping with Pain" and "The Anguish of Separation" describe the resultant journey of grief which she went through with her husband and daughter.

The four subsequent chapters, "Accepting Reality," "Tears and Healing," "Goodbyes are Not Forever," and "The Hope of Resurrection," depict the

---
1. Pastoral Concern Series 1. Edited by Siga Arles. Bangalore: Centre For Contemporary Christianity, 2007.

journey of coming to the end of the dark tunnel by coping with the reality of death, finding support from family, friends, and community, and looking forward with faith in the risen Christ and the resurrection of all believers. In "Superstitions and Christian Life and End of One's Physical Journey," the author extends invitations to her readers. The first is an invitation to understand the impact of grief on one's life and to respect the various ways of expressing it. The second is an invitation to understand that Christ has conquered death (1 Cor 15:55–57) and therefore Christians are and should be people of hope, because their God is the God of hope. The book concludes with letters written to the author by her friend, her mother, and her brother, in which they share their condolences with her and comfort her. These offer practical guidance for individuals and faith communities on how to respond to suffering from loss.

Response
On the Summary

This book is not easy and comfortable reading. Pain, frustration, and sorrow from a broken mother's heart and a suffering family can be felt on almost every page of the book. However, the reader cannot but admire the author's courage in writing her own sad story while at the same time expressing her hope in the midst of pain.

The author's biography states that she is an experienced teacher. This was clear in her writing style. She is careful to share facts, feelings, and emotions, aiming to help the reader benefit from her own experience and journey. In addition to much advice throughout the book she dedicates a whole chapter, "Suggestions for Family and Friends," to offering practical tips on how to grieve and how to help people who are grieving. Although I understand and appreciate the marvellous faith and strong hope of the author, it is hard for me to agree with her statement, "I am so grateful to the Lord for the experience of going through the separation of my son because if I had not gone through it I would have never been so equipped in ministering to people who had lost loved ones."[2] While her experience is valid, this attitude is often used to condemn those who are still in the midst of grief or anger in response to abuse, persecution, or even the loss of a loved one.

---

2. Kumar, *When Time Stood Still*, 48.

Our Commitment

Take time to reflect on these questions.

- Have you experienced a recent loss of a loved one? What are the things that helped you cope with the tragedy of loss?
- "Time heals." Do you agree with this expression? Why?
- How is grief expressed in your community, church, and society? What is your role with those who experience grief and sorrow?

Reflection

The faculty and students of the Union Biblical Seminary, Pune, India, where the author and her family lived, read this poem at the funeral of the author's son. Please take few minutes to read and reflect on the poem.

God's Garden[3]

Flowers in your garden,
Bloom of rarest hue
Fragrance so delightful,
Sweetness all day through.

Flowers in God's garden,
Oh! Can that be true?
What grows in God's garden,
Beyond the portals blue?

Little ones HE sent down,
Briefly to dwell here
Summoned back to Heaven,
Plucked from earthly sphere.

Sounds the beckoning trumpet,
To meet Him in the air,
We'll stroll around God's garden,
Amidst those blossoms fair.

God is planting gardens
For His family
To bloom in full profusion,
Throughout eternity!!

---

3. Kumar, *When Time Stood Still*, 64.

Japan

Theology of the Pain of God:
The First Original Theology from Japan[1]
Kazoh Kitamori

Contributed by Alfred Sebahene (Tanzania)

Summary

Can the Almighty God feel pain and suffer from it? Is our God really suffering? How could this be? How could my Creator be in a state of agony? Can the suffering God I know, he who in his sovereign grace humbled believers like me in our pain, sustain our faith? These questions are appropriate and significant if one wants to know what pain and suffering are all about. They lay a foundation for believers to understand who God is and what it means to be the child of this suffering God.

In his book *Theology of the Pain of God*, Kazoh Kitamori (1916–1998) addresses the issue of pain and suffering by rereading and reviewing the classical doctrine of the nature of God. In doing so, he aims at clarifying how the fusion and tension between wrath and love cause God's pain. *Theology of the Pain of God* is about God's love embedded or rooted in the concepts of suffering and pain. Kitamori's interpretation of God's love and God's pain finds its origin on the cross, where he believes the pain and suffering is an act within God himself within redemptive history, the central theme of the Christian faith.

Kitamori's articulate display of the dynamic link between pain and the cross demonstrates how important this is today. This linkage cannot be separated from Christ's calling, extended to believers to follow the way of the cross and to identify with him in his earthly shame and humiliation. Christ's call is good news because he assures that we suffer together with the whole of humankind as we share in the suffering of creation. The good news does not end here. Its

---

1. Eugene, Oregon: Wipf and Stock, 2005. First edition: Louisville, Kentucky: John Knox Press, 1965. These editions are a translation of *Kami no Itami no Shingaku*. 5th revised edition. Tokyo: Shinkyo Shuppansha, 1958; first edition published in 1946.

culmination is best explained in terms of the bigger picture of the suffering of creation being on its way to liberation and freedom in the Spirit. Thus, we are assured that, having suffered, we will be glorified with Christ. St. Paul's summary fits in well with Kitamori's analysis: yes, we will suffer. But suffering in this present life is nothing when we compare it with the glory and splendour which is in store for us.

Response
On the Summary
Refreshingly, although the book has a long history, having first been published in Japan in 1946 and in America in 1965, *Theology of the Pain of God* remains richly relevant to us. Personally, this book reminds me to look around myself and to truly see the pain, the suffering, and the distress of so many people I meet every day in my country, Tanzania. Here and elsewhere, human suffering in all its forms continues to escalate. But suffering in this world is an inevitable part of life on earth. Jesus Christ spoke clearly: "In this world you will have trouble. But take heart! I have overcome the world" (John 16:33a). And St. Paul reminds us in 1 Thessalonians 1:6–7, "and you became imitators of us and of the Lord, for you received the word in much affliction, with the joy of the Holy Spirit, so that you became an example to all the believers in Macedonia and in Achaia." Most upliftingly, their conversion produced both suffering and joy (v. 6). Kitamori's *Theology of the Pain of God* speaks to our context today, reminding us that in the midst of violence and oppression, our duty should be to adopt the role of "suffering servants" of God and humanity. We can participate in Christ's redemptive work through the suffering which he undertook. While Christ's work is complete and sufficient, and his work on the cross and in his resurrection was done once for all people and for all ages, nonetheless we ourselves can add to it as we participate in Christ's redemptive work. What then is our duty? There is suffering which we Christians can missionally take part in so that we can also take part in the mission of Christ. In the same spirit, and as an African theologian, I want to raise several issues.

First, while the book engages in difficult theological questions and parts of it are not light reading, it is still worth reading by ordinary people. It is written clearly, even though the subject matter is difficult, and speaks plainly to everyday and global questions of pain and suffering.

Next, I want to remind my readers that pain speaks, even though we naturally do not want to hear it. We all experience pains which speak to us, more especially about some specific area of our lives. The same pains bring to us the memories of the things we know and that are in need of caring attention. Whether in the midst of our own pain, or from Kitamori's own sad experience of Hiroshima and Nagasaki, the easiest responses to pain and suffering are either to suppress or to react in anger. Kitamori avoids those choices because those who follow Jesus know that violence has its teeth removed not by retaliation but by patient, innocent suffering.

Third, *Theology of the Pain of God* is a good resource to help believers remember that we are called to bear the marks of what it took Jesus to sacrifice for us and our fellow believers. In today's common language, this can best be understood as a call to build a better world, something which is done at a high price. Whatever the circumstances, it is the pain of the suffering of our fellow humans which should encourage us to reach out and take some of that pain and suffering off their shoulders.

In My Context

It is clear that Kitamori's work and theology revolve around the problem of suffering. He uniquely reflects on the suffering of God and human suffering. More broadly, he wants his readers to value the understanding of divine suffering and of the Japanese and the wider global churches' participation in divine suffering in their imitation of Christ. Kitamori took a positive approach to Japanese culture during the post-war period when Japanese culture was disregarded. Similarly, we in Tanzania, and in Africa at large, should both embrace our cultural identity and heritage with their ethics and values and also learn how to authentically engage with Scripture on its own terms. This will allow us to refine biblical teachings on suffering and to understand the nature of the African believers' church as a covenant community whose suffering is for the perfection of the church. The accomplishment of the church's mission can be found in the day-to-day sharing of fellowship with Christ. For Kitamori, suffering, pain, the cross, and witness are inseparable. By understanding what the pain of God means, the body of Christ, acting in unity and purity, can be a powerful witness to the love of God. In addressing community pain and suffering, the church will give a practical demonstration of that love. This is how Christians can bear witness, even in the face of suffering, and thereby live in redemptive, Christ-worshipping communities in the church's call to transform the world. This is how we continually keep our witness to the presence of God open until the promised coming reality, as clearly testified by John.

Then I saw "a new heaven and a new earth," for the first heaven and the first earth had passed away, and there was no longer any sea. I saw the Holy City, the new Jerusalem, coming down out of heaven from God, prepared as a bride beautifully dressed for her husband. And I heard a loud voice from the throne saying, "Look! God's dwelling place is now among the people, and he will dwell with them. They will be his people, and God himself will be with them and be their God. He will wipe every tear from their eyes. There will be no more death or mourning or crying or pain, for the old order of things has passed away." He who was seated on the throne said, "I am making everything new!" (Rev 21:1–5)

Our Commitment

1. Kitamori writes that "to follow the Lord of the cross means to serve the pain of God; believers are supposed to respond to God's suffering with their own suffering." Should Christians be concerned about standing in their peoples' pain? Should they always respond to the things that affect them? If so, why?

2. In what area can you, as an individual, contribute to addressing human suffering caused by the violation of people's rights and dignity? Which of the common problems in your area do you see yourself as having the potential to help with, and which responses do you need to cultivate?

3. How can we better reflect the suffering of God in our own lives and avoid causing or increasing pain and suffering within our own family, in our relationship as husbands and wives, and in our relationship with our children? Give examples using at least five Bible verses on the subject.

Reflection

A Teen with Albinism Who Was Mutilated Due to Superstition

In Africa, people with albinism are often subject to persecution. While statistics are not available on this phenomenon in Tanzania, it has been happening in various areas in the country. In my view, such Tanzanians are still in danger because persecutors believe that the particular body features of people with albinism have the potential to convey magical powers.² Until such superstition disappears, especially in Africa's Great Lakes region, Africans with albinism will remain at risk.

Prayer

Heavenly Father, I read and understand your words in Proverbs 31:8–9: "Open your mouth on behalf of the mute, and for the rights of the destitute; Open your mouth, judge justly, defend the needy and the poor!" Thank you for reminding me about my responsibility to remember others, especially those facing persecutions and who are in precarious situations. Lord, I pray that our fellow human beings, people with albinism in our villages, will not be persecuted. I pray that persecutors would turn to you, confess their sins, and understand that the skin of all people with albinism is your creation and has no magical properties. The same skin carries with it your glory, as does all human skin. I pray that people with albinism will not be killed, dismembered, nor their body parts used in magic potions. Lord, I call upon you to teach your people that people with albinism are not cursed neither do they bear bad luck. Protect them, Lord I pray.

In your name, Amen.

---

2. Madenge, "Albino in Tanzania – Statistics, Persecution, Superstition," United Republic of Tanzania (https://unitedrepublicoftanzania.com/government-of-tanzania-and-the-society/education-in-tanzania-system/laws-of-tanzania/albino-in-tanzania-statistics-persecution-superstition-hunters-people-children-hunting-killings-documentary-killed-how-to-help-albinos-of-what-happens-why-are-there-so-many-is-albinism-so-common-attac/), 2 July 2022.

Japan

Silence[1]
Shūsaku Endō

Contributed by Dimitrios G. Oulis (Greece)

Summary

The translator of this edition of *Silence*, William Johnston, states in his preface that "in the course of discussions on his book, [Endō] often protested that he was writing literature, not theology. Yet on these occasions many of his remarks showed that he was not indifferent to the theological implications of what he wrote."[2] This observation not only legitimizes a theological reading of the novel, but also allows us to highlight the three most important theological questions around which Endō's narrative is articulated: the question of Christian mission, the question of ecclesiology, and the question of theodicy – or rather, God's "silence" in the face of evil.

In relation to the first question, *Silence* reflects Endō's lifelong effort to reconcile his Japanese cultural origins with his Christian faith and outlines the inherent possibilities and limits of Christian mission. To satisfy its claims to universal applicability, every Christian mission must no doubt pay a painful price; but, even if this price is paid, Endō seems to suggest that there will always be a part of the Christian faith which can never be assimilated by its host culture. In the book, Cristovao Ferreira argues in his conversation with Sebastian Rodrigues that the "swamp" of Japan has never been able to assimilate the Christian faith in all its fullness and depth. He argues that even the most ardent among Japanese Christians were led to martyrdom for a God completely different from the one preached by the official church dogma – a God which the Japanese distorted to fit their own religious and cultural presuppositions. Such a claim has grave implications for mission, insofar as it points to a fundamental cultural mismatch between the "West" and the "East"

---

1. Translated by William Johnston. New York: Taplinger Publishing Comp, 1980.
2. Endō, *Silence,* xviii.

which makes it impossible to transplant Christianity into cultural environments other than the "Western." If this were indeed the case, then mission would be understood as a betrayal of Christianity, for what is supposed to be gained in range and magnitude would be lost in doctrinal accuracy and authenticity.

The second question posed by *Silence* concerns the anthropological foundations of the church. Judging by the ending of the novel, we would say that Endō proposes a martyric ecclesiology of the body of Christ over an ecclesiology of the priestly office. Early on, in the second chapter, we read that the small Christian community of Tomogi managed to survive without a priest for six whole years: "with neither priests nor brothers and in the throes of a terrible persecution at the hands of the government, they secretly made their own organization for the administration of the sacraments; and so they kept alive their faith."[3] When the Japanese Christians finally meet the missionaries Garrpe and Rodrigues, they are overwhelmed with joy and gratitude, not so much because they make the survival of their church dependent on them, but because in their faces they recognize the universality of their faith: they feel they belong to a larger Christian family and that the two priests will serve as a link between Japan's many broken and scattered flocks. It is interesting to note, however, that as the relationship of the local community with the two priests is consolidated, not only do the priests shepherd the community, but the community also "shepherds" the priests: it provides them with shelter and food, protects them, helps them flee when necessary and is even willing to sacrifice themselves in order not to betray their presence. The relationship between the flock and its pastors, in other words, is not hierarchical, but dialectical, complementary, and interdependent. This fact presents the reader with the idea that if the theological foundation of the church is Christ, then its anthropological foundation is no other than the martyrdom and testimony of the community of believers.

Speaking in terms of patristic theology, we would venture to assert that Endō's narrative seems closer to the ecclesiology of Tertullian (c. 155–220) and St. Cyprian of Carthage (c. 210–258), according to which the unity and universality of the church rests primarily on martyrdom, confessional rigour, and fraternal charity and less on the ecclesiology of St. Ignatius of Antioch (early 100s), according to which the unity of the church is manifested primarily in the person of the bishop. The final outcome of the novel is particularly suggestive at this particular point: Christian martyrs glorify the church by enduring their martyrdom to the end; priests, on the other hand, are crushed

---

3. Endō, *Silence*, 45.

by the anguish of insurmountable moral dilemmas – and eventually defect to the enemy's camp.

It remains to explore the novel's third question: God's "silence" in the face of human suffering. This question keeps coming back like a leitmotif and finds its answer only in the penultimate chapter of the book – in a moment of borderline pain and despair by the protagonist priest, Rodrigues. Christ invites Rodrigues to trample on his *fumi-e* and "betray" him,[4] in order for the community of believers to live.[5] We could say that Christ is willing to sacrifice himself once more in the name (and for the sake) of his people, which is another way of saying that God breaks his silence only to be "crucified" and brought to extreme humiliation as another martyr among martyrs. It is evident, however, that by martyrically breaking his silence, God becomes propitiation and mercy not only for the victims of history, but even for the perpetrators: his traitors and crucifiers. We could conclude therefore that Endō's answer to the question of God's silence is its martyric assumption by the community of believers and its transformation into a perpetual act of love, mercy, forgiveness, and service for the others. If the silence of God constitutes – and indeed is – a scandalous void for the life of the church, this same church is called through her martyrdom and testimony to fill that void and understand God's silence as the preeminent transcendental basis of her responsibility vis-à-vis history and the world.

Response
On the Summary

Reading *Silence* has been a mesmerizing experience for me for three main reasons: first, because the questions around which the novel is articulated are not abstract or meticulous but touch the very heart of the Christian faith. I have good reasons to believe that the answer the church will give to these questions – its mission, foundation, ministry, and discipleship – will to a large extent determine its present and future.

Second, because as a teacher and religious educator myself, I am indebted to wrestle on a daily basis with the question of the "cultural translation" of

---

4. Editors Note: During the anti-Christian persecutions of the Tokugawa or Edo shogunate (1603–1868) of Japan, authorities required suspected and known Christians to trample upon a *fumi-e*, an image of either Jesus or Mary placed on the ground. Those who refused or who seemed too reluctant were arrested and tortured and, if they refused to recant their Christian faith, executed. The *fumi-e* were first used in 1629 in Nagasaki.

5. Endō, *Silence*, 220.

Christianity: how am I supposed to introduce the content of Christian faith to younger generations, who have grown up with completely different perceptual, moral, socio-political, and cultural premises than my own?

And third, because I read *Silence* as Endō's special appeal to every local Christian community – and also to the Christian church as a whole – to reaffirm the martyric character of its faith (and the Greek term "martyric" should be taken here in its twofold meaning: as *martyrdom* and as *testimony*). I read his novel, that is, as a plea for the Christian faith to regain its confessional dynamism and socio-political relevance – and stop being strictly a "matter of the heart," hidden from the public eye, as the ending of Scorsese's 2016 film adaptation of *Silence* suggests.

In My Context

I am a member of the Orthodox Church of Greece – that is, a church that enjoys all the comforts and privileges of an "official" state religion. The centuries-long coexistence of Orthodoxy with the State – which goes back to the Byzantine political ideology of *synallilia*[6] – has contributed to people in my country perceiving Christianity more as a kind of customary and cultural heritage, than a martyric ministry addressed to the suffering brother and sister. It would even be worth noting that, due to its hegemonic status, it is not uncommon for Greek Orthodoxy to take on fundamentalist elements or be understood in strict ethno-racial terms – hence the notorious slogan circulated among zealous religious circles "Ellas simainei Orthodoxia [Greece means Orthodoxy]." In the face of such an understanding of the church, I believe that Endō's account can serve as a serious counterweight, insofar as it reminds us of a non-hegemonic ecclesiological model, which does not embrace the authoritarian and secular ideologies of this world but aspires to demystify – through martyrdom – their power and sovereignty.

Our Commitment

- Whenever you practice evangelism, pay special attention to the cultural contexts that mediate between you and your audience. No

---

6. Editors Note: Synallilia, a transliteration of the Greek word *sunallēlía*, means *reciprocity, mutual understanding,* or *solidarity*. This concept defines the church and State relationship as a relationship between two independent equals who engage in mutual assistance and coordination. It was first clearly articulated by Justinian, who ruled as the Byzantine emperor from 527–565.

evangelism has ever been accomplished through plain "copy-paste" processes.

- Whether you are a pastor or a simple member of a church community, try not to think only in terms of how the community "fits" your needs, but also what you can offer to it. What exactly do you "sacrifice" to be a member of a church community? What is the cost of your being a disciple of Christ? Try to give yourself clear answers to these questions.
- When you feel that God is "silent," try to listen to his voice in the voices of your brothers and sisters in need. Consider the possibility that maybe God silences himself deliberately, so that their voices can be heard more clearly and motivate you to a dynamic public expression of your faith.

Reflection

The Forty Martyrs of Sebaste[7]

---

7. These were believers martyred in AD 320 in or adjacent to the city of Sebaste in Lesser Armenia, then a client kingdom within the Roman Empire. Now the city is called Sivas; it is in central Turkey. Illustration source: https://orthochristian.com/138136.html.

Japan

Silence and Beauty: Hidden Faith Born of Suffering[1]
Makoto Fujimura

Contributed by Myrto Theocharous (Cyprus)

Summary

How do you examine persecution when your own country has been guilty of one of the most brutal campaigns of persecution against Christians in history? How do you find beauty in that culture without rejecting it altogether? How can you find corrective proposals from the West when, in fact, more Christians died in the atomic destruction of Nagasaki than in the severe persecution of Christians that followed the deaths of the twenty-six martyrs in Japan in 1597? How do you negotiate your identity between such starkly different models of Christian faith and culture when you feel at home in both, but also in none?

The author of *Silence and Beauty*, Makoto Fujimura, a Japanese American artist living in New York, embarks on an exploration of his own journey of faith, "journalling" his thoughts on the beauty and pain of the history of Japanese Christianity. When Fujimura first started his studies at Tokyo University of the Arts, he stepped into an exhibition room where he saw various tablets laid flat on the floor. These were the *fumi-e*, the stepping blocks of the seventeenth century which were produced in order to be used for Christian persecution. These were images of Jesus or Mary with her child carved on wood or cast in bronze; Japanese villagers were forced to defile them by stepping on them in order to renounce their Christianity. What really impressed the author was that these images were flat from continuous use, smoothed out due to the many feet that stepped over them. This was Fujimura's first encounter with Japanese Christianity. He had already become a Christian before going there, through his wife, but this was his true baptism, as he calls it.

Fujimura is attempting to understand his own journey into Japanese culture and Christianity by using Japanese Christian novelist Shūsaku

---

1. Downers Grove, Illinois: IVP Books, 2016.

Endō (1923–1996) as a guide and his work *Silence* in particular. The author is fascinated with how Endō was obsessed with a part of history that was largely silenced or hidden. After observing the smoothed out *fumi-e* tablets and realizing how many people had been stepping on them, Endō became obsessed with the failures of faith rather than triumphant Christianity. Thus, in *Silence*, he decided to "talk" through a Portuguese missionary priest, Father Rodrigues, who is basically an outsider going into Japan and seeing things from his own perspective. Endō wants to show that Japan is not so easy to read, but it is, in fact, a Christ-hidden culture, as he calls it, which is haunted by the past and which managed to develop a mechanism of hiding what is most valuable. Silence is a virtue in Japanese culture and what is most important is kept completely out of sight, not advertised. What an outsider would call "children of a failed faith" are, in fact, people who have been hiding their faith really deeply but without actually abandoning it. One of the heroic or key characters in Endō's writings, Kichijiro, functions as Endō's critique on the imperialistic confidence of the Western God of Christianity, the God who wants to overcome the pagan religions of Japan. Things are not as clear as Western Christianity makes them appear – that all these cultures are weak and have not been able to suppress their pagan past. According to the author, Endō is trying to redefine the hero and even calls himself "Kichijiro." Father Rodrigues, on the other hand, symbolizes the male imperialism of the Christian West that is brought into Japan.

Fujimura sees in Endō a deep understanding of suffering. Endō finds that it is easier to understand Christ's suffering for our sake, but it is much harder to see his followers, in a gruesome graphic depiction, tormented and to digest their suffering. Fujimura explores this aspect through the issue of suicide as something that has been widely respected and honoured in Japanese culture because of the *seppuku* ritual.[2] Suicide is beautified as a moral way of dealing with injustice, so it is very hard to convince a Japanese person that suicide is bad. It is a reality for many people in Japan, and at least the contemplation of suicide exists in multiple artists. This gives insight to the understanding of death in Japanese culture: the cross is very honoured, even though it is something cruel, because it overlaps with the *seppuku* ritual. The Japanese see nobility in this kind of death; therefore, the way to extinguish Christianity

---

2. Editors' note: *Seppuku* was a form of Japanese ritualistic suicide by disembowelment. It was originally used by samurai who performed it voluntarily in order to die an honourable death rather than fall into the hands of the enemy. It was also used in order to restore their honour when any of them had committed a serious offence.

in Japan is not by giving them a cross, because this would make them more honourable and would in fact increase the attraction of Christianity. Instead, the way to extinguish Christianity in Japan is not by death, but by exposing the scandalous and ignoble character of a leader. Making a leader betray his people and bring shame to himself is the way to extinguish Christianity. For this reason, the persecutors chose to push Christians into this path of betrayal of their own people in order to extinguish Christianity.

Endō, as well as Fujimura, honours the crucified people of Japan who did not surrender but died for their faith, but their focus is on the unseen masses that kept Christianity in hiding. While the *fumi-e* tablets witness to the brutality and darkness of Japan, as well as to the failure of Christianity at the surface level, Fujimura notes that persecution was not able to eradicate Christianity because, after more than two hundred years of isolation, there were still groups discovered that called themselves *Kakure Kirishitan* (hidden Christians). These were people who maintained their faith, developed rituals and prayers to pass on from one generation to the other, had hidden altars, took communion with rice cakes and sake, and who utilized local statues that they had baptized as the "Virgin with Child." To a Western observer, true Christians are only those who died. What the hidden Christians were doing could very well be called "syncretism" rather than the means to maintain a faith in isolation by utilizing the local material available. However, when the borders opened, Catholic priests went to convert the villages back to Catholicism, but the villagers refused and claimed that they were the real Christians because they were the ones who were persecuted and preserved their faith for three hundred years. This example makes one wonder what the mark of authentic Christianity is and who is able to pass this judgement.

Fujimura, like Endō, critiques homogeneity. The Christian in Japan was the oddity, the anomaly that had to be hammered down for the sake of homogeneity. This group-think culture that excludes everyone who is different is an artificial reality, not the truth. Even a Buddhist temple Fujimura had visited in Japan had functioned as a refuge for Christians, something that testifies to the reality that Buddhist attitudes towards Christians were not monolithic. He says that just as estuaries – the mixing points where rivers carrying sweet water connect to the sea – are essential to biodiversity and the health of the environment, the diversity of voices is essential and healthy for cultures as well as for the Christian faith. While we proclaim the unnegotiable exclusivity of Christ, this exclusivity is an exclusivity of the *centre* that holds all the diverse parts together, a centre that leads us to mystery, humility, and the surrendering of power. It is a costly exclusivity. With Endō, Fujimura critiques our overdependence on rationality that can lead to the reductionism of faith, to a simple decision-based faith, black and white judgement, culture wars, and a faith lacking the mystery of grace and compassion.

Father Rodrigues ends up serving in hiddenness. He remains a "priest," undercover to the end of his life, with a buried former identity and only then, through his defeat, is he able to serve the people. He accepts confession by Kichijiro and absolves him while a secret Christian community survives in his household. For Fujimura, Rodrigues's "public death" is the death of the chrysalis. It is not suicide nor betrayal but a death that will bring life, a seed that falls into the ground to bring fruit. For many, this way of life would be considered a betrayal to the Christian faith. However, this way of living out faith is a growing reality for many, worthy of acknowledging and studying, especially for contexts of brutal persecution. Today's parallel may be the so-called "insider movements," especially in Muslim countries, where believers remain integrated in their natural community while at the same time living under the lordship of Jesus Christ.

Response
On the Summary

This work brings to light the suppressed reality of the "failed" Christian. Above all, Fujimura portrays how one may evaluate Christian life in other contexts, other cultures, or even other ecclesiastical groups. He goes into great depths to understand the meaning of key concepts in Japan, how these may have coloured the way Christianity was lived out, and why thousands of Christians responded to persecution the way they did. His example is extremely useful for any of us attempting to understand other forms of Christianity.

The author speaks of one of the harshest persecutions in history and, while there is much to be learned, we must keep in mind that these were extreme and unique circumstances. While one may feel the pressure today to keep their faith private in secular contexts, I would be reluctant to draw a direct analogy between the persecution of Japan and pressures faced in the secular West. It was humbling for me to read the story of two boys dragged all the way to the hill of Nagasaki to be executed and, looking up at the lined-up crosses upon arrival, the words that came out of their mouths were, "Show me my cross." For this reason, it was uncomfortable to read on the next page,[3] as if of equal measure, about the pressures faced by the author to hide his Christian

---

3. Fujimura, *Silence and Beauty*, 47.

identity in the art world at the cost of a more mainstream career. The author would probably not equate the two types of suffering, but I would have liked the awareness of the dissimilarity to have been more explicit.

In My Context

Believers in Greece grow up with the *Synaxarion*, a collection about the lives of the saints and martyrs and a book relating how saints remained faithful, confessing their Lord at the cost of their lives. It is therefore very difficult to shift attention to these "unseen" people who betrayed their faith, make an effort to understand why they acted this way, and discern whether their betrayal marked the end of their faith. There is no religious persecution in Greece so I do not think analogous conditions are to be found in my context but, as I mentioned above, this attention must be paid to the growing phenomenon of "insider movements" in the Middle East.

However, I find that in this book Fujimura warns against making superficial claims about the authenticity or "orthodoxy" of faith expressions which are different from our own. He also indirectly warns about the careless use of the Western descriptor, "syncretism." Living as an evangelical in Greece, with 98 percent of Greeks being Greek Orthodox, it is easy to dismiss the local faith as syncretistic. Fujimura's careful study of the importance of Japanese culture in understanding local faith in its context was an inspiring example of how one should explore deeply in order to comprehend ecclesiastical differences. Greek Orthodoxy has had a long and difficult journey, of both faithfulness and betrayal. Its journey should be studied, understood, and respected.

Our Commitment

Let us repent for suppressing the realities in our world that are not successful, triumphant, or exactly like the image we have created of the victorious Christian. We have not embraced failure, we have not looked deeply beneath the surface to see what treasures have been hidden, but we have dismissed superficially and quickly.

Let us encounter the one who is different, the Christian who does not follow our own ways and practices. Let us learn from them about their faith, their values, why they express their Christian faith in the way they do.

Let us isolate syncretism in our Christian faith. Does our faith include Western cultural elements that are adopted as indispensable to faith? Do we read the Scriptures with rationalist eyes? How do I think a Middle Eastern, an

Asian, an African Christian would read the same text? How would a homeless person read this text? How would a black refugee woman read this text?

Let us begin by assuming that our way of reading and understanding faith is not true for everyone and that I may be enriched by what others see and experience.

Reflection

Fumi-e to Expose Christians[4]
by Tokugawa Shogunate,
Meiji period print (c. 1870)

---

4. Source: Wikimedia Commons. https://commons.wikimedia.org/wiki/File:Fumi-e_to_Expose_Christians_by_Tokugawa_Shogunate.png

Pakistan

Suffering for Christ[1]
Shahbaz Masih Boota

Contributed by Riad Kassis (Lebanon)

Summary

Boota's book aims to help Christians understand the reality of suffering as they live their faith in Jesus Christ. It also offers practical guidance for individuals and faith communities on how to respond to persecution.

The book is divided into ten chapters. Each chapter addresses a question related to the book's overall purpose. The ten questions are:

1. What is persecution?
2. Why do some people decide to persecute Christians?
3. Why does God allow his people to be persecuted?
4. How should Christians respond to the threat of persecution?
5. What should I not do if I face persecution for Christ?
6. Can anything good come from suffering persecution?
7. How should I lead a church that is being persecuted?
8. What is the role of Christians in countries where there is little persecution?
9. What is God accomplishing through allowing persecution?
10. How should I respond to the challenge of persecution?

The author makes it clear several times in his book that he is not dealing with every kind of suffering which Christians may experience in their lives. He focuses on suffering which is experienced by Christians because of their faith in Christ and cites Acts 17:1–9 as a New Testament example. He adds

---

1. Knowing the Christian Life, edited by Ian Shaw. Darvel, East Ayrshire, UK: Overseas Publishing and Literature (OPAL), 2022.

that "preaching and sharing the message of God awakens hostility"[2] which could come from governments, political and religious groups, communities, and even family members.

Boota mentions six reasons from the Bible why God allows his people to experience suffering and persecution. He concludes with a call to his readers to read and reflect on James's exhortations (1:2–4, 12; Acts 4; 8:1) as they face persecution. He encourages them to pray and persevere. However, this is not the only way to behave while encountering persecution. The author outlines with three basic responses by the faith community: flight, fortitude, and finding legal redress. Flight is permissible if the Christian mission is threatened by persecution (cf. Matt 10:23; Acts 14:5–7). Therefore, it is crucial to have the right motive and to prayerfully consider whether flight is appropriate or facing suffering is necessary.

In addition to the three main responses to persecution, Boota refers to other responses such as praying for the persecutors and understanding them, trusting in God, praying for wisdom, rejoicing as the persecuted share in the suffering of Christ, and looking ahead to the glory. On the negative side, the author refers to three responses which Christians should avoid when facing persecution: they are not to renounce their faith, not to hide their faith, and not to respond with violence or antagonization of the authorities.

Paul is presented as an example of how a church leader should help his church during persecution. Boota cites the letter to the Ephesians which Paul wrote while in prison and in which he shows how Christ's followers should respond to persecution (Eph 3:1, 13; 4:1). Boota also refers to Paul's letter to the Philippians as another example, written from Paul's prison, on how persecuted Christians are to behave. They should stand firm and be bold in their faith (1:14) as they view death for Christ to be regarded as gain (1:21). Finally, Boota sees in the second letter to Timothy a call to view persecution as a reality (1:8; 4:14–15) and to be assured of the crown of righteousness at the end of life (4:6–8). Boota invites church leaders to educate their congregations, to preach on the subject, to encourage memorization of the Bible, and even to plan ahead for alternative meeting places when persecution intensifies.

It is interesting that the author provides practical advice on how Christians who reside where persecution is limited or non-existent are to extend help and support to persecuted Christians in other regions. This support could take several forms: prayer, education, seeking justice by writing letters to politicians, advocacy, and by showing mercy and compassion.

---

2. Boota, *Suffering for Christ*, 6.

According to Boota, God allows persecution to accomplish his purposes because through persecution God brings blessings to the believer (Matt 5:3, 10), spreads the gospel (Acts 8:1–25), strengthens the church (1 Pet 1:6–7), increases commitment to prayer (Acts 2:42), deepens interest in mission (Matt 16:24; Phil 1:12–26), and brings an eternal perspective to our outlooks (Phil 1:21; Rev 22:12–14).

Response
On the Summary

This book comes from someone who lives and works in a country where freedom is limited for Christians (i.e. Pakistan). Therefore, the book brings a genuine and authentic voice to the topic of Christian suffering and persecution. However, I was hoping that the author would cite real life events and practical examples from his own context about how Christians understood and faced persecution.

Boota states that in the two thousand years of the Christian faith an estimated seventy million believers have been killed for their faith.[3] This is alarming and necessitates more teaching and education on this important topic to help Christians to be prepared well as they face persecution.

At several times the author seems to be too idealistic, even as he quotes Bible verses on the proper response to persecution by asking Christians to love the persecutors, pray for them, understand their motives. I had hoped that he would bring the vengeance psalms into this discussion. However, while Boota rightly dwells on the benefits of persecution for persecuted Christians, he does reflect realistically on the negative impact on the Christian community. What about the social and psychological tragedies that persecution brings to the lives of individuals, families, churches and communities?

Our Commitment

As you read this book review, please take time to reflect on the following:
- Is teaching on, and education about, persecution relevant in your own context? Why?

---

3. This startling statistic is confirmed by well-known demographer Todd M. Johnson, "Christian Martyrdom: A Global Demographic Assessment," unpublished paper delivered at the University of Notre Dame, November 2012, https://mcgrath.nd.edu/assets/84231/the_demographics_of_christian_martyrdom_todd_johnson.pdf.

- What are two matters that attracted your attention in this book? How are they relevant to your context?
- If you live in a country that does not face persecution, what are practical steps that you or others should be taking to help those who are persecuted?
- Share this review with one of your friends and spend time conversing about its importance.

Reflection

It seems that with all our attempts to understand suffering we fall short in comprehending its depth and impact. The author concludes by saying,

> There is always an element of mystery about God's dealings with us especially in suffering. This mystery can cause struggles in our lives. We are not called to solve the mystery but to embrace the wonder of it with faith. It should cause us to fall down in awe and worship.[4]

---

4. Boota, *Suffering for Christ*, 51.

Philippines

How Long, O Lord?: The Challenge and Promise of Reconciliation and Peace[1]
Athena Gorospe and Charles R. Ringma (editors)

Contributed by Adrian Paul P. Morales (Philippines)

Summary

In a world marred by conflict and division, the aspiration for reconciliation and peace is a constant yet rarely satisfied need for many people. Strife persists every day in every layer of our society, from the personal to the national and the international levels. While this decaying condition may have already been largely accepted with reluctance, this book dares to confront this issue and presents biblical frameworks and practical steps for becoming effective bearers of peace, inspiring the body of Christ to take part in God's ongoing ministry of reconciliation.

The first section in this collection of essays, "Biblical Perspectives," examines how peace is defined in Scripture. Christopher Wright highlights reconciliation and peace as the overarching themes of the whole Bible. The Old Testament's concept of peace, or *shalom*, goes beyond mere freedom from violence. It also includes total well-being and living in a restored relationship with God, others, and creation. In Psalm 85, the psalmist declares that this vision of peace cannot become a reality without a commitment to God's standard of righteousness, truth, and compassion. Wright's essay, "'Righteousness and Peace Kiss One Another' (Ps 85:10): Biblical Perspectives on Peace and Reconciliation" weaves this theme with God's work of cosmic (Col 1:15–20) and ethnic (Eph 2:11–22) reconciliation in the New Testament. Wright encourages believers as we put our human efforts into peacebuilding despite how small those efforts may seem to be against the wide-scale conflicts of today. We must understand that our efforts are not in vain because we are struggling between "the victory of the cross and the coming of a new creation." Peacemaking is an integral part

---

1. ATS Theological Forum Series. Carlisle, Cambria: Langham Global Library, 2019.

of the church's mission, and our lives reconciled to God and others are proof of the power and effectiveness of the gospel which we preach.

With this in mind, we can see that the path to reconciliation and achieving peace is multifaceted and complex. Such nuances are explored in Takamitsu Muraoka's essay "What's Your Name? Biblical Perspectives on Memory and Reconciliation" which takes inspiration from key biblical passages (Gen 32:1–32; Jer 31:27–34; Mark 5:1–13) on reconciliation and his reflections as a Japanese on his country's responsibility towards the nations it colonized during World War II, including the Philippines. Muraoka emphasizes the need for both the perpetrator and victim to face their histories in order to arrive at genuine reconciliation. It is a precondition for the perpetrator to have humility, to pay a material price, and to experience a sense of guilt and remorse. Only then are perpetrators able to sincerely ask for forgiveness. Similarly, victims should remember their past and not become the "victimizer of tomorrow." Alvin Molito's essay illustrates the same theme and develops a biblical model for reconciliation from the Jacob and Esau narrative (Gen 32–33). Molito points out that Jacob went through a process of liminality, a "state of statuslessness and ambiguity," which allowed him to become aware of his own weakness and vulnerability before God. This ushered him to his individual transformation and also led to the creation of a national identity when his name was changed to Israel in Genesis 32:32. This experience enabled him to see "the face of God" in the face of his estranged brother Esau. Molito challenges us to appropriate this narrative in resolving conflicts by recognizing our own vulnerabilities and weaknesses, seeing the "face of God" in the face of others by considering the worth and dignity of other people as important as our own.

Reconciliation and peace are indeed fundamental to the Christian faith, but what do they mean in the context of non-Christian communities deeply fractured by social structures or situations that breed and perpetuate discrimination, oppression, and marginalization? The second section of Gorospe and Ringma's book, "The Ways of Peace," tackles the challenges to peacebuilding and practical strategies drawn from grassroots-level experiences in various local communities. Salim Munayer's essay gives a picture of their work in Musalaha, a non-profit organization that seeks to promote reconciliation between Israelis and Palestinians by building relationships through their reconciliation encounters. Fermin Manalo's essay also makes a rich resource for peacemaking as it zooms in on the people affected by the armed conflict in Mindanao, the second largest island in the Philippines. Given the extreme violence and diverse religious influences in the region, this author underscores the role of evangelicals in interfaith peace movements, advocating for a spirituality that goes beyond sectarianism and respects the dignity of each person regardless of ethnic or religious backgrounds.

To foster true reconciliation, another dimension we should address is trauma healing. The third section, "Healing and Forgiveness," sheds light on the significance of addressing trauma and the restoration of individuals and communities affected by violence and oppression. Annabel Manalo shares her experiences in providing psychosocial services to survivors of organized political violence and explains how unhealed trauma can fuel the cycle of violence. The trauma healing processes that facilitate reconciliation in her essay serve as a roadmap to peacebuilding in the context of war and displacement. She also calls on us to reconceptualize our understanding of trauma healing by integrating psychosocial and spiritual factors with restorative justice, human rights, community development, governance, and policy-making aspects of peacebuilding.

Conflicts will continue to be a reality in this fallen world, yet we are called to respond without reluctance. Just as Jesus, the Prince of Peace, steps into this unjust world to reconcile it back to God, we are also to enter fully into it and be bearers of peace by promoting justice, fighting for truth, and loving others unconditionally.

Response
On the Summary

The authors of the essays in this book collectively present a distinct vision of reconciliation and peace drawn from biblical narratives, theological reflections, and on-the-ground engagements in the work of peacebuilding. The majority of the chapters covered in this review focus on the context of the Philippines, a country which is divided by geography (it is composed of over seven thousand islands), political beliefs and affiliations, philosophical differences, and religious and socioeconomic backgrounds. As a Filipino, I can strongly identify with the cry, "How Long, O Lord?" as an expression of the immense and long suffering of my people from violence, neglect, armed conflicts, displacement, discrimination, and marginalization.

In My Context

From 2012 to 2020, I ministered to our local church in Santa Ana, Manila, which is situated in a impoverished urban community. The majority of our members were young people who came from poor families and resided in cramped spaces with limited access to basic necessities like clean water and sanitation. A huge number of our youths were incapable of continuing their education at the college level because of financial constraints; their narrow opportunities often eventually lead to unemployment. Some were forced to do manual labour at an early age to help sustain their families' needs. Some sadly resorted to self-destructive behavioural patterns such as alcoholism and the use of illegal drugs to cope with the stress of poverty. One of the most depressing experiences for me was hearing "Sara," one of the youths, tell us about how her older sister, who was still a teenager at that time, offered sex in exchange for two packages of instant noodles and one kilogram of rice, and how she was also tempted to do the same just to alleviate their family's hunger.

Reflecting on all their experiences, I was confronted with the question, "What does the gospel of peace that they hear in church even mean when they go back to their broken families and poverty-stricken lives?" It was a call to review my disposition and recalibrate the scope of my mission as a follower of Jesus. The difficult living conditions that they have cannot be resolved with mere dole-outs. Peace in their context means protecting them from predators who would take advantage of their vulnerability. It requires serious attention in fighting against marginalization and social orders that promote inequalities and helping them develop the life skills which will both lead to a higher quality of life and destroy the cycle of poverty. *How Long, O Lord?* challenges the way we do ministry and offers practical insights on being peacemakers in our societies.

Our Commitment

In the past, I believed that being peaceful only meant not causing harm to others, and as long as I am not hurting anyone, I have fulfilled my responsibility as a peacemaking Christian in this world. Because of my ignorance, I was uninvolved in dealing with social issues and was unbothered by rampant environmental abuses, political repression, marginalization of the poor and of members of indigenous groups and of other minorities, and by extrajudicial killings that are happening in my country.

This book is one of the instruments God has used to change my beliefs and transform my approach to ministry. It has widened my view of reconciliation and peace and kindled my desire to re-engage with my local community. I commit to immersing myself in peacebuilding initiatives, both at the grassroots level and in broader societal contexts, and continuously praying for God's mercy and healing for individuals affected by all forms of conflict and violence.

Reflection

Where is Christ?

Where is Christ?
She is waiting in line in a public hospital, old and shaking
still unsure if she can make the cut for today's check-ups
Her knees are getting weaker
But she needs to stay in line if she wants to live longer

Where is Christ?
He is the dead body lying on the street
with his head wrapped in packing tape
and left with a cardboard sign saying,
"Adik ako, wag tularan" (I'm a drug addict, don't imitate me)

Where is Christ?
He is roaming in the city obliviously
while still wearing his tribe's traditional clothing
a member of the indigenous group who is now homeless
because a large company took over their land for business

Where is Christ?
He is at an eatery, shaking out of hunger
buying what he can afford with his last fifteen pesos,
one plain rice and lots of water
tired from walking for six straight days to the city
to find a job only to fail from being employed

Where is Christ?
He is on the table as an empty plate, waiting to be filled.

Philippines

Why, O God? Disaster, Resiliency, and the People of God[1]
Athena Gorospe, Charles Ringma, and Karen Hollenbeck-Wuest (editors)

Contributed by Adrian Paul P. Morales (Philippines)

Summary

The Philippines is considered to be one of the countries that is most vulnerable to disasters. Filipinos have suffered tremendously from some of the strongest typhoons, earthquakes, volcanic eruptions, and other catastrophes in history. These unfortunate events took countless lives and left survivors traumatized, homeless, and widowed. To make sense of this painful reality, the people wrestle with the question, "Why, O God?" This book seeks to navigate through this question in light of the Bible and offers practical approaches to how the church can better respond to natural disasters as part of her calling in today's context.

Christians may take different positions on why God allows disasters to happen. A popular interpretation ascribes the suffering borne of disasters as God's punitive judgement over a sinful people. On the other hand, Fretheim's essay suggests looking first on the history of nature as far as the pre-existence of humankind on earth. The first chapters of Genesis show that God's approach to creation is not a "do-it-all-by-myself" attitude. Rather, he involves what he has already made in the creative process. "God invites the earth and the waters . . . even the natural disasters" to take part in the "becoming" of the world. Although this creative process goes through a messy phase which poses danger to humans and non-humans alike, God allows all of his creation to move with their creative potential towards order and beauty.

Similarly, God involves humanity in the creative process. The mandate in Genesis 1:28 is an invitation to contribute to bringing order to the continuing disorder in creation but it is often misconstrued as a licence for violent domination. In effect, humanity's destructive actions intensify the existing dangers of an already dynamic world. Peñamora's essay (chapter 8) furthers this

---

1. Manila, Philippines: OMF Literature, 2017.

notion by providing narratives about heavy landslides and floods in Quezon, a province in the Philippines, due to increased illegal logging activities. It calls for an emphasis on the *Kapwa* ethics that aim to understand the position of humanity in a larger creation, not just in the context of one's fellow human beings (*kapwa-tao*), but also in the context of animals, nature, and the rest of creation (*kapwa-nilalang*). Furthermore, Mendoza's essay (chapter 4) explores the theme of risk and randomness by analyzing the divine speech in Job 28–31 which speaks of a creation with chaos as an integral part of its design. Not all who suffer from natural disasters are stricken by God's judgement in the same way that not all who are spared are innocent of sin. With all these in mind, it is inappropriate to claim that disasters are God's retribution to human deeds.

Nonetheless, this still begs us to ask, "Does God care when we suffer from the dangers of this creative process or when our suffering is worsened by humanity's greed?" Fretheim's essay (chapter 3) deconstructs the view of an impersonal God detached from the suffering of his people. God is deeply affected by the agony of human beings, choosing to suffer with and for them even when their sufferings are a result of their own actions. However, his redemption does not come in an instant. It follows his way of creation in the sense that he wants his people to participate in his work, too. As Fretheim puts it, "While God suffers with the people, God is not powerless in the suffering. But instead of wiping all the problems at once, he chooses to enter into the situation and work towards resolution from within." God is in the vocation of suffering with and for others – and invites his people to do the same.

But how do we practically suffer with and for others? Alexander's essay says that the question, "Why, O God?" is a cry for justice to a personal God, and that by paying attention to questions like this, we allow the Spirit of God to transform us from within. Picking up on the same theme, Villanueva's essay explains how Filipinos are generally uncomfortable asking God, "Why?" due to a preconditioned belief that was historically used by our foreign oppressors to abuse us. Nevertheless, just as the Bible and Jesus affirm the use of lament, we should also allow people to experience *pagtatampo* (a cultural appropriation of lament in the Philippine context) towards God in the face of disaster. We need to give people who are suffering space for asking questions to help them adapt, heal, and rebuild. In addition, as the church continues to find creative ways to alleviate suffering in disasters, it is equally important to provide post-event physical and psychospiritual support and be a part of disaster risk management movements.

It is the poor who suffer the most during these times of crises. Their socioeconomic status limits their capacity to take precautionary measures against disasters. Lacanilao's essay (chapter 13) proposes that churches situated in ultra-poor communities can serve as immediate response providers during disasters and that pastors, as part of their "kingdom work," should be trained to help prepare their communities for future calamities. Cross's essay (chapter 15) stands on the same principle. Local churches should facilitate workshops on disaster risk reduction among the residents of impoverished areas and partner with them to form community-based organizations which will prepare for the most common type of disasters that may hit their community. We must not forget that the mission of the church is to transform the community. This cannot be done without addressing the power imbalances that perpetuate poverty and disrupt the proper distribution of services and resources. Perhaps this is what it means to suffer with and for others. It is to protect the environment from individuals and corporations who use their economic power to lobby and connive with officials in creating unfair policies that allow them to prey on our natural resources. Maybe it is to be the voice of the poor when their pleas for safety and security are ignored, to fight alongside the marginalized when their rights to their own lands and decent housing are trampled upon – leaving them no choice but to settle in areas most vulnerable to disasters.

Response
On the Summary

The authors of the essays in the book provide rich theological reflections and practical insights that resonate deeply within me as a Filipino. I know firsthand the struggle of living in a country where the occurrence of a disaster is not a matter of "what if," but "when." Reading through the stories of victims overcoming their trials and people trying to find the best ways to help others in times of crises brings me hope and peace.

In My Context

I currently live in Manila, the capital city of the Philippines, but my family migrated from the province of Bicol (southern part of Luzon) where typhoons, floods, cyclones, and volcanic eruptions commonly occur since our land faces the Pacific Ocean and has an active volcano, Mount Mayon. Some of my relatives are still there. They have shared stories of how their houses were torn down to pieces many times by strong typhoons that yearly pass the region. On top of surviving the extreme weather conditions, my people lived through the deadly eruptions of the volcano in 2006 and 2009. When my family and I visited our place months later, I saw one village turned into a cemetery as an entire town was buried in the ashes of Mayon, killing more than a thousand people in it. It was devastating for me back then. Today I can still vividly picture planks of wood tied together to form crosses that were put on top of the mountain of ashes to identify where people are buried.

I still struggle with doubts and questions for disasters continue to take lives and cause heavy damages in our country. Making sense of suffering is not easy even when you have the resources to reason or theologize with, but the narratives and reflections in the book helped me find a way to grasp the difficult matter at hand.

Our Commitment

This series of essays challenged me to re-examine and reshape my understanding of ministry. It inspired me to participate in organized works that protect and develop creation, and heightened my sensitivity to the cry of the vulnerable and the marginalized as they continue to fight for their lives in disaster-prone areas. God made me realize how complacent I have become in just doling out to charities whenever calamities strike and not trying to address anymore the underlying systemic issues that put people's lives at a greater risk.

Our faith communities and/or local churches can use this book as an inspiration for preparing prayer gatherings and liturgies of lament for all those affected by the calamity. The topics/essays can also be a reference to develop a church curriculum for small groups which would be discussed over a span of time to create awareness and a sense of urgency in the congregation about disasters and how the people of God should respond. Furthermore, appropriate trainings on disaster-preparedness can be given to pastors and church volunteers and eventually be extended to the residents of our respective communities as part of the calling of the church today.

Reflection

A Prayer of Lament

Why, O God?
Why did a good God like you make his people suffer like this?
You said that you will protect us
But why did you leave us in the middle of a storm?
Where were you when the super typhoon ravaged our place?

Did you not hear the wailing of the six-year-old girl who lost her mother to the flood?
Did you not see when the sixty-seven-year-old man got buried in the remains of his own house?
Did you not smell the stench of 10,000 rotting corpses floating in the flood?
Did you not feel anything at all when all these were happening?

Why did you allow some people to take advantage of the environment?
Are you unaware of how their selfish actions put us in danger?
Why were they safe in their fortresses during the disaster while we were struggling to survive?
Where is justice in that? Until when will you let evil prosper?

We cried out to you with all our hearts
But you remained silent
Why did you ignore us? Why didn't you do anything?
Why, O God?
Why, O God?
Why, O God?[2]

---

2. This lament in the form of a poem was inspired by the narratives of the survivors of the 2013 super-typhoon.

Philippines

It's OK to Be Not OK: Preaching the Lament Psalms[1]
Federico G. Villanueva

Contributed by Myrto Theocharous (Cyprus)

Summary

Villanueva's main concern is about Christian responses to suffering and persecution. He begins his book by sharing his experience of the 2009 Typhoon Ondoy in the Philippines that destroyed countless lives, houses, and villages. What Villanueva observed was that the church's subsequent worship made no mention of this unspeakable tragedy that people from his congregation had just experienced. Their songs and prayers continued to be joyful, and people did not feel comfortable acknowledging the sorrow, anger, doubt, and other "negative" emotions they were feeling. Only triumphant experiences counted as "testimonies" to God, but unanswered prayers and "failures" were not permitted to enter the public gathering. It is a characteristic of Filipino culture to not be transparent with one's struggles, but another part of the problem is that Filipino worship, as experienced by the author, is mostly comprised of songs from the West which means that worship is not born organically from within the people's local experience.

Responding to this, Villanueva presents thorough research showing how biblical characters, including God in the Old Testament as well as Jesus in the New Testament, express a wide range of emotions. Through the study of the lament psalms, the author explores these so-called "negative" emotions as elements essential to the worship, healing, and restoration of the community. He believes that without proper and truthful lament, the church will be ill-prepared to face the present and future suffering. Lament is not popular in the church because people often equate it with complaining or moaning, but avoiding lament is essentially a form of teaching people to suppress or deny truth. We forget that the Scriptures are filled with lament, in the Psalms and

---

1. Carlisle, Cumbria: Langham Preaching Resources, 2017.

elsewhere, and lament is there to give us words for the unspeakable and to make room for the one who is in pain, not only in acts of mercy outside the church, but in the centre of communal worship.

The book includes eight "It's OK" sections: It's OK to be down, be sad, cry, be afraid, struggle, be angry, question God, and fail. The first victory for the Christian is to admit he or she is *not* OK, says Villanueva, even though we have created a system of blocking such "weak appearing" individuals from ministry and leadership positions. Mourning in itself is "embarrassing" or useless at best, so these days even funerals have been turned into opportunities for evangelism, rather than a space to mourn. Standing on the shoulders of great theologians and saints of the past, Villanueva shows that they all felt the absence of God and wrote about it, while not elevating "being down" to a virtue. There are different seasons, according to the author, and different appropriate responses for different circumstances and different times – a time to dance and a time to mourn. If we do not honour each stage, if we rush it, we cannot travel towards healing. This movement from joy to sorrow should not be feared as if it reflected a change in God. What it does reflect is the truth about the reality of human life. The author illustrates this by sharing a moving story of how while he was singing, "You are the everlasting God, you never grow weak or weary," during Sunday vespers, he broke into tears, sat down and wept, crying, "Lord, you never grow weary, but me, I am so tired!"[2] The truth about God and the truth about us must *both* be expressed and acknowledged for both can be true at the same time.

In the Scriptures, a position of power and control is never good for the Christian. Instead, the best position to be in is a position of need before God. The first is an illusion, the second opens our eyes to the truth. The author speaks of the rich and the poor and how pain is a universal experience for all classes, but the way we deal with it will differ. He quotes Gracia Burnham after she was rescued from the Abu Sayyaf in Mindanao:[3] "Here [in the USA] when you are thirsty you just open the faucet, and there is water. If you are hungry, you just open the fridge and get something to munch. But in the mountains, when you are thirsty, you cry out to God."[4]

When it comes to anger, the author warns against hypocrisy. Of course, we are called to forgive and love our enemies, but often rushing to forgive

---

2. Villanueva, *It's OK to Be Not OK*, 52.

3. Mindanao is the second largest island in the Philippines. Abu Sayyaf is a jihadist group affiliated with the so-called Islamic State.

4. Villanueva, *It's OK to Be Not OK*, 68.

becomes a means of avoiding confrontation and "keeping the peace." As a result, anger is not succeeded by forgiveness but is instead suppressed and becomes destructive for both ourselves and the others.

The author recommends honesty. One should share their feelings of anger with wise and trusted believers who can actually "take it." Looking at the imprecatory psalms, we feel uncomfortable saying such strong words against our enemies and such psalms are usually censured. But while many refrain from uttering those words, they may wish those things in their heart. These psalms give us permission not to pretend before God and not to be dishonest about our embittered hearts. This is the only way to process our anger, and as we begin being honest in prayer, only then do we come to know what is actually present in our hearts. The author also notes how psalms that would start with imprecatory prayer will often end in praise, which means that the process of expressing one's anger can effect change.

How do we pray for our leaders when these are corrupt? Villanueva says that continually praying for them to be blessed betrays that we do not care about all those suffering as a result of these leaders' corruption, and we do not really believe that God is just. Instead, wishing and praying for the transformation of these leaders means praying that God brings them down. Being brought down is a necessary step to their transformation. At the same time, the imprecatory prayers require us to have a just life. The Christian is robbed of his or her boldness in prayer when they themselves are practicing the very things they are praying against.

The hardest part of all is praying "against" God, questioning his ways. God is the "supreme court" we go to when other courts fail, but when it is God we are complaining about, where do we go? Villanueva examines the examples of Abraham, Moses, Habakkuk, and others who expressed how they were not pleased with God. They were not "yes men" for God does not want "Yes, Lord, yes, Lord" Christians; rather, God wants "covenant partners who are able to express what they think and feel."[5]

We may never find a solution to suffering, but Villanueva says one answer to suffering is lament. Lament is a sign of hope, a mechanism of coping with our sufferings, an umbrella that cannot stop the rain but can enable us to stand in the rain.[6] Lament is what helps us grow in our intimacy with God and it is an act of faith. It is given to us by God so that we know that this God is able and desires to be touched by a suffering and broken soul.

---

5. Villanueva, *It's OK to Be Not OK*, 102.
6. Villanueva, *It's OK to Be Not OK*, 123.

Response
On the Summary

This book, written in a very approachable way and animated with multiple examples from the author's context, fills a huge gap in our treatments of church worship, theology of suffering, and coping biblically with real struggles. The author teaches us through becoming vulnerable himself, portraying before us a powerful way of doing theology from a position of weakness that licenses readers to do the same: to condemn the silencing their own contexts have imposed on those who suffer, to critique what their own churches have imposed on their members, and to renounce the silencing the readers themselves have imposed on their own experiences. Drawing from a wealth of scriptural texts, the author leads us to a healthy process of truthful reading and embracing pain with eyes wide open.

In My Context

The author's thoughts are relevant beyond his context. The propensity to joyful worship, triumphant stories of success, and ostracization of doubt, complaint, and anger is true for many congregations. This is especially so for evangelical churches who are the product of Western missions, import songs and theologies from the West, and lack indigenous expressions of worship and thought on local challenges and tragedies – all of which adds to the need for this book to be heeded. In my own context, local folk songs and poems of lament have been handed down throughout Greek history and the evangelical church could learn a lot from their style and themes.

With the increasing environmental catastrophes, rising prices of basic necessities, unemployment and social fragmentation, we see people drowning in anger, depression and despair. Lament is an antidote. First of all, it is a form of resistance to the dismissal of harsh realities and to being fugitives from the truth. Second, it is a form of public condemnation of evil and its naturalization in the lives of all human and non-human creation. Unfortunately, communal lament is absent from my ecclesiastical context in Greece, and I share the author's view for the necessity of introducing this element as primary to our church gatherings.

Our Commitment

- Let us acknowledge that we are guilty of suppressing the truth of pain and suffering in our churches, in the experience of others, and in ourselves.
- Let us find a wise and spiritually mature brother or sister to share our pain, anger, and struggles with them. If others come to share with us, let us listen without attempting to add "happy notes" or "bright sides."
- Let us weep with those who weep. Let us produce songs, poems, and liturgies of lament.
- Let us think of how we can structure public services of lament that do not "police" people's pain nor give in to chaos, but weave together a liturgy that leaves room for lament and communal catharsis.

Reflection

Tough Years: Lament of Women[7]
by Telemachos Kanthos
Woodcut on paper, 33 x 30 cm. 1976.

---

7. Source: https://www.ucy.ac.cy/publications/wp-content/uploads/sites/54/2022/03/Telemachos_Kanthos_Skliroi_Xronoi2009.pdf

Singapore

Hope for the World: The Christian Vision[1]
Roland Chia

Contributed by Adrian Paul P. Morales (Philippines)

Summary

With all the pressing issues that the world struggles with today – poverty, economic inequality, social exploitation, terrorism, violence, and all other things that depreciate and destroy life – one could easily fear and feel paralyzed. Yet, there is one essential thing that enables us humans to move forward in life: hope. This book surveys hope as a pervasive theme in the Bible and offers ways it can empower followers of Jesus to face the threat of suffering and evil in the present.

Christians and other religious communities do not claim exclusivity to hope. It is a universal phenomenon which every human being experiences as a reaction to life's difficulties. However, hope is often confused with blind optimism. Chia draws the line between the two. He says that the latter is naïve; it embraces triumphalism and ignores the reality of pain and suffering, while the former "confronts the world as it is" and responds proactively by imagining new possibilities.

Hope has indeed fuelled humanity to progress in civilization. It has inspired the modernization of societies and advancements in science and technology. Unfortunately, attempts to create alternatives are not always beneficial to all. In many instances, a false sense of progress has paradoxically made life more difficult for others, such as those who are victims of wars and unjust social policies. Is this the same "hope" that the Bible speaks of? To define what "Christian hope" really means, the author explores different passages from the Scriptures.

Chia says that for Christians, "God is not just the object of hope but is its basis," and that true hope centres on who God is, and not on human powers.

---

1. Global Christian Library. Carlisle, Cambria: Langham Global Library, 2012.

In the Old Testament, the creation account in Genesis depicts Yahweh as the ultimate Creator of the universe. Also, the exodus story tells us that when Yahweh saw the suffering of the Israelites in Egypt, he rescued them from slavery and brought them to the Promised Land. This experience of deliverance, which became central to Israel's history, taught them that Yahweh is the one who "creates and continues to work among men in recreating and renewing their lives."

The author explains that the faith of Israel in Yahweh, the Creator and Deliverer, led to an understanding of God as the ultimate king. However, a huge challenge to the belief of God's kingship is the continuous existence of sin and evil in the world. From this point, hope for Israel starts to come in the form of a future kingdom wherein God's reign is absolute, where justice and righteousness prevail, and where evil no longer exists. Moreover, the Israelites start to associate this kingdom with a coming king from the line of David – the Messiah who will completely establish the kingdom of Yahweh. This is the hope shared by the Israelites up until the beginning of Jesus's ministry.

In the New Testament, the coming of the kingdom of God is the central theme of Jesus's message (Mark 1:15). It is tied with Daniel's vision of the coming of the "Son of Man" out of the clouds of heaven. However, this raises a question: If the Son of Man already came in the person of Jesus, the Messiah that the world awaits, why does he still speak of the coming of the kingdom as a future reality? Chia suggests that the coming of the kingdom dawned upon human history when Jesus was born and still awaits its completion upon his return.

The concept of the "already" and "not yet" has been discussed repeatedly in Paul's epistles. In his writings, he exhorts the followers of Jesus to continue living in hope as they wait for the "glorious appearing of our great God and Saviour, Jesus Christ" (Titus 2:13). He encourages the church that suffering in this world does not compare to the glory that will be revealed in the future (Rom 8). Paul's concept of the coming of the kingdom is anchored on the resurrection of Christ which constitutes victory over death. With this in mind, Chia says that believers should not fear for death is not final and it will be eradicated completely in the fullness of the kingdom.

Some may argue that this belief fosters an unhealthy attitude, encouraging believers to avoid dealing with the challenges of today and focus solely on the afterlife instead. However, what really are the implications of the hope for a future kingdom on Christians living in the present age? In his biblical survey, the author presents that all forms and themes of eschatological hope in the Scriptures are mainly concerned with overcoming wickedness. On the same note, Paul's epistles emphasize the transformative power of Jesus's resurrection and its significance for humanity. It fulfils the promise of deliverance from evil in the Old Testament and marks the start of "a new community of the redeemed and the new world," in accordance with Israel's expectations on the coming kingdom and the Messiah.

In essence, Christian hope is active hope. It does not call the church to run away from this fallen world. Rather, it invites us to step into it with "profound realism" as we follow the footsteps of Jesus. It creates in us a deeper sensitivity for justice in the middle of injustice and oppression. It inspires us to take radical actions to promote the values of the kingdoms on Earth. It enables us to share in the sufferings of Jesus as we continue to struggle against evil and pain in the present with the assurance of the resurrection and God's absolute reign in the finality of things.

Response
On the Summary

The author speaks from a Southeast Asian perspective. As a Filipino, I can attest to the book's depiction of how the majority of the people in our region are poor due to various social factors. Many disadvantaged individuals are trapped in the cycle of poverty and injustice in developing countries such as the Philippines. In our context, hope is not just a desirable feeling but a necessity we are desperate for to continue living.

In My Context

The book highlights the coming of the Lord to establish his kingdom and judge both the living and the dead as the overarching event in human history. This concept is one of the most dominant theological voices in the Philippines. It is used by fellow believers in the evangelical community to explain why suffering and unfortunate events take place. They say that these hardships are signs of the end times and, in response, the believers should not be afraid, for soon they will be taken to paradise.

This is articulated in the creeds of the church but there is a specific undertone in the proclamation of this belief in our country that roots deeply in our experience as Filipinos.

According to the Philippine Statistic Authority, in 2021 there were around twenty million Filipinos who lived below the poverty line with a monthly income of PhP 12,030 or 215 USD for a family of five. Many factors contribute to the worsening social challenges in the Philippines. Although it is not the only reason, the long and harsh periods of colonization by Spain, the US, and Japan have undeniably delimited our progress. Colonization has passed on the legacy of unequal distribution of power, wealth, and land – allowing a certain few, often affiliated with our historical oppressors, to take control of our resources while the masses continue to live in poverty. Colonialism still persists in the Philippines, only now in the guise of capitalism and the exploitation of our local workers.

In addition, there are issues of corruption that are evident in the national infrastructure projects that only serve the interests of people in authority or their associates, unfair government policies on taxation, labour, agriculture, housing, limited access to healthcare and education services, etc., which make it more difficult for the poor to improve their quality of life. On top of all these are the thousands of extrajudicial killings related to the controversial war-on-drugs campaign that targeted marginalized communities, the harassment of journalists, and the enforced disappearances of some indigenous leaders and human rights activists.

Most of the time, when Filipinos speak of Christian hope, of Jesus returning, it does not mean that we want to disappear magically from this world. It just means that our people have already experienced too much suffering and we are crying out to God for justice.

Our Commitment

For the past years, the socio-political climate in the Philippines became too hostile for a quality life. I personally felt hopeless. I temporarily disengaged from my commitments in our local ministry and community. I grew tired of our efforts being easily overturned by the systemic injustices in our country. However, this book reminds me that true hope lies not in human powers but in God alone. I was humbled and, at the same time, inspired to continue living my life before God while facing disappointments. Furthermore, this book allows me to understand the works of the kingdom on a scale larger than myself. Now, I want to participate more proactively in the work Jesus has already started in recreating and renewing life in this world as he establishes his kingdom in its fullness.

Reflection

A Prayer of Hope

Where can we go when death surrounds us, O Lord?
Either we die of disease, hunger, disaster, or the violence of others
What can we do now that we are being killed in our own land?
The arms that are supposed to protect us are already pointed against us

O God, we have nothing but you
We are powerless, voiceless, and restless
Please hear us and answer to our distress
You are our only hope

How do evil people keep getting away with their corrupted ways?
They play with the lives of the vulnerable like chess pieces
Who do we call if our leaders are already the ones taking advantage of us?
Our people are easily being abused and silenced

O God, we have nothing but you
We are powerless, voiceless, and restless
Please hear us and answer to our distress
You are our only hope

When will justice, truth, and peace prevail, O Lord?
Grant us your grace to face evil and suffering in the present
And the courage to confront issues that require our collective attention
Remind us of the hope that we have in your resurrection.

Singapore

When Christians Face Persecution: Theological Perspectives from the New Testament[1]
Chee-Chiew Lee

Contributed by Chee-Chiew Lee and her student, T. Lee (East Asia)[2]

Summary by Chee-Chiew Lee

Why do Christians face persecution, and how should they respond to persecution in a way that is faithful to Jesus? These questions are relevant not only to the New Testament (NT) Christians but also throughout church history across the world. This book describes the NT's teaching regarding persecution as a basis for God's people to reflect on how to respond to persecution in their own contemporary contexts.

In the introduction, I define what constitutes persecution to distinguish its nuance from opposition to Christian faith and suffering for Christ in general terms. Also, I adopt a methodology which not only describes the NT's unifying teaching on persecution, but also highlights each NT author's distinctive perspective or approach in encouraging their audience to persevere despite facing persecution.

In chapter 1, I show why Christians were persecuted and by whom. By introducing the first century's Greco-Roman and Jewish religious worldviews, I identify those beliefs that clashed with Christian beliefs and how the NT and other Greco-Roman historical sources reflect these. I also show that some factors are held in common with persecuted non-Christian groups. Besides the spectrum of human opponents (individual/group opponents, various authorities), the NT portrays Satan as the instigator of persecution. I analyze the reasons for persecuting Christians from both the insiders' and the outsiders'

---

1. London: Apollos, 2022.
2. I, Chee-Chiew Lee, live in Singapore – a place where there is barely any religious persecution. However, my students come from surrounding regions in Asia with varying degrees of religious persecution. This short video explains why the book was written: https://www.youtube.com/watch?v=q3uF04_fdp0.

perspectives, as this relates to understanding why NT Christians respond in certain ways (these are discussed in chapter 2). I summarize four reasons from the outsiders' perspective: a threat to dearly held traditional values; a threat to economic losses; (alleged) vilification of opponents; and a threat of social unrest.[3]

In chapter 2, I describe the various forms of persecution and the diverse responses of early Christians. In Acts, Luke portrayed both Jewish and pagan opponents as frequently instigating others to join them in opposing Christians. To stop Christians from propagating their beliefs, they would bring charges against Christians to their local or regional authorities, who would sometimes punish the Christians for causing unrest. These opponents also verbally and physically abused Christians through mob behaviour. Christian responses to persecution in the NT may be generally classified as "resistance and perseverance," "apostasy and assimilation," and "accommodation and adaptation."[4]

Positive examples of "resistance and perseverance" abound in the NT. There are also some negative examples of apostasy, such as those whom Jesus predicted would fall away (e.g. Mark 4:17), and assimilation, such as those who advocated that it is all right for Christians to eat food sacrificed to idols or participate in pagan/imperial worship (1 Cor 8–10; Rev 2). While the gospels clearly portray that denying Jesus under the pressure of persecution is not the desired response, the biblical authors also seem to accommodate those who are weak but repentant (e.g. Peter), and John seems to accommodate certain disciples' secret behaviour (e.g. Joseph of Arimathea). Paul and Peter adapted current practices, such as "good works" (Rom 12–13; 1 Pet 2–4) and praying for all people and the authorities (1 Tim 2:1–2), as a response to accusations that Christians are a threat to society. First Timothy 2:1–2 is an important example of adapting the practice of imperial worship by honouring the imperial authorities through prayers without compromising the Christian faith.

In chapter 3, I explain in detail how the NT authors persuade their audience to be faithful to Christ despite facing persecution. First, the NT authors used common rhetorical techniques, such as exhortations, exemplars, logical reasoning, and the stirring up of emotions (e.g. hope, fear, empathy, honour, shame) to deter compromises of faith and to motivate perseverance. Second, the honour-and-shame culture and Christian eschatology were powerful in shaping people's values and lives. The NT authors redefined what

---

3. Lee, *When Christians Face Persecution*, 40–50.
4. Lee, *When Christians Face Persecution*, 63–89.

was "shameful" in the dominant culture's perspective as being "honourable" in God's perspective (e.g. suffering shame for Christ). It is better to bear with "shame" temporarily than to be shamed eternally at the final judgement. God will bestow eternal glory to Christians who now suffer shame for Christ. He will also avenge the wrongful persecution of his people. Third, a few of the distinctive motifs are noteworthy here: the reality of Jesus's promises in Luke-Acts – the disciples experienced his promises to empower and deliver them; empathy for community perseverance in Hebrews – Jesus's empathy is a motivation for his people to seek his help without fear, and the author stirred up his audience's empathy so that they may help those who suffer for Christ; and, while John and Hebrews acknowledge the reality of fear, they also address how it may be overcome.

In the conclusion, I summarize the causes of persecution, diverse responses to persecution, and various persuasions towards perseverance. Finally, I encourage contemporary readers to reflect on their own contexts and consider how the NT authors' theological perspectives could be relevant to them.

In the epilogue, I demonstrate how contextual reflections could be relevant by providing examples and asking questions, but without claiming these to be absolute. The prime ways contextual reflections could be relevant are as follows. First, understanding what constitutes persecution is important to avoid trivializing or exaggeration. Second, it is important to note contextual differences and adjust accordingly when applying biblical principles. The different views among NT authors on certain issues remind us not to judge others who may differ from our opinions. Third, understanding the perspectives of our opponents is important for us to formulate responses that address their concerns. The factors causing persecution (see chapter 1) are similar throughout the ages, though they may take different forms. Fourth, the NT authors' proper use of emotions reminds us that empathizing with the persecuted is important in encouraging them to persevere, not just telling them what to do. Finally, I encourage contemporary persecuted Christians to share their reflections with fellow Christians, whether in similar or different contexts, so that we may bring "fresh insights" to help one another respond to persecution in a manner faithful to our Lord Jesus.

Response by T. Lee, translated by Chee-Chiew Lee
On the Summary

The diverse perspectives on the issue of persecution in the NT that Dr. Chee-Chiew presents caught my attention. Why were Christians persecuted, and by whom and how? How did Christians respond to persecution? How did the NT authors admonish their audience? As Dr. Chee-Chiew's research shows, there is no single, stereotypical answer. This book describes the persecution narratives of the NT using a biblical-theological approach. In the past, the East Asian mainland (EAM) church's reflections and discussions on this issue are mostly "theological-philosophical." For many years, we have been adept at choosing a certain system for our position, thinking that there should only be a single, standard, and universal way to shape the Christian view of persecution. This book tells us that the diverse persecution narratives in the early church constitute a rich resource for God's people in different situations to delve into and apply.

In My Context

This book is a particularly good reference for the churches in EAM and even in greater Asia for its multi-faceted persecution narratives. The contexts of the Asian church are very different from the Western Christian world. In many ways, Asian Christians resonate with the early church in their experience of persecution. For example, for Christians living in some parts of East Asia under the rule of a government that promotes anti-religious ideology, persecution is the norm. The persecution of these Christians varies distinctively from time to time, province to province, and church to church. Even within the same country, political leaders of different periods can vary in their religious policies; provinces differ in their religious controls due to the differing proportion of Christians and their historical influence; churches are impacted differently due to the diverse nature of their members, causing assorted kinds of tension. In all of these, the persecution contexts these Christians face (though within the same country) are very different. Therefore, the churches in EAM and even in greater Asia need to refer to multi-faceted persecution narratives.

Our Commitment

What I learned most from this book is to respect those who are different and to love those who are weak due to persecution. EAM churches often have too homogeneous an attitude toward persecution, either the traditional separatist/martyrdom model or the non-violent confrontational model that urban churches have tended to advocate since the turn of this century. Regrettably, there are antagonisms and recriminations between advocates of these different models. This book helps the churches in EAM to respect the diversity in persecution narratives, and even encourages the churches to listen to the different plights of different groups. Of particular importance, this book shows us some important spiritual qualities, such as John's accommodation of those who are weak due to persecution and the empathy demonstrated by the author of Hebrews in his rhetoric and exhortations. These qualities provide us with greater dimensions of the higher goal of Christian communion.

Reflection

Easter in Lanlin[5]

---

5. Source: Jiang, *It All Begins with the Dark-faced Christ and Not Cannibalizing* (yi qie cong mo mian ji du he bu chi ren kai shi), Poetic Drama (Hong Kong: Typesetter Publishing, 2017), Fig. 2, page 3. (Used with permission.)

Remarks

The following poem illustrates the need to practice an empathetic theology of facing persecution, as shown in the Gospel of John and the book of Hebrews. Its content does not represent the views of the reviewers. Special thanks to A. Hwang who alerted us to this poem.

What Have You Lost? (ni shi qu le shen me)[6]

When your country's flag is burned,
    You sneered, "It's only a piece of cloth."
When your mother is reviled,
    You sneered, "It's only a sentence."
When your cross is demolished,
    You sneered, "It's only an external symbol."
O you, I see that,
    You are only a prattling mouth . . .

O mindless people,
When humiliation befalls, you have endured much, have you?
    "But there is no need to see it as glorious."
When persecution befalls, you shout,
    "Great! There shall surely be revival!"
Just that I would like to see,
    Have you ever lifted your finger?
    Have you ever wriggled your toes?
    Does revival come by shouting from your home?

O, a generation that has lost its mindfulness,
    Will also eventually lose its substance.
O, a generation that has lost its glory,
    Will also eventually lose its faith.

---

6. Anonymous (c. 2014–2015), translated by C.C. Lee.

Sri Lanka

Sarah's Laughter: Doubt, Tears, and Christian Hope[1]
Vinoth Ramachandra

Contributed by Nathanael M. Somanathan (Sri Lanka)

Summary

In *Sarah's Laughter*, Vinoth Ramachandra, a Sri Lankan theologian, provides both an intellectually stimulating and deeply moving reflection (or meditation as he calls it in the last page of the book) on the existential reality of pain, suffering, and doubts. Having lived through a bloody civil war in Sri Lanka and the personal loss of his dear wife, Ramachandra is no stranger to the acute pain of loss, injustice, and tragedy.

Skipping the need for an introduction Ramachandra dives straight into the first chapter of his book. He begins by acknowledging and elaborating the serious disparities that exist in the world despite popular rhetoric to the contrary. The rich, powerful, and elite position themselves as paragons of compassion and saviours even though "people in rich countries are directly linked to communities in poor countries where lives are being devastated by conflict."[2] The "selective amnesia" (as Ramachandra calls it) found in history books and media discussions facilitates and upholds false narratives like the superiority of American political institutions and their "anti-imperial 'essence'" despite their complicity in creating conflict.[3] For Ramchandra, the inequalities, the pain wrought by conflict and injustice, and the overall grief, compel questions about God's hiddenness and apparent silence in the face of such evils.

Moreover, according to Ramachandra, the questions asked of God amid overwhelming grief like, "Why, Lord?" and "How long, O Lord?" are perfectly consistent with the lament tradition that runs through the Scripture. Lament,

---

1. Carlisle, Cumbria: Langham Global Library, 2020.
2. Ramachandra, *Sarah's Laughter*, 3.
3. Ramachandra, *Sarah's Laughter*, 4.

says Ramachandra, is not only a form of catharsis but also a mode of political protest against injustice for those who lack agency. Lament is not complaining about God but complaining to God. As a chiding word at the end of the chapter, Ramachandra rebukes churches that "suppress the biblical lament tradition in their preaching and liturgies," because in so doing they "are very much part of the status quo, having invested massively in the preservation of exploitative and oppressive social relations."[4]

Intriguingly, before even getting to the meaty chapters, a perceptive reader of *Sarah's Laughter* can discern right off the bat that Ramachandra is writing within a particular theo-philosophical tradition – one which challenges classical conceptions of God and "traditional Christian doctrines such as the 'sovereignty of God' or the 'providence of God.'"[5] Chapter 2, aptly titled "Job and the Messiness of Theology," tries to show that theology is messy in a suffering world. Here, Ramachandra focuses in on the epistemic value of experience and the "creative tension" that exists between beliefs and experiences. Most often, lament mediates this tension: in the words of Scott Ellington, "To lament is to risk the move towards newness, a move that is certain to reshape both our beliefs about God and our most formative experiences of him."[6] Ramachandra expounds on this dialectic in the rest of the chapter by offering an exegetical reflection on the quintessential scriptural text on suffering and lament, the book of Job.

Chapter 3 is by far the most riveting chapter in the book with its provocative title, "The Tears of God." Here, Ramachandra joins the likes of Adolf von Harnack in charging patristic theology of syncretizing Christian theology with the presuppositions of Greek philosophy.[7] Challenging the metaphysical attributes espoused to God, such as immutability and impassibility, Ramachandra argues that the classical theologians of the early church were more interested in preserving the "divine perfection" of God and Creator–creature distinction than concerned for the inadvertent chasm they were creating between "God's being from his creation" as a result.[8] Instead, Ramachandra argues emphatically for a view of God in relation to the world wherein "he has humbly and freely chosen to be in a personal (that is, mutually

---

4. Ramachandra, *Sarah's Laughter*, 21.
5. Ramachandra, *Sarah's Laughter*, 7.
6. Ramachandra, *Sarah's Laughter*, 24.
7. Editors Note: What von Harnack and others fail to recognize is that *all* theologizing is culturally contingent, be it German, Greek, or Sri Lankan. What looks like syncretism from the outside may well be the honest, if messy, work of Christian conversion in a given cultural context.
8. Ramachandra, *Sarah's Laughter*, 45.

responsive) relationship with his world."[9] In using references and examples from psychology and philosophy to make his claim, Ramachandra suggests that the

> only ultimately satisfying mental response to the problem of unmerited and disproportionate suffering is to believe that our Creator, through a wonderful and incomprehensible act of self-limitation, is present in the darkness of affliction, shares our pain, bears our sorrows and sustains us through it all, creating good in spite of evil, so expressing the true nature of divine power.[10]

What better picture of this is there than the "the Trinitarian event of the cross" where "there is a 'giving-up' and a 'being-given-up,' God present in God-forsakenness?"[11]

Furthermore, what is quite surprising in *Sarah's Laugher* is the breadth of issues that Ramachandra addresses in a 130-page reflection. From "horrendous acts of human cruelty and deceit" to "the callous slaughter of animals and habitats," Ramachandra's overall outlook diverges from typical Christian meditations that limit suffering in the world to personal loss or hardship. Ramachandra devotes the entire fourth chapter to grappling with the subject of "natural evil," a matter of profound concern not only for Buddhists in Sri Lanka but for numerous young Christians worldwide because of the escalating ecological crisis. His answer to the problem, however, is to reject the notion that the natural world fell alongside humanity in the Fall. Ramachandra suggests that natural disasters and natural events are the means by which God brings about "ecological changes and biodiversity on the planet." Finding some commonality with deism, Ramachandra also strives in the chapter to jettison the notion that God is behind every event in the world working it toward an end. This removes culpability on God's part in every "accident, mishap and tragedy" that happens and highlights God's providence that works "in and through the regularities and contingencies of the world."[12] Ramachandra, however, rejects a full-fledged deism for what he calls a "'control' model of divine sovereignty" wherein God foregoes total control of the world to truly make room "for the response and cooperation of created humanity."[13] This

---

9. Ramachandra, *Sarah's Laughter*, 47.
10. Ramachandra, *Sarah's Laughter*, 65.
11. Ramachandra, *Sarah's Laughter*, 60.
12. Ramachandra, *Sarah's Laughter*, 92.
13. Ramachandra, *Sarah's Laughter*, 92.

then also means that "God knows perfectly the past as past, and he knows perfectly the future as future."[14] In sum, the term "natural evil" is somewhat of a misnomer since "it is human sin that is the great evil and from which flow all the other kinds of evil and misery" that sometimes also wreaks havoc in the natural world.[15]

In the fifth chapter before the final epilogue, Ramchandra's reflection on suffering culminates on the appropriate Christian theme of hope. He does not leave the reader merely with the brute fact of a suffering world and the consolation of a suffering God, instead he brings the true meaning of the gospel to the forefront: that the Triune God brings about "something astonishingly new, something which is not merely a development of the inherent potentialities and possibilities of the historical present."[16] Therein lies the Christian hope, "upon the action of the creator God who summons forth life out of death in the resurrection of Jesus Christ."[17]

Response
On the Summary

There is no doubt that *Sarah's Laugher* seamlessly blends emotional depth with intellectual rigour. One is both called to solidarity with the sufferers and to repent for complicity in causing suffering at the same time. But all the while looking to Christ as the pattern for true humility and to the Triune God as the power for compassion and hope.

What is particularly insightful in Ramachandra's reflection is his identification of the ways in which human practices that contribute to systems of evil in ways go unnoticed. This aspect of the problem of evil and suffering is often overlooked in contemporary Western evangelical discussions on the subject. This is because for majority world Christians the problem of evil and suffering is not a philosophical conundrum to overcome, it is an existential threat to everyday living. Ramachandra exposes how selective amnesia, elitist politics, and even academic (contextual) theologies do not always address the conspiracy of human actions with the works of darkness in consistent manner because many do not want to give up power. Resurrection is not seen as the vindication of Good Friday suffering; it is often seen as a triumphalist

---

14. Ramachandra, *Sarah's Laughter*, 93.
15. Ramachandra, *Sarah's Laughter*, 95.
16. Ramachandra, *Sarah's Laughter*, 99.
17. Ramachandra, *Sarah's Laughter*, 100.

replacement. All in all, Ramachandra brings to the surface important resources in the lament tradition and the majority world experience that can be a balm to many today.

In My Context

Ramachandra's writing style and choice of ideas and thinkers he engages with do not shield him from all criticism. Even though his Sri Lankan context contributes much to his reflection, he seems to be writing predominantly to a Western audience. This is particularly evident in the lack of consideration of the theme of suffering in dominant Asiatic spiritualities, such as Hinduism and Buddhism. Such a treatment may have required more space, but it would have certainly proven more beneficial to Asians and other majority world worldviews that do not approach the problem of suffering in the same way as the West. Regardless, Ramachandra's insight has something to offer Western Christianity: those who have ears, let them listen.

Our Commitment

In reading *Sarah's Laughter*, my own convictions about lament as a Pentecostal have been challenged and enriched. As a pastor, I was deeply struck by the importance of recovering and incorporating practices and liturgies of lament in regular church services. Ramachandra's emphasis on the resurrection as a sign of new possibilities and new horizons through the "Spirit who groans, empowers, and sanctifies"[18] has brought new direction to my ministry towards the downtrodden and the marginalized.

---

18. Ramachandra, *Sarah's Laughter*, 125.

Reflection

A Poem[19]

How long will we wait – O Sovereign Lord,
How long will we wait?
How long will we wait for those who killed
and destroyed us to repent?
How long will we wait?

We lived by farming – helped
Many poor to live.
Why did the missiles detonate? – Why did they
Finish us off? – How long . . .

We lived by fishing – provided
Many with their food.
We were arrested – we did
Perish to the ground – How long . . .

We were teaching – became the
Instruments of learning
Got struck by the land mines – became
Corpses in an instant – How long . . .

---

19. Fr. Selvan an Anglican clergyman wrote this poem "from the killing fields of Jaffna, northern Sri Langa . . . during the height of the war and based on Revelation 6:10," quoted in Ramachandra, *Sarah's Laughter*, 17.

Sri Lanka

The Call to Joy and Pain: Embracing Suffering in Your Ministry[1]
Ajith Fernando

Contributed by Nathanael M. Somanathan (Sri Lanka)

Summary

Ajith Fernando, a world renown speaker and a Sri Lankan theologian, brings an important resource, especially for those in ministry, in his book *The Call to Joy and Pain*. Fernando reveals that the book is written to address the growing false conception that Christians must not suffer. However, in addressing the theme of "pain," he did not want to leave out the blessings of it. Therefore, this book emerges as an encouraging biblical study to uphold the twin realities of ministry: joy and pain. Fernando suggests that "something is seriously wrong not when Christians suffer but when they do not have the joy of the Lord."[2]

Fernando begins the book by asserting the call of God as both a call to joy and to pain. He states that both joy and pain/suffering are necessary and essential parts of the Christian life. Thereon, he observes that Christians often exchange joy for cheap satisfaction or pleasure. But the true joy of the Lord that is a product of Christian deliverance and liberation is what God intends for the believer. However, as he shows in chapter 3, this does not mean there is not a place for pleasure. He affirms that Scripture validates and promotes "bursts of pleasure" which we all experience in mundane life. For the married couple, this can be sex and for the young person, it could be playing a sport. However, these bursts of pleasure must be based on the "joy of the Lord." Fernando calls Christians to actually "show how joyful joy is. . . . Then people, in their mad quest for pleasure in this hedonistic age, will realize that what they are searching for is found only in the way of life ordained by their Creator."[3]

---

1. Wheaton, Illinois: Crossway, 2020.
2. Fernando, *The Call to Joy and Pain*, 10.
3. Fernando, *The Call to Joy and Pain*, 30.

The second element he identifies as necessary for joy in pain is faith. Faith in God's essential attributes of love and care as revealed in Scripture. Fernando reminds the believer, in the words of Martyn Lloyd-Jones, to "stop listening to our self-pitying conversation and start preaching the deeper realities to ourselves."[4] The third element is surrender. Fernando believes that for "a biblical Christian, rather than being something to dread, surrender can become a gateway to an exciting adventure."[5] In this way, the Christian holds nothing but God as supremely important and experiences God's comforting presence in the departure of a loved one.

Nevertheless, Fernando rejects any notion of seeking after suffering or "being gluttons for punishment." He encourages pursuing discernment when "we should turn the other cheek and we should stand up for our right to practice Christianity."[6] Yet many Christians, due to an undeveloped theology of suffering and theological blind spots, resist any instance of suffering.

In the second part of the book, Fernando moves to the theme of suffering as a means for fellowship with Christ. Here, he shows how suffering can mature intimacy with Christ. So much so that this knowledge can remove the sting of suffering and one does not need to fear it. Additionally, suffering not only deepens intimacy with Christ, Fernando intimates that it also conforms us to being like Christ. That is, in doing the things that Christ did, we are assured to experience his promises of intimacy.

In the third part of the book, Fernando brings attention to suffering in relation to the church. Here Fernando argues that suffering Christians "help create situations for the gospel to go out."[7] Acts 8 and 9 serve as examples for Fernando's point here, where the scattering of the church served God's gospel purposes. A second way that suffering Christians help the church is in demonstrating the gospel. When Christians are faithful and endure in the midst of suffering, it shines a light on the truth of the gospel.

In the final part of the book, Fernando focuses on church ministry. He encourages those in church ministry to see themselves as servants and stewards. But this service is neither of self-will nor sustained by one's own strength. Fernando urges that we "make sure that all our service springs from grace."[8] However, this understanding of grace is supplemented by an understanding of

---

4. Fernando, *The Call to Joy and Pain*, 41.
5. Fernando, *The Call to Joy and Pain*, 46.
6. Fernando, *The Call to Joy and Pain*, 48.
7. Fernando, *The Call to Joy and Pain*, 86.
8. Fernando, *The Call to Joy and Pain*, 138.

the riches that are in the gospel of Christ. Fernando is careful to not "present the cost of service without the underlying confidence that is accompanied by joy and a reward that outstrips the cost."[9]

The final chapters of the book explain that the ultimate Christian message is Jesus Christ himself. Therefore, his followers must "follow the path of radical obedience to Christ and sacrificial service to humanity" in the process of Christian discipleship.[10] As difficult as discipleship might be, it is indispensable to the life of the church and gospel service. Fernando concludes by highlighting the paradox of the Christian life, which is a running theme in the New Testament: Christ promises both suffering and joy as inherent to the Christian life in this world.

Response
On the Summary

The Call to Joy and Pain is clearly an outflow of Fernando's long-term ministry in Sri Lanka. His pastoral and gentle tone is palpable in every page. The many anecdotes, scriptural references, and hagiographical snippets are bound to inspire readers to approach the Christian life and ministry for what it is: joy in pain. As such, Fernando's book is a relevant resource for those in ministry and who may be even struggling to retain the passion for serving God. However, where Fernando's style and his understanding of God may have some weakness is in how the complex and varied experiences of suffering sometimes seem to be flattened out. Much ink has been spent in recent decades addressing the various gaps in Christian literature, specifically addressing how trauma and involuntary suffering has sometimes been glamourized by the church to the detriment of victims. While Scripture is an incredible source of encouragement and inspiration for sufferers, the biblical authors do not always address suffering with a monotone voice nor do their contexts directly correlate to every contemporary experience of pain. Therefore, Christian books on suffering require meticulous nuances to distinguish what is in the purview of God's will and what are the works of darkness.

---

9. Fernando, *The Call to Joy and Pain*, 41.
10. Fernando, *The Call to Joy and Pain*, 160.

In My Context

Fernando brings attention to the importance of lament in the Christian life. He identifies this as one of three things which are needed to experience joy in the midst of pain. Reflecting on his own ministry challenges and the tragedies of Sri Lanka such as the 2004 tsunami, Fernando recounts his own experience with lament. He notes that these were moments in which he experienced God's comfort but also ways in which bitterness was disposed. Prosperity theology, Fernando suggests, is directly contradictory to the lament tradition of Scripture

Our Commitment

Fernando also highlights the importance of how Christian suffering can be a sign of solidarity with those who live in dire circumstances. Fernando sees this as the precedent set by the incarnation of the Son of God. Accordingly, this also means that suffering can be a sign of true Christian witness. Those who seek to live godly lives are often persecuted. But Fernando also notes that unwillingness to suffer is also associated with a lack of commitment. Here, he reinforces the importance of staying true to commitments to the church and to the people we serve.

Fernando's book is a beautiful tribute to what ministry can be. Many Christians, including myself, would prefer a comfortable and easy life. But Fernando challenges the spiritualizing of material prosperity and shows how Scripture's and Christ's call is different. Fernando emphasizes that the Christian life is hard and yet joyful. To forfeit ministry for the sake of worldly treasures and an apparent sense of prosperity is actually a poor trade-off. In reading Fernando, one is convicted to reevaluate their commitment to Christ and his service and also, more importantly, to seek joy in the midst of pain.

Reflection

Fisherman in Sri Lanka[11]

---

11. Source: https://picryl.com/media/fishing-fisherman-sri-lanka-travel-vacation-a7ba72. This image is from Pixabay and was published prior to July 2017 under the Creative Commons CC0 1.0 Universal Public Domain Dedication license https://web.archive.org/web/20161229043156/https://pixabay.com/en/service/terms/

Thailand

A Christian Theology of Suffering in the Context of Theravada Buddhism in Thailand[1]
Satanun Boonyakiat

Contributed by Nathanael M. Somanathan (Sri Lanka)

Summary

In this important contribution to Christian theology, Satanun Boonyakiat attempts to develop a theology of suffering that is relevant to the context of Theravada Buddhism in Thailand. The impetus behind the project is based on the inadequacies present in Western reflections on suffering that focus on the philosophical issue of theodicy. While Boonyakiat does not dismiss the need for theodical enquiries, he observes that in the Thai context and, by extension, the South Asian Buddhist context generally, sufferers "do not merely seek to understand, but to be freed from, suffering."[2]

Furthermore, Theravada Buddhism, and particularly the four noble truths, characterizes the lens through which people in Thailand, including Christians, understand the reality of human suffering. Therefore, for Christians in Thailand to construct a theological framework for understanding the nature, purpose, and mitigation of suffering, it cannot simply be a Western import, they must do so in dialogue with Buddhism. And so Boonyakiat begins his endeavour by establishing his methodology in the first chapter; all the other chapters are ordered and based on the precepts of the four noble truths – truth of suffering (*dukkha*), cause of suffering (*samudaya*), extinction of suffering (*nirodha*), and the way to extinction of suffering (*marga*).[3]

---

1. Carlisle, Cumbria: Langham Monographs, 2020.
2. Boonyakiat, *A Christian Theology of Suffering*, 159.
3. Editors' note: These terms are in Pali, an ancient language of India, and are ultimately derived from Sanskrit cognates. It became the sacred language of Theravada Buddhism. *Dukkha* means "unease" or "suffering," *samudaya* means "origin" or "cause," *nirodha* means "cessation" or "confinement," *marga* means "way" or "path", both literally and figuratively.

In the first chapter, Boonyakiat argues that a "Christian theology of suffering that is relevant to the context of Theravada Buddhism in Thailand, yet is faithful to Christian belief, must be grounded in both a trinitarian theology of religions and trinitarian comparative theology."[4] In agreement with other comparativists, he suggests that theology in contexts with religious pluralism must necessarily be comparative. However, comparative theology does not replace a theology of religions, but complements it wherein both give a Christian account of other faiths and the Triune God's work in and through them. Boonyakiat also proposes that the trinitarian framework overlain on the two not only enables theological engagement with other religious traditions while remaining faithful to one's own home tradition, but also "make possible a Thai Christian theology of suffering that is more relevant to the Buddhist context, as well as a global Christian theology of suffering that is more applicable to the radically pluralistic world."[5] Here, Boonyakiat also draws on Martin Luther, Kazoh Kitamori, and Jürgen Moltmann to show how a trinitarian framework for a Christian theology of suffering points to the cross of Christ. The cross "reveals that the triune God of Christianity is a suffering God who actively participates in human suffering."[6]

In the first chapter, reflecting on the first noble truth (acknowledgement of the existence of suffering), Boonyakiat identifies that both Buddhism and Christianity affirm the reality and complexity of suffering and that even some "forms of suffering can be part of human nature."[7] However, Christianity can learn from Buddhism in how to respond to this concrete challenge: not merely as an intellectual problem, but as an existential crisis to be overcome. Furthermore, Boonyakiat notes that Christians must reject the notion that all suffering is a result of sin and embrace a new perspective that some suffering is an inevitable part of the created order.

This leads to his second chapter on the second noble truth on the cause of suffering. Here, Boonyakiat states that a Christian theology of suffering in the context of Theravada Buddhism in Thailand refuses to generalize causes of suffering. He provides three categories of suffering to explain this further: suffering as the result of sin, as caused by oppression, and as a mystery. In

---

4. Boonyakiat, *A Christian Theology of Suffering*, xi.
5. Boonyakiat, *A Christian Theology of Suffering*, 51.
6. Boonyakiat, *A Christian Theology of Suffering*, 51.
7. Boonyakiat, *A Christian Theology of Suffering*, 160.

this, Boonyakiat also challenges the law of *kamma* (i.e. karma)[8] as an all-encompassing framework for understanding the cause of all forms of suffering. In reflecting on the third and fourth noble truths, Bonyakiat argues that a Christian theology of suffering for one's context acknowledges that right action and attitudes can help alleviate and even prevent unnecessary suffering. However, the Christian affirmation goes further: that Christ is the only true way (*marga*) to salvation from sin and from suffering (*dukkha*) and the one who will bring ultimate extinction (*nirodha*) to suffering itself.

Response
On the Summary

Finally, Boonyakiat ends his exploration with the affirmation that a Christian theology of suffering that is relevant to the Thai Buddhist context cannot be limited to academia. He states that the question must not only be, "What is God's response to suffering?" but also, "What is the response of Thai Christians to suffering?" This must entail "faith" in addition to repentance and solidarity. Christian faith is faith in the Triune God, but Christians can learn how to sustain faith in the midst of suffering from Buddhist meditation practices. He notes that, "Buddhists practice meditation to empty their minds so they will be freed from all attachments, but Christians engage in the various activities of Christian spirituality to empty themselves so they will be filled with the fullness of Christ."[9] Boonyakiat also emphasizes solidarity and repentance as appropriate responses to suffering that find grounding in the very ministry of Christ.

In My Context

Boonyakiat's overall thesis is relevant and enormously helpful to my context of Sri Lanka, which is also home to Theravada Buddhism. His experimental endeavour in daring to shift theology that has been dominated by Western assumptions and methodological biases to the Asian context in the study of suffering is not only desirable, but existentially necessary. The trinitarian theology of religions and comparative theology that is proposed in his work has

---

8. Editors' note: The more familiar term karma comes from Sanskrit; *kamma* is the Pali equivalent.

9. Boonyakiat, *A Christian Theology of Suffering*, 166.

potential to undergird Christian theology in general and also assist provincial theologies in exploring other areas of theology as well.

Boonyakiat has also successfully shown that dialogue with Buddhism is necessary and possible for theologians in Buddhist countries like Thailand and Sri Lanka. The rich output from such an endeavour is not subordinate to western theology, but the norm for how Christians in these parts of the world can decolonize their theology and be unfettered from Western theological paternalism.

Our Commitment

Boonyakiat's concluding comments on spirituality and spiritual practices that overlap with Buddhism are noteworthy. The importance of meditation as emptying is striking. As is often said in Russian Orthodoxy, "there is no *theosis* without kenosis."[10] This is a needed reminder that Christians must not merely pursue intellectual reasoning to address suffering that may remain in the abstract; rather, we must also learn to sit, wait, ask, and hear so that our faith may increase as seen in the lives of the saints of old and in the monastic traditions. Solidarity is also a Christian communal response to suffering. Just as God is present with the weak, downtrodden, and destitute, the Triune God invites his people to be his hands and feet in the world, providing consolation and relief to sufferers. Finally, repentance is a key response that Boonyakiat highlights in order to bring important attention to our complicity in the systems and structures that perpetuate and exacerbate suffering. God requires repentance that we might become instruments of peace and trees of shade to the broken and marginalized. Boonyakiat's book, although academically styled, is an important development in South Asian and Southeast Asian constructive and comparative theology that both serves the academy and the church alike.

---

10. Editors' note: *Theosis* is the ancient Christian teaching which expresses Peter's language of our becoming "partakers of the divine nature" (2 Pet 1:4), that "the Son of God became human so that we might participate in God" and "just as the lord, putting on the body, became human, so also we humans are made to participate in God through his flesh, and henceforth inherit eternal life," as stated by Athanasius in *On the Incarnation* and *Against the Arians*. It is similar to Lutheran and Wesleyan concepts of sanctification. In *theosis*, we remain created beings and do not ourselves become God or gods, but in Christ we become ever closer to God and ever more realize the "image and likeness of God" in which we were created. *Kenosis* means "the act of emptying" and refers to the "self-emptying" of Jesus; see Philippians 2:7.

Thailand: *A Christian Theology of Suffering* 135

Reflection

Photo by Javier Saint Jean on Unsplash[11]

---

11. Source: https://unsplash.com/photos/man-in-black-shirt-sitting-on-brown-rock-mountain-during-daytime-TuBi9rFQJVY

Central and South America

Bolivia

A Nazarene Church: Theology from the Insignificant[1]
Víctor Codina, SJ.

Contributed by Riad Ghobrial (Egypt)

Summary

From the midst of today's pain and misery, in *Una Iglesia Nazarena: Teología desde los Insignificantes* [A Nazarene Church: Theology from the Insignificant], Víctor Codina opens for us a window of hope. He says, "Nazareth is a mystery, a sign of contradiction: for some, it is a sign of scandal; for others, it is the good news of salvation." For Codina, Nazareth is not a mere geographical location, but a mystery which he invites us to explore. Nazareth is the place where Jesus was raised and spent most of his life. Nazareth was the angle from which Jesus built up his worldviews and grew in wisdom and stature, and in favour with God and humans. Nazareth is where the seed of the kingdom of God sprouted and began blossoming. Jesus identified himself with the people of Nazareth, as shown by the inclusion of "of Nazareth" both in the identifying notice placed on the cross (John 19:19) and the proclamation of the resurrection (Acts 2:22–24). In sum, Nazareth became a mystery when the Incarnate Word of God was called Jesus of Nazareth.

In the times of Jesus, Nazareth was a small insignificant town; it did not shine on the religious, social, or economic map, and no one expected that the people of Nazareth would be of any benefit to society. Codina confirms that the same thing is happening today where the "people of Nazareth" are the poor, suffering, and marginalized masses of people who live and die unnoticed. The Nazarenes today are those who stay in the peripheries of our interest and whose flourishing or disasters are unimportant to us. The Nazarenes today are the sectors or nations which we regard as culturally or theologically far lower than ourselves. In different ways, we echo what Nathanael expressed in the past, "Can anything good come out of Nazareth?" (John 1:46).

---

1. Santander, España: Sal Terrae, 2010. [Spanish]

In response to Nathanael, Philip answered, "Come and see." In the same way, Codina encourages us to enter what he calls "the school of Nazareth" and to experience what we could not see from the outside. At the school of Nazareth, the poor and the oppressed are not objects of study but rather teachers and mentors. The suffering people of Nazareth are the closest to the mystery of the cross. Thus, we cannot approach the cross without passing through the school of Nazareth. In their humility, Codina says, the poor recognize their sinful life; hence, they are often closer to repentance than the high authorities of the church. No surprise, then, if we see that the poor suffering ones were and still are the true bearers of the message of the gospel.

What is then the secret power of Nazareth? On his way to lead us in discovering the poor's treasures, Codina asks the following questions.

- Why do oppressed people not commit suicide collectively?
- Why do the poor get married and have children?
- Why do the marginalized buy flowers and dance?
- From where do they get strength and hope to continue struggling every day?

The poor suffering Nazarenes have faith in the God of life and his proximity to their very painful/enjoyable life. The poor face their sufferings with greater faith than anyone else. They have hope in a better world; they simply believe in the resurrection. Therefore, Codina finds no difficulty in applying the description of the church in Smyrna to the Latin American disenfranchised masses: "I know your works, tribulation, and poverty but you are rich" (Rev 2:9). Yes, the poor are rich, because they believe in God, while the rich are poor because they believe in Mammon, the cause of all kinds of evil. It is evident that the strongest factor behind suffering and wars is greed. Accordingly, the poor are the least responsible for and the most influenced by the tragedies of today's world and the tyranny of rich countries, corporations, and individuals. The Latin American experience shows that popular religiosity, which was often despised by many, had the strength to face persecution and suffering. Codina demonstrated that the poor people of Latin America, and Bolivia in particular, exhibited genuine Christian values like solidarity and hospitality in the face of catastrophes (such as the destructive flooding in 2008) more than many other populations of the so-called Christian First World. Their profound living doctrine sustained them during their sufferings which can be summarized in the popular saying, "Diosito nos acompaña siempre," that is, "Our little God[2] is always with us."

In the school of Nazareth, prayer has a special place. Against today's secularized and dry spirituality, the prayers of the poor are worth exploring. In Nazareth, prayers of authentic faith arise from the depth of distress (see Psalm 130). Poverty is an endless state of suffering thus it is from the school of pain that fervent prayers are produced. Codina saw that the Nazarenes' cry, their prayer, is the prolongation in history of the cry of Jesus of Nazareth on the cross, who mysteriously identifies himself with all the crucified of this world (Matt 25). It is the cry of the groaning Spirit passing through them for the birth of life. Codina tells us that their prayers are often connected to their actions, especially their solidarity among themselves. Therefore, Codina encourages us to adjust our rhythm of prayers with those in pain as we all form one chorus of humanity.

Speaking of Nazareth, it is essential to mention the women of Nazareth represented by the Virgin Mary. In this regard, Codina helps us to look at Virgin Mary, not only as the *Theotokos* (the "Bearer-of-God") but as Mary of Nazareth – the anonymous young orphan living in a highly conservative community who was accused of extramarital pregnancy; the wife of a simple carpenter, who accepted by faith one of the most complex theological mysteries, her son being the Son of God; the woman who in such low social conditions did not passively accept injustice but prophesized against the powers of this world; the mother who raised her son on the hope of a just kingdom of God to come, whose son in his thirties unjustly died in front of her eyes, and who celebrated the victory of life over death by the resurrection of her son. She is the exemplar for all women struggling for their place and dignity in today's world and church. This closeness of Mary of Nazareth to the condition of the poor in Latin America makes her present in their life; she is not just an idea but is a living present person. If she is the mother of Jesus, she must also be their mother. From another perspective, she is for the Latin American simple people the personification of the Pachamama, that is, Mother Earth, as the people have no difficulty in symbolically identifying Mary and Mother Earth.

While acknowledging all the possible critiques – theological, biblical, and doctrinal – to these ideas and affirming the necessity for these practices to continuously be enriched and even purified with the Scriptures and ecclesial tradition, Codina points out the importance of the existence of such a character

---

2. *Diosito* in Spanish literally means "little God," but it is used as a relational diminuitive, indicating the nearness of God; it does not indicate littleness in terms of importance or hierarchy.

in the lives of the poor suffering people in Latin America. Moreover, Mary of Nazareth symbolizes the poor church that does not take advantage of her position as the mother of the Saviour to exploit the weak and gain riches, social privilege, or authority over others, but lives humbly in service of the other and voluntarily or involuntarily offers her own son for the salvation of the oppressed. In fact, Mary of Nazareth is a prophetic voice against all ecclesiastical outward manifestations of greatness and luxury.

Codina summarizes the mystery of Nazareth by reminding us of what the young man said to the women at the grave, "The resurrected one is the crucified one, the crucified one is from Nazareth."[3]

Response
On the Summary

When reading the Gospels, we usually tend to jump from the manger to Jesus' ministry, to his crucifixion and resurrection. In his book, Codina encourages us to look at the longest silent part of Jesus' life on earth, Nazareth. In fact, Codina made it clear that because he was from Nazareth, Jesus was rejected, and ultimately crucified. We are then in danger of missing the mystery of the cross if we do not pay attention to the mystery of Nazareth. For us, it is both a challenge and an invitation, to have, as Codina says, "a faith linked to life"[4] – a faith that walks in the streets and markets where the marginalized struggle to survive, that leads us to humble ourselves and learn from the poor and the oppressed at the school of Nazareth.

We should enter the school of Nazareth, not only as individuals but also as a church. It is where we will learn solidarity and unity in our divided communities, acquire a faith "that is vulnerable to the suffering of the people and that knows that the glory of God goes through the defense of the lives of the poor people,"[5] as Codina says, and practice a life of true prayer according to the will of God and in full dependence on God.

Codina compels us to rethink the way we perceive and practice theology in Egypt. The position where we stand matters significantly. Before we talk about God, we must ask ourselves, are we identified with the poor, oppressed, and marginalized? Are we on the side of the Nazarenes or against them? According to Codina, a third position does not exist. Doing theology this way will help

---

3. Codina, *A Nazarene Church*, 213.
4. Codina, *A Nazarene Church*, 77.
5. Codina, *A Nazarene Church*, 155.

us be more humane and sensitive to humans' conditions and sufferings, as Jesus of Nazareth was.

In My Context

In Egypt, the main cities enjoy more social and ecclesial privileges than the rural villages. What Codina proposed earlier describes well the conditions of those whom we can call the Egyptian Nazarenes. The poor villagers are usually regarded as an object of compassion by the urban churches. Unfortunately, their religiosity and wisdom are often overlooked by those in the centre. We should then remember, according to Codina's advice, that God reveals his mysteries to the insignificant ones (see Matt 11:25).

Indeed, Egyptian rural villagers, women and men, are the bearers of genuine spirituality and profound wisdom. Consequently, we must realize that they are the subject of potential transformation, in other words, they are God's agents for building his kingdom. Moreover, the type of relationships they have between one another and with nature can rarely be found in the cities. As Codina described them, "These profoundly human relationships, which are like an ancient heritage of the wisdom of the peoples, *persist* even in the midst of all the difficulties, ruptures, violence and daily abuses."[6]

For Your Commitment

- We must look around us and detect where Nazareth is and who the Nazarenes are in our context. This is where our treasure is hidden and where our focus should be directed.
- In repentance, we should confess our role in marginalizing the Nazarenes and augmenting their sufferings.
- We should learn from the Nazarenes' prayers how to pray as a community and not enclose ourselves in individualistic-oriented prayers. From wherever we are, we can be in solidarity with the suffering people by joining their prayers that are already coming out of their anguish.

---

6. Codina, *A Nazarene Church*, 72.

Reflection

The Nobodies[7]

The nobody's children, owners of nothing.
The nobodies: the no ones, the no-bodied,
running like rabbits, dying through life,
screwed every which way.

Who are not – but could be.

Who don't speak languages, but dialects.

Who don't have religions, but superstitions.

Who don't create art, but handicrafts.

Who don't have culture, but folklore.

Who are not human beings, but human resources.

Who do not have faces, but arms.

Who do not have names, but numbers.

Who do not appear in the history of the world,
but in the police blotter of the local paper.

The nobodies, who are not worth the bullet that kills them.

---

7. Eduardo Galeano, *The Book of Embraces*, tr. Cedric Belfrage; New York: Norton, 1992, 73.

El Salvador

Witnesses to the Kingdom: The Martyrs of El Salvador and the Crucified Peoples[1]
Jon Sobrino, SJ.

Contributed by Riad Ghobrial (Egypt)

Summary

During the last century, El Salvador passed through difficult years where more than 80,000 people were killed or disappeared, more than a million were displaced or escaped the country, and countless lives were oppressed brutally in various ways. Along with this tragedy, there were Christian witnesses who condemned these injustices and lived in solidarity with the oppressed people – defending them and ultimately killed by the oppressors. Jon Sobrino, a wounded Christian, theologian, and Jesuit, who lived through (or rather, survived) these events, wrote *Witnesses to the Kingdom* from amid the sufferings. The book is composed of articles, written over a span of almost twenty years, in which Sobrino tries to theologize and conceptualize what he and the poor Salvadorians experienced. In doing so, he discusses one of the most difficult topics of all times: the death of the innocent.

Sobrino begins his book by justifying why we should remember the martyrs. In doing so, he responds to those who say that keeping alive the subject of martyrdom is masochistic and a glorification of suffering. First, these views often come from other places in the world where martyrdom is not a reality. Second, it is not about presenting pure spiritualism, triumphalism, or tragic existentialism. Third, remembering the martyrs keeps alive "a deep and massive human and Christian reality."[2] Fourth, theologizing martyrdom today will significantly help people understand "the most important question: why did they kill Jesus?"[3] Fifth, failing in remembering them means letting them

---

1. Maryknoll, New York: Orbis Books, 2003.
2. Sobrino, *Witnesses to the Kingdom*, 1.
3. Sobrino, *Witnesses to the Kingdom*, 108.

die forever, to kill them again in a different way. Theologically, forgetting them may lead to a certain form of Docetism (a heresy that asserts that Jesus did not have a real body but only assumed an apparent one). Sixth, martyrs are proofs of the incarnation of the gospel, and there is no incarnation without a cross, and no cross without resurrection. Remembering the martyrs as a humanizing task is one way of believing in the resurrection. All martyrs should rise again in history, each in their own way, says Sobrino. In other words, the martyrs make the church's message of salvation credible.

Throughout the book, Sobrino presents two types of martyrs:

1. The anonymous martyrs, or passive martyrs, the masses who are killed unjustly and without remembering their names, and
2. The Jesuanic martyrs,[4] or active martyrs, those who die for standing on the side of the oppressed and defending the poor.

Regarding the first type, they are the poor children, elderly, women, peasants, and those who are killed simply for being poor, and to prevent them from being anything else. For such people "we often do not know what to call them,"[5] exclaims Sobrino. They do not meet our theological, religious, or ecclesiastical standards of martyrdom – perhaps because they never had the opportunity to accept their death at will. Not only that, but neither did they show (or have the opportunity to show) the "conventional heroic virtues required for sainthood, because of the socioeconomic conditions in which they live."[6] Here, Sobrino invites the church to reevaluate its conception of modern sainthood and martyrdom; thereby, he adopts Ignacio Ellacuría's expression: they are the "crucified people."[7] The *crucified people* are the majorities who are unjustly bearing the burden of the sin that destroyed them slowly in life and annihilated them forever in death. Sobrino repeats quite often that the most real reality – in El Salvador as well as in other places of the majority world – is the life and death of the poor. In addition, Sobrino recalls how Ellacuría reflected theologically on the presence of the crucified Christ in the suffering people; hence, it is the reality of sin that makes these people suffer without being able to escape, it is the anti-kingdom that kills more people every day.

---

4. Sobrino introduces the term Jesuanic martyrs to refer to those who imitate Jesus' martyrdom (to be explained below).

5. Sobrino, *Witnesses to the Kingdom*, 4.

6. Sobrino, *Witnesses to the Kingdom*, 109.

7. Ellacuría (1930–1989) was a Spanish-Salvadoran Jesuit priest who was assassinated/martyred near the end of the Salvadoran Civil War. "Crucified people" – *los crucificados* and *gente crucificada* in Spanish – is an important theme of his theology of liberation.

Jesuanic martyrs refers to those who lived and died in the same way Jesus died and for the same reasons, those who, like Jesus, expressed their identification with the poor by their words, deeds, and ultimately their blood. As in the times of Jesus of Nazareth and now again in El Salvador, men and women in every capacity – pastoral, social, academic – did not escape the cruel death executed by the orders of the idols' priests. The crucified Jesus is in the assassinated archbishop, the murdered Christ is in the person of four women missionaries raped and killed, and the suffering Son of God is in the tortured and shot Jesuit fathers. Their love for God drew the Jesuanic martyrs closer and closer every day to the suffering poor. Sobrino believes that they found God crucified in the crucified people. For Sobrino, this idea is central, that God is loved *in* the poor. As he mentions elsewhere, there is "no salvation outside the poor."[8]

Sobrino insists that this type of martyrdom does not come suddenly. It begins with a radical conversion: to move to the side of the oppressed and to prefer losing friendships with the powerful and their benefits and gaining the affection of the poor. This detachment and attachment are then followed by a commitment to the "ministry of accompaniment,"[9] which eventually will lead to their cross. In other words, their love for the poor and their solidarity with the victims were gradually becoming their cross of martyrdom. In fact, Sobrino points out that "it is the necessary reaction of the idols of death toward anyone who dares to touch them."[10] And the martyrs, like Jesus, touched the idols of wealth and power; thus, they had to die.

Finally, Sobrino makes it clear that the poor and the martyrs offer the church both challenge and hope. Through their wretched life and unjust death, the poor set to the church the greatest challenge that tests its authenticity, and the church has no excuse to ignore their cry. The church either listens and will be saved or disregards and will die. On the other hand, the church owes the poor and the martyrs the hope to move on amid such a sinful and cruel world. Through their life and death, the poor and the martyrs stand as reminders for the church that "God is hidden but nevertheless present."[11]

---

8. Jon Sobrino. *No Salvation Outside the Poor: Prophetic-Utopian Essays* (Maryknoll, N.Y.: Orbis Books, 2008).
9. Sobrino, *Witnesses to the Kingdom*, 28.
10. Sobrino, *Witnesses to the Kingdom*, 74.
11. Sobrino, *Witnesses to the Kingdom*, 97.

Response
On the Summary

Although Sobrino speaks of what for some may seem alien or extreme, I believe that he brings to light some crucial issues that need to be addressed in every context. "Oppression is not a fashion,"[12] argues Sobrino. The situation of global poverty, oppression, and marginalization is getting worse every day, and numbers show that it will not get better soon. This makes the words of Sobrino even more valid for us.

One key theme that comes to mind is responsibility. First, we must take responsibility for keeping the crucified people on the cross. Sobrino reminded us that "all those who seek to accumulate wealth and only think about living better and better, should look at themselves in the mirror of the victims of this world and see plainly the evils they are causing."[13] Living with an individualistic mentality like this one, no matter where we are, is anti-evangelical. In supporting the worship of wealth and power, we contribute to the crucifixion of the poor. Second, we need to take up our responsibility in bringing them down from the cross. After we realized that in this world, "there are idols, and they produce victims, there is sin, and it produces death,"[14] what would be our duty in face of such reality? How can we repent and act toward their liberation? This is a challenge that Sobrino leaves us with.

Sobrino offered some answers as well through the lives of the Jesuanic martyrs. Each one of these martyrs, or witnesses to the kingdom, was given a life, and they chose to spend it for the love of the most vulnerable ones. And this creates another challenge: how do we want to spend the life that each of us has received?

In My Context

According to Sobrino "doing theology means raising reality to a theological concept."[15] In *Witnesses to the Kingdom*, Sobrino was able to theologize the reality of martyrdom and make it heard by the rest of the world. He extracted from the Salvadorian experience concepts that can help other Christians around the globe in their path. Because we have martyrdom in Egypt, this work is of much help for us to reread our context theologically.

---

12. Sobrino, *Witnesses to the Kingdom*, 93.
13. Sobrino, *Witnesses to the Kingdom*, 80.
14. Sobrino, *Witnesses to the Kingdom*, 83.
15. Sobrino, *Witnesses to the Kingdom*, 105.

On another level, the kind of commitment that the Jesuanic martyrs demonstrated shows a deep consistency in all their decisions and complete fidelity to the path they have chosen. In minor and major steps, they took sides with the poor, always having the impoverished in their minds. This attitude gave them credibility in the eyes of the poor. Sobrino affirms that "in practice, it is clear that the poor of this world listen to and trust the people who risk their lives for them to the point of martyrdom."[16] In the same way, Sobrino recalls what Oscar Romero had said,

> How sad it would be, in a country where such horrible murders are being committed, if there were no priests among the victims! A murdered priest is a testimonial of a church incarnate in the problems of the people. . . . A church that suffers no persecution but enjoys the privileges and support of the powers of this world – that church has good reason to be afraid! But that church is not the true church of Jesus Christ.[17]

These words can strongly describe the condition of the Egyptian church, where the leaders of the church are not exempt from the cruelty of the oppressors, and their blood is mixed with that of the poor.

Our Commitment

- To repent from the sin of forgetfulness and ingratitude to the martyrs, whether passive or active ones.
- As a church, we must pay attention to the true reality (the suffering of the poor) and stop occupying ourselves with a fabricated reality (historical, cultural, religious, or virtual).
- To criticize and fight against neoliberalism in all its disguises knowing that God and the poor will hold us accountable for our failure to act and for our silence.

---

16. Sobrino, *Witnesses to the Kingdom*, 115.
17. Sobrino, *Witnesses to the Kingdom*, 37.

Reflection

> Dark centuries ago,
> it is told, a bishop died
> by order of a king,
> spattering the chalice with his blood
> to defend the freedom of the church
> from the secular might.
> Well enough, surely. But
> since when has it been told
> that a bishop fell at the altar
> not for the freedom of the church,
> but simply because
> he took sides with the poor –
> because he was the mouth of their thirst for justice
> crying to heaven?
> When has such a thing been told?
> Perhaps not since the beginning,
> when Someone died
> the death of a subversive and a slave.
> – José María Valverde[18]

---

18. Quoted in Sobrino, *Witnesses to the Kingdom*, 44

Europe

Germany

Christian Persecution in Antiquity[1]
Wolfram Kinzig

Contributed by Brent Hamoud (USA/Lebanon)

Summary

While many books about Christian persecution and martyrdom can be characterized as impassioned works by passionate writers, Wolfram Kinzig's *Christian Persecution in Antiquity* seems to intentionally stand in the field as a different, more measured type of resource. The text is packed with facts and information about suffering, persecution, and martyrdom in early Christianity, but semblances of sentiment are noticeably restrained. This is purposeful; immediately in the introduction Kinzig mentions the problematic nature of many writings on the subject due to their propensity to valourize and romanticize testimonies of those who have, and presumably do, suffer for their Christian faith. (The fact that he makes critical note of Martin Mosebach's *The 21* hints that this book aims to deliver a contrasting inquiry.[2]) Just as the title suggests, *Christian Persecution in Antiquity* is a straightforward report of the dynamic experiences of Christian persecution during its first four centuries. Kinzig sketches the lines of this history but leaves it up to readers to fill in the colour as they process account after account of trial, tribulation, and martyrdom. Persecution was certainly central to the roots of Christianity; however, Kinzig makes implicit that we must hold this position critically, and he appeals to credible, reliable, historical facts to do this.

As a scholar of Christian history, Kinzig is highly concerned about methodology. He describes at the start of *Christian Persecution in Antiquity* how he goes about handling historical accounts of Christian persecution. In doing so, he speaks to concerns about the tendencies to exaggerate and inflate

---

1. Translated by Markus Bockmuehl. Waco, Texas: Baylor University Press, 2021.
2. Editors Note: Martin Mosebach's *The 21* is reviewed by Brent Hamoud in the following chapter.

the degree of violence that was unleashed against Christians. This also works to validate the historicity of early Christian accounts by making a case for why they cannot be dismissed as fictitious, which is often supposed by historians and scholars. Kinzig's sincerity to the subject is seemingly rooted in his academic credibility, not emotions or theological convictions. This is evident in the way he underlies a technical, even surgical, approach to scholarship when stating that "writing about the persecution of Christians resembles the work of an archaeologist: one very carefully has to remove one layer after another of later additions and embellishments to the texts in order to get to the precious artefact."[3] Though readers exploring this topic may respond more to affective rhetoric, the scholastic nature of the book is precisely what makes it a valuable contribution to literature on Christian persecution and martyrdom.

Christian Persecution in Antiquity's organization is informative though not particularly innovative. Starting at the period of Christian persecution within Judaism, the book carries out a mostly chronological survey of Christian suffering from the time of the apostles to the post-Constantine Roman Empire rule in the mid-fourth century. Thus, while the title refers to Christianity "in Antiquity," the book is primarily limited in scope to happenings within the Roman Empire. The very short ninth chapter provides merely a token summary of persecutions outside of the Roman Empire in Germanic territories in Europe and in three areas of Asia – Armenia, Georgia, and Sassanid Persia. The chapters form a Christian history built around the ways in which resistance to the early church was mustered and inflicted.

Kinzig addresses the religious persecution endured at the hands of Jewish leaders by recounting well-known accounts of the Gospels and the Book of Acts. The material is familiar to Christian readers, and the book offers little in the way of new insights or commentary. His interest in the Bible here is more for its historical offerings rather than its meditative value. Interestingly, Kinzig does caution that the reliability of stories about persecution by Jews should be viewed critically. He asserts that the burgeoning church had good reason not to accuse the powerful Roman authority of wrongdoing (doing so would be detrimental), but Christians did in fact have compelling motivation to annunciate Jewish harassment since doing so works to conform the faith community's narrative to that of the crucified Christ. Additionally, the book notes how Christians and Jews outside of Palestine were both minority groups, therefore the likelihood of the latter persecuting the former at a significant scale beyond the traditional heartlands of Judaism is low. We can gather that

---

3. Kinzig, *Christian Persecution in Antiquity*, 7.

despite being amplified in Scripture, Kinzig believes Jewish hostilities against Christ-followers should not be seen as something phenomenal.

The chapters then examine Christianity's movement from a breakaway Jewish sect to a religious movement throughout a pagan empire. Here Kinzig traces the ebb and flow of persecution by Roman rulers. Different periods (usually marked by particular emperors) and different geographic locations ushered their own moments of Christian treatment, sometimes leading to the favourable situations for the church and other times leading to brutal crackdowns. The second and third centuries reveal an apparent trend as persecution moved from localized incidents to empire-wide initiatives. Kinzig explains how reasons for Roman aggression varied. Sometimes it was a response to Christian rejection of paganism (and the threat it posed to social order and political rule) and other times it was a reactionary measure of scapegoating Christians for the misfortunes befalling the empire, such as environmental irregularities or natural disasters. Additionally, antagonism against Christianity developed ideologically as well as physically; anti-Christian polemics emerged at certain points to counter Christian teaching just as adherents themselves were oppressed and crushed.

Kinzig not only describes Roman assaults against Christians but also explains the legal procedures and measures employed to convict groups and individuals. This gives a window into the legal dimensions and cruel "civility" entangled in persecutions. As remembered in traditional Christian narratives, the treatment of Christians under the reigns of emperors Nero and Diocletian stood apart for their waves of intensity against the church. Even so, *Christian Persecution in Antiquity* is careful to avoid sensationalizing notions of a "high point" of Christian suffering and instead casts these rulers within the grand tapestry of persecution. The conditions during Emperor Marcus Aurelius's tenure, which is noted for its own brand of ruthlessness, is particularly interesting given his reputation as contemplative philosopher. Throughout these chapters, Kinzig substantiates the oft-evoked stories of Christians being thrust into the gladiator games, fed to wild beasts, burned alive, and destroyed in an array of tortures. The book in its reporting proves that colourful writing is not needed to convey the gut-wrenching harrows of such mistreatment.

The final part of the book's discussion on Christian persecution is particularly noteworthy. Following Emperor Constantine's recognition and validation of Christianity in the early fourth century, we see the status and orientation of the church change dramatically in its move from a marginalized faith movement to a dominant state religion. Here Kinzig's subjectivity is evident. He is softly sceptical of Constantine's motivations suggesting that political utility was at the heart of the emperor's decision to elevate Christianity. The impact of this Constantinian moment is profound. He makes a startling comment that, "from then on, Christians sided with the winners of history."[4] The move from Christians being persecuted at the hands of non-Christians to Christian groups persecuting one another is quite unnerving. In his brief concluding thoughts, Kinzig points out the irony that a religion rooted in suffering intolerance and persecution has proven throughout history to manifest power and inflict intolerance to other religions. This final statement is a startling punctuation to a sobering study.

Response
On the Summary

Throughout *Christian Persecution in Antiquity* Kinzig seemingly prioritizes information over analysis. The pages are packed with facts about people, places, and events addressing violence against early Christianity, but little is presented in the way of thick description or narrative. The book does not explicitly defend a thesis nor advance a theory. As such, personal thoughts of the author come across as muted. This is no weakness; the intention of the text is not to promote a perspective per se, but rather to present historical data "excavated from the field" in ways that allow readers to affirm or critique their own theses. *Christian Persecution in Antiquity* reads much like a massive encyclopaedia entry or official report, and the force of the book's ideas is in its commitment to textual evidence and academic integrity rather than in how it tells a dynamic story, casts theological reflection, or promotes ethical considerations.

Surprisingly, Kinzig's absence of personal persuasion comes across as somewhat unusual for a book in this field. I expected the text to delve at some point into case studies or reveal overarching theories accentuating the author's philosophical orientation. In fact, it is surprising to see how understated Kinzig is in his arguments and how quickly he moves from one point of investigation to the next. (Or in the conclusion of the book, how suddenly he wraps up his own personal reflections to end the work.) This may buck a trend in literature about Christian persecution, but it is welcome. The approach allows readers to consider raw data about the church in antiquity and formulate their own thinking. For some, it will mean levelling down judgements about the quantity and severity of early Christian persecution, while, for others, it may lead to

---

4. Kinzig, *Christian Persecution in Antiquity*, 139.

fuller admission that the trials of the church in antiquity are not only profound in their meaning but unquestionably extensive in their volume.

The lack of vivid pathos may prove a challenge when reading *Christian Persecution in Antiquity*. Everyone is wired differently, and some require a degree of emotional weight from literature to stir their hearts and minds. Others, like me, find cognitive-heavy approaches highly effective when engaging a topic. Though the discussion would benefit from more analysis by Kinzig, it is understandable why he chose not to include this in the study. The analysis that is done is efficient and educational. *Christian Persecution in Antiquity* demonstrates how a well punctuated statement can leave as strong an impression as any elongated prose.

Two additional elements of the book worth mentioning are its length and language. *Christian Persecution in Antiquity* is noticeably short for an academic work, coming in at under two hundred pages including the appendences. This is a strength. It makes the text more accessible and increases its general utility. It also helps readers when ingesting information since the presentation of facts is dense but not lengthy. One can even describe the book as breezy. Concerning language, the book was originally written in German and later translated into English. This does not detract from the text, but it does help explain aspects of its diction and writing style. *Christian Persecution in Antiquity* is a reminder of the importance of translating academic literature to make ideas more available to a wide audience.

In My Context

Christian Persecution in Antiquity is clearly a history book. As explained earlier, Kinzig aims to uncover the early church experience first and foremost, though he focuses on Christianity within the Roman empire. This directs its focus to particular times and geographies. Little is done to relate the Christian experience of antiquity to current times or apply the research to ethical considerations for church and society today. This is not to say that the book has little relevance to us now; it fits squarely within a catalogue of writing on Christian persecution. One area where relevancy is evident is academic relevance. Kinzig strives to steer the way we critically think about Christianity's persecution roots by filling knowledge gaps (and perhaps correcting attitudes) with solid, credible historical evidence.

For Middle Eastern Christians, concerns about religious persecution largely revolve around the treatment of Christian minorities under Muslim domination. That said, it is important to note that Christian attitudes towards

Islam differ across the regional Christian tapestry. (Too often the most amplified voices on the issue are from those outside the region.) And in extreme cases like Palestine, Christians and Muslims suffer alongside one another against a dominant religious power. Kinzig naturally concludes his study centuries before the emergence of Islamic rule in the region. However, it is feasible to use this text within a type of comparative study between Christian persecution during antiquity (when it was an emerging, fringe minority sect) and during the first centuries of Islamic rule (when it was an established religion moving from position of dominance to one of marginalized status).

Two themes stand out as informative to our understandings of Christian persecution today. The first is how contextualized dynamics of religious persecution play out at both particular and general levels. Kinzig shows that complex forces led to periodic ebbs and flows of persecution during antiquity. Situations were fluid throughout political developments of the Roman world, and Christians in different places experienced varied measures of mistreatment and indifference. This does not lead us to lighten our assessment of the cruelty endured by the early church, but it does require our judgements of persecution to be thoughtful and nuanced. In our current times, as we seek justice and rights for Christians in the Middle East by empowering followers of Christ to live in security and dignity, we must resist wrapping blanket assessments around the challenging conditions endure by Christians in the region. Drawing attention to suffering is important (and there is far too much of it taking place) but it is imperative to remain mindful that persecution is complex and subjected to contextualized factors.

Secondly, Kinzig mentions at numerous points how politics were at the core of Christian persecution in antiquity. Simply put, Roman antagonism of Christianity was largely fuelled by political anxieties about the movement's threat against imperial authority and preservation. Peering through political lenses is crucial when thinking about Christian persecution today. We can easily distil issues to components of religious doctrine, belief, and zeal, but oftentimes politics is at the heart of the oppression against religious groups (though politics cannot be divorced from its religious components). Therefore, it is imperative when considering the political dimensions of the Middle Eastern context today to comprehend how politics at national and international levels apply gruelling pressures on local Christian communities. Omitting politics from our understandings of persecution is a rampant folly we often make in our evaluation of religious persecution. I too admit, when reflecting on the ways in which Christians maintain firm grasps on political power in places from Lebanon to Europe to North America, it is possible to figure that ignorance of politics is actually an intentional decision taken to avoid exposing the extent to which Christians are more interested in maintaining their positions within power dynamics rather than they are in advancing solidarity with the religiously marginalized.

Our Commitment

Christian Persecution in Antiquity in its succinctness and academic rigour dutifully challenges people of faith to utilize all methodologies for comprehending the struggles bound up in our faith tradition. This involves commitments to grounded research aiming to uncover authentic pictures of what has happened in the past. For studies on Christian persecution, our interests in the present and desires for the future can easily influence how we hold our history (or histories). Kinzig provides a thoughtful reminder that we need not resort to sensationalism nor exaggerated emotional appeal when crafting narratives of the church's suffering and fidelity. Seeking understanding built on facts is part of being truthful thinkers, and when it comes to testifying to the treatment of our brothers and sisters in faith, truthfulness is paramount. High-level scholarship is vital for evaluating Christian persecution, and we should intellectually receive and disseminate contributions like this to shape our own intellectual and spiritual orientations. That said, Christian persecution is never a case of raw numbers and qualifying variables; it is always a matter of human lives and the individual people who have been dehumanized because of their commitments to Christ. As our critical thinking is bolstered by knowledge and insights served to us in resources like *Christian Persecution in Antiquity,* our commitments to compassion for the oppressed and solidarity with the marginalized must increase as well.

Reflection

St. Erasmus Flogged in the Presence of Emperor Diocletian[5]
Byzantine artwork from the crypt of the church of Santa Maria in Via Lata in Rome

---

5. Source: https://en.wikipedia.org/wiki/Diocletianic_Persecution#/media/File:Flagellation_St_Erasmus_Crypta_Balbi.jpg

Germany

The 21: A Journey into the Land of Coptic Martyrs[1]
Martin Mosebach

Contributed by Brent Hamoud (USA/Lebanon)

Summary

In February 2015 the world witnessed a true horror as ISIS released a video showing the gruesome beheading of twenty-one men on a Libyan beach. The victims were Egyptian Copts (and one Ghanian) who had been working in Libya before their capture. Hailing primarily from the Samalut area of Upper Egypt, the video showed individuals full of poise and courage as they faced certain death. Though meant to spread terror, the ISIS media production had a different effect on many by testifying to a Christian commitment to martyrdom and a deep willingness to die for one's faith. The Coptic Church quickly recognized the men as saints, and the killings evoked both mourning and pride among their families and faith community. The video garnered amazement around the world – both for its brutality and beauty – stoking newfound curiosity in the Egyptian Coptic religious tradition and stirring discourse on Christian martyrdom. Moved by the death of "the twenty-one," German novelist Martin Mosebach set out on a journey to visit their homeland, engage their religious heritage, meet their families and acquaintances, and discover the people behind the powerfully tragic story. The result of this venture is his 2019 book, *The 21: A Journey into the Land of Coptic Martyrs*. It is a unique text that manages to illuminate the lives of these men and explore their Coptic Christian heritage in heartfelt ways. But, in doing so, it also demonstrates unfortunately narrow thinking as it tries to make sense of places, cultures, and a faith clearly foreign, and, oftentimes, confounding to the author.

Mosebach is a fiction writer who entered a new literary genre with *The 21*. The book is a passion project, the result of an intense personal response to the ISIS killing video. Shaken deeply by the event, Mosebach expresses a sense of

---

1. Translated by Alta L. Price. Walden, New York: Plough Publishing House, 2019.

perplexed admiration when trying to understand how the twenty-one martyrs could conduct themselves with such calm as if "lambs being led to slaughter." While the world was transfixed on their deaths, Mosebach became intensely interested in their lives and set out on a journey to discover it for himself (and presumably to write a popular book). Over the course of twenty-one chapters (one dedicated to each martyr) he presents semblances of the men's life narratives and assesses the complexities of their homeland.

The 21 is an unconventional text that does not fit neatly into any particular literary category. In some regard it is an ethnographic study, yet it does not attempt to follow the rigours of human subject research. In other ways it is a theological inquiry, though it does not aim to advance any type of biblical or theoretical framework. At times, there is a sense that Mosebach takes on the role of investigative journalist gathering firsthand evidence to unlock the identity of the individuals, and, at other times, he positions himself as an analyst of religion, politics, and society providing broad interpretation of the sweeping forces shaping Egypt and its Coptic community. There are even times when he pulls from his fiction writing background to set up rhetorical dialogues between fabricated characters. The book reflects many types of literatures and different elements manifest at different points. Interestingly, if I had to put *The 21* under some type of label then I would categorize it as travel literature. Mosebach, in both pleasant and problematic ways, essentially describes a journey, a pilgrimage, through an exotic land of wonders. Along the way he conveys fascination, inspiration, and concern as he records his experiences.

As a type of firsthand travel account, the narrative presents its stories as seen squarely through Mosebach's European Christian eyes. While many interlocutors lend their voices to the subject matter, the book's ideas are filtered exclusively through the author's mind. The approach is inventive but flawed. Though it manages to garner insights on a Christian community that is too often overlooked and misunderstood by the wider global church (and perhaps especially by the Western church), Mosebach displays yet another example of someone discussing a people, place, and faith tradition while standing firmly outside of the culture of inquiry. It is apparent that Western Europe constantly remains in the author's mental background.

Martyrdom is the front and centre motif throughout the book. The killing of the twenty-one men at the hands of ISIS and their subsequent elevation to Coptic sainthood is used as a gateway to approach a challenging element of Christian faith: religious persecution. (This topic can be all the more confounding to those from Christendom contexts.) Mosebach is intent on exploring issues in a way that confronts brutality head on. His description of the killing scene, including detailed analysis of the video's editing, is truly gut-wrenching. The sheer inhumanity of the act is presented in raw terms that would be guilty of sensualizing were it not for the fact that the ghastly footage exists. The video is essential here since it directed the author to uncover the story of the martyrs' lives. Each part of the conversation comes with both scepticism of Christian martyrdom and a sincere reverence for those ready to take the ultimate sacrifice in devotion to Jesus Christ. It is as if Mosebach cannot believe Christians would ever head to their deaths with such meekness and grace, and he is compelled to uncover the reasons for this. His interactions with the Coptic community testify to a tradition wholly comfortable with martyrdom as a hopeful means of strengthening faith rather than a force crushing individual and collective spirits. As such, the book aims to give a fresh, deeply humanized look at the gravity of religious persecution.

While many of us are familiar with the twenty-one men from their highly publicized deaths, Mosebach takes extensive measures to reveal their personalities. This is something that had not been previously presented to the wider world. He visits their village, Samalut, and draws from the memories and recollections of those who knew them. Without fail, each individual is presented as someone faith-filled, righteous, and fully willing to give his life in testimony to Christ. (That said, the author is keen to include comments giving some alternative perspectives.) Though structured to include each of the twenty-one martyrs, not everyone is profiled while some are given more attention than others. None are given a full biographical treatment, and they are mostly presented through snapshots and quips about the men's lives. Even so, the approach provides meaningful contemporary perspective on "the lives of the saints." Particularly interesting in the text is the account of how their high-profile martyrdom and sainthood tangibly impacted their families and home communities. The celebrity status of the twenty-one attracted wide-reaching attention and concern, leading the Egyptian government to build new houses for the victims' families and a large church in their memorial – the Church of the Martyrs of the Faith and Homeland. A look at these material implications of the event provides compelling and informative dimensions that have likely not been previously addressed.

One element of the twenty-one mentioned by Mosebach time and again is the nature of their poverty and economic destitution. This point is easily overlooked when memorializing the martyred, and the book concentrates on it to explain why they were in Libya at a time of great insecurity. The link between poverty and Christian faith and fidelity is also touched upon. At times, Mosebach's reading of rural, working-class lifestyles comes across as accusing folks of backwardness, and some comments made in the book are downright offensive. This is unfortunate. It seems, at times, as though the materialistic conditions of the twenty-one's family members left an impression on the author nearly as impactful as their spiritual condition.

The book does well to note how not everyone killed on the Libyan beach were Egyptian Copts. One of the twenty-one is Matthew Ayariga from Ghana, a companion of the group who insisted on declaring his own Christian faith to ISIS and therefore subjecting himself to the same death. His story is a fascinating element of this martyrdom and the way he has been embraced into Coptic sainthood alongside the others is meaningful on different levels.

As the title suggests, the book uses the twenty-one martyrs as a type of entry point to tell a larger story of Egypt and the Coptic Church. Throughout the text Mosebach weaves discussion of the experiences of the Copts today and historically. He attempts to frame conditions that have made the Coptic Church what it is now and explain how martyrdom is not only a part of the tradition but a core element of their witness and beliefs. In the latter chapters he moves on from the twenty-one martyrs by taking readers to desert monasteries, urban slums, and luxury city developments (New Cairo) while considering the fate of the country and its Coptic presence. Though he addresses it only indirectly, his commentary on Egyptian politics is rather critical. Likewise, he addresses Islam at numerous points but avoids getting into the weeds of analysis and critique. (The intentionality of this decision is stated explicitly in the text.) Even so, his position on Muslims and Islam is evident via sentiments which can be characterized as mistrusting and pessimistic. This is conveyed eerily in the closing of the book when Mosebach wonders ominously if Coptic Christians can continue to embrace martyrdom if (or when) tested to new limits of persecution. He then suggests that the contemporary status quo will give way to a much more confrontational arrangement for Christians within Egypt. It is an unsettling conclusion to what could have been a meditative wrap-up.

Response
On the Summary

The unique literary approach of *The 21* makes it an intriguing text for a study on Christian persecution. It's unlikely that a similar writing project about martyrdom, the Coptic Church, and victims of the 2015 ISIS killings is available elsewhere. It is a distinct perspective that moves beyond literatures of theology, Christian history, religious studies, Islamic studies, and human rights and advocacy while tackling the topic of Christian persecution. Likewise, the extent to which Mosebach goes on to present individual people demonstrates a meaningful way to humanize tragedy. That said, the book remains a singular reading of Egypt, Copts, and martyrdom. Mosebach is open about his obvious limitations for conducting this kind of project. He admits to having absolutely no Arabic abilities, limited cross-cultural knowledge, a paralyzing reliance on translators and local guides, and significant difficulties in locating the family members of all the victims (which he failed to do). Likewise, he makes no claim to be a scholar in any field related to this study. All of this makes it a bit curious as to how he figured himself qualified to write such a text. One of the key issues with this is that he does not seem apprehensive about making concrete assessments. Mosebach frequently makes certain claims about people, places, and events as if he is an authoritative voice on the topic. Despite being packed with much information, the book fails to offer a single work's citation. Nothing that is stated in the text is supported by academic referencing. We are expected to accept every point of fact and analysis as if written by a credible, expert source – but is it? Even as Mosebach carries senses of scepticism towards his subjects, the reader is compelled to be sceptical of the interpretations conveyed and the conclusions reached throughout the book. In the end, it is often painfully clear that the text is an example of a European speaking from Christendom while trying to make sense of a world, and even a faith, that he does not understand. There are certainly good points to garner from the book, but the aims of the project – that of discovering people, cultures, and places – demand something more incarnational than what the author provides in these well-intended musings.

In My Context (The Middle East)

The Coptic Church is a fascinating point of exploration for Middle Eastern churches, and the worldwide church in general. Middle Eastern churches' position within the Eastern Christian tradition is particular; they embody religious characters both reflecting and contrasting other Eastern Christian traditions. Sadly, numerous Middle Eastern traditional churches claim to be "churches of the martyrs" due to the extent of hardships they have endured under years of Muslim domination and modern political upheaval. The Coptic experience can certainly contribute to discussions about the minoritization of Christian communities in the region. What stands out in this text is the church's firm confidence in its traditions and rituals. Hardly a trace of religious uneasiness is evoked from any religious perspective included in the book, which testifies to the deep foundations of a centuries-old religious heritage sustaining the Coptic community during times of tragedy. As Christians in the region continue to face uncertain times (many of which are not related to aggressive forms of Islam), the text provides a reminder of our need for robust church life and traditions.

Furthermore, the book's discussion of spiritual remembering and memorializing is noteworthy. The twenty-one were instantly recognized as saints and their deaths were quickly etched into the collective Coptic conscious. Some church traditions, like Protestants, have grave uneasiness with notions of sainthood. This can result in a thin approach to remembering those who have lost their lives for their faith. Though the scale of the twenty-one's memorialization is exceptional, due in large part to the dramatics of their deaths, the means by which Copts embrace martyrdom is something of value for other churches grappling with questions about the blatant evil inflicted against God's faithful.

Our Commitment

For all his flaws in the venture, Mosebach demonstrates something extremely meaningful in *The 21*: he seeks to look beyond the headlines of religious persecution and attempts to uncover people, places, and traditions behind the story. Too often our response to the "death of the saints" is to pause in momentarily sadness before simply resuming life. It is rare for a soul to be truly disrupted by persecution to the extent that it drives them to action. Mosebach allowed his inner disruption to lead him on an actual journey to Egypt, and we can use this as an example of choosing direct ways of responding to another's suffering. It is essential that remembrances and reflections about persecution are always about individual people and their stories. As such, the commitments arising from this book should be to:

- Allow evil to truly unsettle us in a way that propels meaningful personal action.
- Move beyond the factual accounts of people and seek their personal stories.
- (Even if done imperfectly,) make the effort to step out of our worlds to try to understand others.

Reflection

The book is another testimony to the way Coptic brothers and sisters demonstrate radical ways of finding spiritual beauty in the terrible and profane. It is a quality that speaks loudly to the hope of the gospel. Mosebach points this out vividly when sharing of the gratitude a victim's family member expressed about the horrendous beheading video. It can serve as an inspiration to us about how to orientate ourselves to enemies:

> We find ourselves in the odd position of being grateful to the Islamist killers for the film with which they documented their acts. Now, instead of relying on potentially contradictory testimonies, we can see it all with our own eyes. Had the killers had any idea of the significance this video would have for the Coptic Church, they probably would not have made it. Far from being intimidating, it gives us courage. It shows us the martyrs' heroic bravery, and the fact that they spent their last moments alive in prayer proves the strength of their faith.[2]

---

2. Mosebach, *The 21*, 47.

Greece

My Sister[1]
Stavros Zoumpoulakis

Contributed by Myrto Theocharous (Cyprus)

Summary

The author wants to tell the story of his sister, not simply in a biographical way, but in the form of a contemplation on suffering and pain. His sister was diagnosed with epilepsy and the doctors were unable to eliminate the seizures nor regulate them through medication. The author felt completely identified with her suffering and states that "as long as my sister is not getting well, as long as her troubles keep growing, my own suffering is also growing."[2]

The author speaks of the unfairness and unevenness of suffering in the world. Even though all may have their share of pain in this life, not all pain is equal. The "levelling" lie that "everyone suffers" is often adopted even by the people who are miserable because they cannot cope with the loneliness which their experience brings.[3] The author says that the pain of collective suffering caused by nature or history is less of a burden than the pain of individual suffering. Sickness is fate singling you out, while collective pain, even the worst of it, is shared. One seeks only to be understood by others, but also to know that others who suffer, even if you have never met them, are out there. The fact that you are not the only one is a comfort in itself.

The greatest question for the author is the harshness of God. How can a God of love, who also demands love from humanity, be so harsh towards his sister? For him, this is the only theological question that there is, the relationship between human pain and the love of God. People struggle in their faith and in their desire for God's response. They expect miracles from this God, and the author has great respect for pilgrims who travel to sacred

---

1. Athens: Polis, 2012. [Greek]
2. Zoumpoulakis, *My Sister*, 16.
3. Zoumpoulakis, *My Sister*, 25.

places in hope that it will bring healing to their loved ones or to themselves. He cannot stand people who mock suffering pilgrims. He acknowledges that the idea of a merciless God is unbearable, so the only exit from the faith that the author accepts is the one based on the inability of the believer to reconcile within himself the pain of the innocent and the mercy of God. This is the only respectable form of atheism the author accepts, and this existential atheism is paradoxically defending or demanding a God of mercy, a God who is identified with goodness as the only acceptable God.

The thought of Simone Weil was very influential to the author. She was someone who completely identified with the sufferers. What she said was no different from what she had experienced, and this is one of the highest values that this book promotes: theology born out of one's actual identification with the pain of the people, experience equal to speech. He admires Simone Weil because she had never spoken of something she had not experienced, while he is critical of theologians, and even church fathers, whose explanations on evil are very theoretical. They usually blame sin and think that suffering is a way of discipline. The author does not believe in the purifying role of evil. He believes that evil does not necessarily work out something good. He cannot accept the necessity of evil, so he finds these explanations inadequate, and he prefers instead the messy voices of contemporary people such as Simone Weil. That does not mean he agrees with her in everything because Weil thinks that God has withdrawn from the world. This is how she accounts for the existence of evil. God withdrew his power and allowed for his creation to exist freely. The author, however, finds it very difficult to love a God who has withdrawn and lets his creatures suffer, even if this withdrawal was done for the sake of their own freedom. Only if one accepts by faith that God's withdrawal is an expression of love can they love this God. This, however, is a great mystery that is revealed or is gifted to those who surrender their power and imitate God in this "withdrawing" from power.

Suffering is an experience that God does not have, says the author, so humans are superior to God in this aspect. An almighty God who is not in pain, who knows no suffering, is lacking in this experience. In Christianity, however, this lack in God is compensated by the incarnation and its end, the crucifixion. His kenosis is calling for our kenosis from power, for our joy in his creation, for the love of the people, for finding beauty in God's world. Only for the person whose experience is pure joy in the world is God's silence not a punishment. Without this kenosis from our ego there is no room for the other.

For the author, the only trace of God in the world is the presence of the mercy of others. The only way for God to exist is through those who demonstrate his love. The merciful are the living presence of God on earth because God is mercy and love. This does not call primarily for the elimination of pain and evil but for the obligation to love the other. This is where the author's quest is leading him: to a faith without theodicy, a faith that assumes responsibility and love for the other. This was a change of perspective in the author. A shift to "what I do" rather than "what God does."[4] He departs from Weil because Weil limits herself to pain as the end. She never speaks of resurrection. She only speaks of Christianity as the cross so for her there is no room for this joy, but the author thinks that Christianity is a religion of joy and that whoever does not have joy cannot be Christian. He says that pain and suffering do not necessarily make a person good, but they can equally make them worse, jealous, or hateful of others. Of course, he says that nobody who has not had pain can really feel compassion and empathy for another person, but the same is true for the person who has not felt joy. A person who has felt joy can be open to others.

The author does not want to think of the problem of evil only within this lifetime. He witnessed his own mother's "eschatology" in her teary prayers and in a note she had written to her daughter. In the note the mother is asking her daughter to wait, not to die first, until the mother goes ahead and prepares the way with flowers at a place where no tears, pain, seizures, or doctors will exist. Then all will be well. His mother is a woman who has not been schooled yet, without knowing the theological terms of "messianism" and "eschatology," her words revealed the deepest possible faith in a coming reality that has kept her surviving and hoping.

Politics has its limits, the author believes. He realises that even in a perfect political system people will continue to get sick, so political involvement is not everything. Any type of political system that lacks the sense of human tragedy is totally out of place and out of this world. The ultimate attention to the truth is listening to the cry of the poor. He says that the person who has not heard the cry of the poor, their despair, and their anger, has never heard the word of God either. God is only found in the face of the poor. Even the most uncomfortable act, that of cleaning a sick person from their excrement in their bed, is an act greater than all the contributions of the titans of theology.[5]

Finally, the author meets Emmanuel Levinas; he feels that he was prepared by the experience of his sister to accept Levinas's teaching that there is no

---

4. Zoumpoulakis, *My Sister*, 40.
5. Zoumpoulakis, *My Sister*, 61.

mutuality in ethics. "I am always in debt to the other."[6] Unfortunately, in his context, the author sees a prevalent form of "civil" Christianity that cares only about having good children, good studies, good marriages, good jobs, etc. But "Don't pagans want the same things?" he asks. There must be something more. Pain frees you from shallowness. In suffering, one begins to focus on the important things, and one gets weary of theological language that is not in touch with reality. The author calls us to know for ourselves that of which we are talking, to stop fooling others, but, above all, to stop fooling ourselves.

Finally, when death approaches, he says, we don't really want to believe in it. It is not a matter of being in denial but a matter of having an excess of love. We refuse to limit loving the other person to a few years. Love always hopes and death is always her enemy. She refuses to become an ally to death. Death will always remain love's eternal opponent.

Response
On the Summary

I resonate with much of what the author is describing. The suffering of the innocent is indeed the hardest reality for one to endure. While it is possible for believers to endure their suffering with faith and trust in God, and we may all have examples in mind of such people, it is much harder to watch your loved one suffer. A mother would prefer to be sick herself than watch her own child in pain. To have joy in such a state would be a spiritual, supernatural gift.

I agree that pain and suffering have no satisfactory explanation. This is reminiscent of the book of Job and the fact that he received no answers to his questions other than a call to trust God and his wisdom. A call to trust and surrender to God is the only response in the face of evil, for those who are able or find the faith to do it.

It is true that, for the most part, the Scriptures attribute evil to sin in the sense that evil was never God's desire nor his plan for humanity and his creation. Attributing all evil to sin is not supposed to make us "witch hunters" and set us on a path of trying to match each calamity to people's faults, even though many self-appointed judges respond this way. Evil being equated to sin simply means that it has no place in God's world, and it is guaranteed to be eliminated by God in his coming kingdom. As the author's mother expressed so poetically, God's ideal is no different from our instinctive ideals of desiring love, rest, and joy for eternity.

---

6. Zoumpoulakis, *My Sister*, 62.

While the author is a prolific reader and mentioned many influential authors, it is clear throughout his book that the formation of who he is, his questions, and his dissatisfaction with certain answers comes from his sister. This goes to show that people are not primarily formed through what they read. The author affirmed, through his reading, a lot of what he had already learned through his sister, but he did not really learn them *from* his reading. He learned them from experience and from watching the experience of his sister and her example.

In My Context

The author's thoughts are relevant not only for believers but also for non-believers. Serious atheism is not the one based on shallow interpretations of ancient texts, but the one based on humanity's frustrated expectations for a just world without suffering and pain. This is paradoxically the same world that a believer desires, with the difference being that the believer places their trust on a God who guarantees its coming.

In a world that is increasingly intolerant to Christianity (or indifferent at best), such as Greece and Cyprus, the author shifts our attention to what *we* are to do rather than being consumed with what God should do. Often God's absence in our world is due to the fact that his people do not reflect him. Demonstrating love and mercy opens a window to God for those we serve.

Our Commitment

Where is God in a world of pain? Let us ask ourselves where God is:

1. God is in those who suffer in our world. How can we approach him in the poor? How can we serve them with joy?
2. God's presence is in the merciful. Do we hide God from the world, or do we bring his presence by choosing mercy and love rather than indifference and hate?

Tough Years: December of '63[7]
by Telemachos Kanthos
Woodcut on paper, 32 x 32.5 cm. 1964.

---

7. Source: https://www.ucy.ac.cy/publications/wp-content/uploads/sites/54/2022/03/Telemachos_Kanthos_Skliroi_Xronoi2009.pdf

Greece

The Enigma of Evil[1]
Christos Yannaras

Contributed by Olga Politi (Greece)

Summary

Professor Christos Yannaras's book *To Aínigma tou Kakoú* ("The Enigma of Evil") discusses the perennial question of what is evil, both physical and moral, with the principles of naturalism and Western theology.

In the first three chapters, Yannaras deals with the naturalistic principles of evil. He summarizes them in two points: (a) natural disasters are part of nature's functioning, which contributes to its proper mechanical operation, and (b) since human beings are solely part of nature, each of their activities derives from the necessities (e.g. self-preservation) given in nature. Yannaras argues against the point, claiming that it deprives nature of a purpose against human understanding. He contrasts it with what we human beings experience as an "absurdity" or a violation of logic: If there is no meaning in the universe, then why is the search for a cause and purpose the given cognitive mode by which human beings can operate ontologically? Against the second point, Yannaras argues that it deprives human beings of responsibility, derived from free will, for the reason that the modern Western civilization excluded any ontological considerations from its interests in the early days of the Enlightenment. There was no room left to realize that freedom is inevitably excluded if mankind follows nature by necessity.

In the rest of his chapters (4–17), Yannaras claims to introduce afresh a pre-modern/allegorical interpretation (flowing from a stream of the Eastern early church fathers) concerning the story of the fall of man in Genesis that offers the Jewish and Christian worldviews on evil in opposition to naturalism. In the narrative of the fall, he highlights the fundamental starting line to his key thoughts about both the origin and nature of evil: God created humanity

---

1. Athens: Ikaros, 2008. [Greek]

free to appropriate either a good mode of existence within the boundaries of a relationship of love between the Uncreated Being and the created beings or an evil mode of existence outside of the boundaries of a relationship of love between the Uncreated Being and the created beings. In their taking of the food which God offered humankind from his garden, they were to receive a life-maintenance blessing which would establish an existential relationship of love between God and humanity. The imagery of the fruit of the Tree of Life embodies a life which would be immortal resulting from the affirmation of God's love. Such a relationship, though, could flourish solely as an event of freedom. That is why with the Tree of the Knowledge of Good and Evil, God offered humanity the possibility to refuse to acknowledge the receiving of food from him as the appropriate mode of existence. By consuming the fruits of this other tree, humankind would be led to an independent mode of existence from the One who is the cause of the existential event. With this regard, death was meant to set the boundaries of a self-centred way of existence. Had it been rendered unlimited, then a second pole of reality would have been brought into being, parallel and opposite to God-centred existence, which would entrap humanity by necessity, not by free choice.

Thus, in the language of Genesis, the contrast between life and death corresponds to the contrast between good and evil. In this context, evil does not form any sort of ontological reality, but it is rather the mode of the independent existence of createdness which is, as a whole, in diametrical opposition to that of the Uncreated Being. Thus, humans are now subjected to limitations of dimensional space, time, decline, and annihilation, which they experience as pain. Gratefully, the narrative of humanity did not end here, but with the historical occurrence of the Incarnation, the Son/Logos enabled the created to participate in the mode of the Uncreated Being to restore the loving relationship with God as a mode of existence.

From the above, it is undebatable for Yannaras that the gospel of the church should be freedom from the independent mode of createdness – that is, from the mode of createdness which sets itself apart from and thus in opposition to the Uncreated – and the pain which that mode necessarily conveys. He repeatedly notes that it should be also preached in radical opposition to the "gospel of the West" that hinders this ontological aspect of humanity. The gospel of the West interprets the legal/juridical language of Scripture literally and not figuratively as he sees clearly from the early ecclesial texts. Thus, the problem with the fall and evil is not a matter of a supposed legal violation of God's divine law that stays on the surface of ethical conduct of life. Such a gospel has cultivated guilt, fear, and terror against God. It is this theology that has led Western civilization to atheism and the naturalistic approaches discussed above.

On natural evil, Yannaras writes that the current functioning of nature is not the result of humanity's fall, which would drift material creation into rebellion and disobedience. Even though nature is hostile to humanity since its creation, at the same time, the manifested wisdom and beauty call humanity to relate with God, the Uncreated. Thus, nature has set the stage for understanding and deciding between good and evil as a presupposition of freedom. In that sense, God did not import evil into nature, but he made it indeed "very good." But is nature meant to remain hostile? Maximus the Confessor's recapitulation theology shows that God would never abandon his "very good" creation to the corruption of createdness or to what men have experienced as evil, regardless of humanity's fall or non-fall. God's purpose for creation has always been to recapitulate it in the person of Christ, who hypostatically unifies[2] the created with the Uncreated through his incarnation. It is a plan which has been destined to include not only the irrational creation but the rational as well.

Response
On the Summary

Professor Christos Yannaras is well-known for demonizing the West for the ills of modern Western society, such as atheism, deriving either from radical reactions against oppressive legalistic theologies or naturalistic interpretations of human existence. Therefore, it is not surprising that, although he joins forces with global Christian apologetics at the beginning of his book to deconstruct the naturalistic principles of natural science against the fall account and the origin of evil in Genesis 3, he becomes far more interested throughout the rest of his book in separating his position from Augustine's legal/juridical understanding of Genesis 3. Against this behavioural and thus superficial account, as he understands it, Yannaras's theology of personhood prioritizes first and foremost a theology of human ontology which locates the problem of evil in the autonomous created mode of existence emanating from the broken relationship between the person of God and human beings. This theological proposal is indeed considerable and undoubtedly valuable in

---

2. Editors' note: The hypostatic union is a theological term that denotes the coexistence of two natures in Christ – a fully human nature and a fully divine nature, both united in the one Person of Christ; *hupóstasis* is an important technical term in Christian trinitarian theology, which understands the one God to exist in three *hupóstases*.

pointing to Eastern patristic accounts and redirecting priorities from outward moral performances to the core of the human mode of existence. However, his exclusion of views regarding an existing parallel juridical understanding of sin in an absolute manner are not convincingly elaborated from critical texts of the Bible. Yannaras instead takes into consideration medieval Western theologians and ignores later theological developments.

In My Context

Yannaras's participation in public discourses through the media has been constant since the 1980s. His role as a public personality has compelled him to comment on social matters according to his theological commitments. His anthropological account based on the relationship between not only God and human beings but humans themselves is not stressed in *The Enigma of Evil*, but it comes as a strong implication, which he elsewhere applies to address evil at a social level in Greece. He is convinced that individualism and the lost collectivity in modern Greek society are the first and most urgent social diseases we ought to address. To eliminate crime and injustice, it's necessary to restore our broken social relationships. Discoursing the constant crimes of a specific notorious region of Athens, he claimed in one of his recent newspaper articles that if we all begin each of our days by merely greeting ten people with "Good morning" as a minimum effort to relate with society, none of us may ever commit murder in our lives.

Our Commitment

Yannaras's book calls for a metamorphosis into a new mode of existence from individuals to communal persons within church and society. To do so, we should first repent from our (a) legalistic approaches to God, and (b) independent self-confidence, both of which may lead to an unconscious autonomy from God. As clichéd as it may sound, each of us, as members of the church, needs to rebuild a spirituality based on the confidence of a loving relationship and in union with God, established on total dependence on the life-giving work of Christ. However, this attitude will be inadequate unless we also put our emphasis on building communities of love and shared worship of God in churches as well as practicing individual worship.

Reflection

Anastasis, Harrowing of Hell and Resurrection
Fresco painting, c. 11th century, Chora Church, Constantinople[3]

---

3. The Chora Church, now in Istanbul, was converted to the Kariye Mosque in the 1500s. Image source: https://en.m.wikipedia.org/wiki/File:Chora_Anastasis1.jpg

United Kingdom

A Theology of Suffering[1]
J. Bryson Arthur

Contributed by Angukali Rotokha (India)

Summary

Arthur offers an examination into the origin and nature of suffering from a theological perspective and its meaning and place in the lives of Christians. His book is divided into three parts. Part 1 (chapters 2–7) explores "The Nature of Suffering." He begins his narrative in Eden where the fall and the resultant curse created an alien and antagonistic environment that necessitated painful struggle to satisfy needs (chapter 2). The author roots the origin of suffering in the argument that God's design for genuine freedom for human beings required the human potential for evil and hence the possibility of sin and suffering. He makes an important distinction between suffering and pain, arguing that pain is intrinsic to creation with positive functions and hence is essentially good – and distinct from suffering caused by sin. The author also looks at suffering caused by the sense of meaninglessness (chapter 3). He highlights the futility of seeking meaning in the created world, asserting that since repetition is meaningless, and repetition is embedded in creation, meaninglessness is in the created order itself. This is because he reasons that meaning is to be found only in the infinite God.

The book then looks at various types of suffering (chapters 4–7) and argues that undeserved suffering has greater meaning. The author emphasizes that for believers the key to enduring undeserved suffering is hope through faith which gives meaning to undeserved suffering. Further, the angst that human beings experience as a result of an awareness of our ultimate return to non-being leaves us with a sense of powerlessness and aloneness. He proposes that for Christians the reality of resurrection and our adoption into God's family brings resolution to our angst. Angst can even be a blessing if through it we

---

1. Carlisle, Cumbria: Langham Global Library, 2020.

recognize the call to live our lives as God intended – seeking the meaning of our existence in God and not in the world.

Part 2 (chapters 8–12), "The Suffering of Biblical Figures," takes a closer look at the Bible's portrayal of suffering in the persons of Job, Jesus, and Paul, as well as the suffering of God and of the persecuted church. Although this section examines biblical figures, the treatment is more theological than exegetical (as the author acknowledges); readers looking for exegesis of biblical texts need to look elsewhere. The author contends that suffering can be woven into God's plan and will for us – suffering can challenge us and lead to a breakthrough in our understanding of God and his ways and our understanding of ourselves, resulting in revelation and closer communion with God, as exemplified by Job's suffering. Job and his friends had preconceived notions about God and how God works in this world, but through suffering Job's understanding was pushed beyond its limits and he was brought to a point of revelation.

Arthur sees Christ's suffering as a means of re-creation or redemption. He asks, "How was Jesus's suffering different from that of the two thieves who hung beside him?" The difference, he says, was that Jesus was the Son of God and innocent, and the Holy Spirit was present in Jesus's crucifixion by virtue of which some were able to recognize him for who he truly was and thus, even today, his crucifixion continues to draw people to God. Further, the book explores the question of the possibility of God suffering and looks at the concepts of *impassibility* (God does not suffer) and *immutability* (God does not change). Chapter 10, "The Suffering of God," gets dense as it delves into classical theological concepts. The author argues that, because of God's omniscience, the course of actions he would take are foreknown to him, there is no essential change in his nature (immutability) despite it appearing to us that he changed. Thus also, his passibility (being subject to suffering) is different from ours. Arthur argues that in Christ's suffering (as God and human), God is "perceived as suffering" but this suffering is in the nature of grace which is God's essential nature (grace being the cost of love borne by God). Since these aspects of God are a mystery to human beings, the answer to the question of God's suffering is not fully provided and the reader comes away with the sense of having understood that not all can be understood.

Turning to the Apostle Paul, the author examines his inner suffering and how it was tied to his task as an apostle in that he suffers for Christ. The author argues that, in receiving a revelation from God, Paul was imposed upon to respond to it and grow from it. This growth in being, the author says, results in suffering as one strives to live authentically according to one's calling. Paul's suffering also authenticated his ministry as an apostle, so that even though

Paul did not encounter Christ or his works on earth as did the other apostles, Paul's inner sufferings and joyful willingness to suffer validated his ministry and his apostolic authority. The author further looks at the healing aspect of suffering in that suffering enables one to comfort others who suffer as well as the fact that healing from suffering reveals God.

Examining the suffering of the persecuted church the author describes persecution as suffering *for* Christ. The author places suffering as a result of persecution within the larger perspective of persecution that has continued from biblical times. He notes that, while in some places, persecution culminates in martyrdom, elsewhere it means living a life of perpetual risks since commitment to Christ in a hostile context is done at considerable risk. However, living a life of such risk can also be considered wisdom since Christians risk what little we apparently have for what is absolute and eternal.

The third and final part is "Trauma and Triumph" (chapters 13–15). Here the author attempts to relate the gleanings from the preceding chapters to understand conflicts and hostilities in different contexts. The author views conflict as a result and reflection of the rebellion which began in Eden as a rebellion against God and which thus resulted in a break of unity in relationships. Further, he notes that the human will, which asserts itself and wants to be independent of and complete apart from God, is a delusion that creates endless striving and strife. The author sees conflict in human relations as being a result of perceived differences in others that are seen as posing a threat to the self. In short, similarity is familiar and reassuring, while differences are mysterious and threatening. Hence sexual, cultural, ethnic, religious, and economic differences become areas of tension and conflict.

Finally, the author concludes by examining the connection between faith and meaning. The author reasons that the meaning of human life is grounded in the command to love, and such love is possible only through faith. In such a life, suffering is to be understood as the pain of growing both in our being and in our capacity to love. As such, while other religions and philosophies may view suffering as destructive, within the economy of God, pain and suffering can be seen as part of sanctification and growth in faith as it increases our capacity to understand God and his ways.

Response
On the Summary

Overall, this book makes a good contribution to the topic of suffering. The distinction the book makes between pain and suffering and arguments for a positive view of suffering are especially useful. The discussion on the potential of suffering to set us free – free from our presumptions about who we are, how the world works, and who God is – can be illuminating and a fresh way of understanding and going through suffering.

Some portions of his theological and philosophical arguments tend to be dense and at times verbose; as such, the book is perhaps more suited for those interested in reflecting on the metaphysical and theological explanation of suffering or who are pursuing some level of theological studies. The book also has numerous sub-headings that can be either distracting or helpful, depending on the reader's preference.

The book's approach to practical issues like suicide, persecution, terrorism, and trauma could have been better. Given that the book is a theological reflection on suffering, it is unfair to expect an in-depth treatment of all issues well. However, for instance, the reference to suicide in a discussion involving references to the noble self and shameful self could have been handled more sensitively (chapter 5). Suicide has a wide range of trauma and mental health issues behind it and self-forgiveness is not possible in all cases. So, to speak of complicated issues, even if in passing, without a caveat and acknowledgement of the nuances involved seemed an oversimplification and could come across as insensitive.

In My Context

The argument for a positive perspective on suffering is helpful, especially in a context like India where suffering is a common sight and experience, and the dominant cultural narrative is that suffering is a consequence of sin (karma). As such, suffering is understood negatively and is associated with guilt, shame, and judgement, adding to the pain of the sufferer. Even within the church, generally speaking, suffering is sometimes perceived as divine punishment, whether stated overtly or understood implicitly. Hence the perspective this book offers can liberate sufferers from the added negative feelings they often feel from within or sense from others.

The author's analysis that the Israelites worshipped the golden calf as something that was made by their own hands or as a symbol of nature/creation seems like a misunderstanding (see chapter 3). While prophets like Isaiah used such language as a critiquing rhetoric, they knew that the idols were supposed to be a representation of a higher power. South Asians are surrounded by idols and it is a common understanding that an idol is a representation of a deity, so when people bow down to idols they are not merely worshipping the man-made thing, they are worshipping the deity it represents, just like the picture of our loved ones is more than just paper and coloured ink, it represents our loved ones and we cherish those pictures. Hence, to put it the way the author has can appear to be ignorant of the religious beliefs of others – which diminishes the impact of the actual critique of the meaninglessness of worshipping that which is not the true God.

Our Commitment

1. Not all suffering is a consequence of sin, so we need to intentionally change the way we think and talk about suffering and not be quick to judge others. This can happen when we are socializing with friends where gossip is shared in the pretext of sharing prayer points, or in the way we talk about others at home and normalize negative talking.

2. Alternatively, suffering can be an avenue for revelation of God and growth of self so wherever possible we need to highlight the positive potential of suffering. We can do this through our teachings in more formal settings like a prayer meeting, a classroom, Bible study, or preaching.

Reflection

> Suffering is a gift, though, like all gifts,
> it depends on how we receive it.
> And that is why we need a pure heart
> to see the hand of God, to feel the hand of God,
> to recognize the gift of God in our suffering.
> – Mother Teresa,
> who served the suffering in India till her last breath

United Kingdom

Faith That Endures: The Essential Guide to the Persecuted Church[1]
Ronald Boyd-MacMillan

Contributed by Angukali Rotokha (India)

Summary

In *Faith That Endures*, Ronald Boyd-MacMillan provides a compelling guide to understanding and engaging with the persecuted church around the world. The author has first-hand experience in working with the persecuted church as well as working with various organizations and bodies that work in this area; his work ranges from meeting immediate needs of the persecuted to long-term policy-making that will change the situation for them. This makes his experience-sharing reliable, and his insights and lessons learned over the years valuable. Instead of looking at persecution from the perspective of an incident – so that recounting incidents becomes the goal of the book – the book examines persecution as a phenomenon in order that its causes, symptoms, and possible remedies can be explored. The author takes a step back to lend his readers a view of the bigger picture of the various forms of persecution around the world and the wide range of underlying causes that motivate those persecutions. He does not sensationalise or try to emotionally move the readers, although the accounts themselves are brutal enough in most cases. Instead, he leads his readers to reflect on why and how persecution happens, what others can learn from the persecuted, and suggests how one can respond to persecution or be of help.

The book has three sections: a description of the persecuted church, strategies of engagement, and lessons from the persecuted. The first section (chapters 1–8) introduces the idea of persecution, the persecuted church, and where persecuted churches are located. He then describes what persecution looks like. By citing examples from various parts of the world, the author shows that persecution looks different in different contexts; for instance, persecution

---
1. Grand Rapids, Michigan: Revell, 2006.

in the Middle East may take the form of physical violence and threat to life, while persecution in the West could take the form of marginalization and relegation of religion into the private sphere. The author also notes that in some cases of persecution, as in India in the 1990s to early 2000s, persecution is systematically orchestrated; there are recognizable stages of development of persecution before a full-scale persecution is unleashed. The author rightly concludes that there is no one reason for persecution but multiple reasons can be at work in religious violence – ideology, government, family, culture, church, corrupt individuals, and over-boldness – and he rightly concludes that more than one factor is usually involved in any specific instance of persecution.

This first section also explains why a consensus on a definition of persecution is difficult to come by, as well as why a legal definition or description of persecution is inadequate: neither reflects the spiritual hatred which drives the persecution of Christians. The book does well in examining the Bible's perspective on what constitutes persecution for Christians, and identifies five groups of persecutors: rulers, religious leaders, merchants, mobs, and family. This is still painfully true today. The author concludes that the term "persecution," applied in a broad sense, has the benefit of enabling us to identify the root cause of persecution, that is, spiritual hatred. It points to where persecution begins to take shape, which if not taken care of can potentially grow till it becomes a full-blown persecution, by which time we will be dealing with the consequences or doing damage control rather than taking care of it at its roots.

The book examines the four biggest sources of persecution – religious nationalism, Islamic extremism, totalitarian insecurity, and secular intolerance. These sources yield persecution of Christians in various parts of the world. Segmenting the world into regions, the author explores the patterns and sources of persecution in Latin America, the Middle East, Africa, Asia, and the West. In each of these regions the reasons underlying the persecution show how varied the root of persecution can be – economic, political, religious, or ideological.

The section on religious nationalism, along with chapter 2, was particularly relevant. The author's analysis on the Indian situation vis-à-vis systematic organised persecution is still quite accurate. The Bharatiya Janata Party (BJP) was in power at the time of the author's writing. (The BJP is the political wing of the RSS or *Rashtriya Swayamsevak Sangh* – a Hindu nationalist, right-wing, paramilitary volunteer organisation with a Hindu fundamentalist ideology.) The BJP has been back in power since 2014 and has picked up powerfully from where it left off in 2004. The vacuum, the villain, the lie, the mob, and the microphones described by the author are all back – and bigger. The

Indian identity is being built around the idea of "one nation, one religion," the rhetoric of racial purity, and land belonging to one religious group. As such, the author's analysis of the situation in India is still relevant and apt. Further, one of the aspects that the book highlights briefly is Buddhist extremism. This is a significant topic. Buddhism is rarely spoken of in the world at large as a violent religion; it is in fact known as the religion of peace. However, in parts of Asia – such as Sri Lanka, Bhutan, and Burma, where Buddhism is the state religion – Christians have suffered much under the hands of the Buddhists and violence incited by Buddhist leaders. Such atrocities belie the image of peace and tolerance that the Dalai Lama (of Tibet) peddles in the West; it is a pity that this side of Buddhism is not talked about more.

The second section, chapters 9–11, looks at a helpful question: How do we provide help to the persecuted Christians around the world in a way that is actually helpful to them, and also does not scam those who want to help? Throughout the book the author brings up methods and ways people have reached the persecuted, some of which worked well and some of which stirred more trouble for the persecuted Christians. However, this section consolidates those methods and analyzes why some of the methods and tactics worked and why some failed. The analysis provides a helpful peek to the readers at how nuanced the landscape of persecution truly is. A method that worked exceptionally well in one context can be disastrous in another simply because the contexts and cultures are different and each values different approaches. It demonstrates the need for various organizations and bodies that focus on the distinct needs of the persecuted church and the need for collaboration among such bodies to share the lessons learned in the process of trying to help the persecuted church. The author recommends seven intervention methods which can be used to help the persecuted church: these include prayers, publicity, legal and illegal interventions, and political pressure.

Response
On the Summary
The book underscores the fact that while religion, especially state religion, is at the root of much persecution in most parts of the world, the other extreme of trying to get rid of religion is also at the heart of persecution in the West. It sheds light on the Western nations' attempts to preserve their secular outlook that have led to increasing marginalization of religions, bans on religious self-expressions (e.g. wearing certain items that identify one's religion), and the

formulation of policies and interpretation of the law in ways that sideline the religious populace.

The third section, chapters 12–14, argues that the persecuted church is not just a recipient but also has much to offer. The author argues that persecuted Christians encounter God and his power in ways that other Christians have not. As such, their lessons and insights are invaluable for Christians who, because of their circumstances, do not get to experience similar testings of faith. The book looks at three kinds of lessons we can learn from persecuted Christians – they model habits of holiness for us, show that a life of faith is essentially a life of trouble, and challenge us to see how big God truly is. The examples cited in the book rightly demonstrate that when we are persecuted we are forced to pare down our faith to the basics – fellowship with God. Service for God and all the other activities we attach to our faith all pale in comparison to the significance of our relationship *with* God. As such, the author argues that the persecuted church models for us the kind of faith life we were primarily called to live. Further, the book makes an important point about getting into trouble. It argues that the gospel speaks truth powerfully into our contexts, and the powerful in those contexts will always react. Hence, if we witness Christ and if we are speaking the truth, trouble will eventually come. As such, the book argues that it is quite impossible to be faithfully living according to the gospel and not see any trouble. This observation strikes home because this is true in the lived experience of Christians, whether one gets into real physical danger or suffers losses in various aspect of life (loss of job or other opportunities) because truth and honesty exposes the falsehood and dark deeds of the society. Moreover, seeing and hearing about God's work among, and intervention on behalf of, the persecuted open our eyes to better grasp the greatness of God and how involved he can be in our lives if we let him.

Lastly, interspersed in the book are several stories of individuals from around the world who have suffered, or are suffering, persecution. Highlighting these stories makes the account of persecution more personal – it's like taking a break from the survey of the world's situation and sitting down to have a cup of tea with them and getting to know them. Their stories and situations are terrifying but they also challenge, encourage, and positively provoke the readers in their faith and deeds.

The book could perhaps benefit from updated information as the data cited in the book is older than 2006; for instance, the heads of countries have changed since the time of writing, which can impact the situation of the country, also the political and religious situations in some countries like Iraq and Iran have changed, etc. Nonetheless, most of the information is still relevant and extremely insightful. Overall, this is an excellent resource to get a grasp of what persecution of Christians looks like worldwide.

In My Context

While I see the merit of the author's perspective that the privatization and extreme suspicion of religion is ultimately harmful to the nation, there is some ambivalence in arguing for religion in matters of the state in the West. For instance, the author criticizes a UK Minister of Education, who is a Christian, for not bringing their religion to bear on matters of the state.[2] As a Christian living as a religious minority, it seems desirable, at least theoretically, to have Christian values informing the state matters. However, to argue that state sponsored religion is bad for minorities like Christians, as the book does, but to then also argue that Christians should bring their religion to bear on matters of the state in the West (where Christianity is the majority religion, if only in name), is slippery ground. One cannot condemn something when some other religions do it and support it if Christians do it.

Within the context of persecution, the line between what is legal and what is illegal is often not simple from a faith perspective. The author discusses the role of illegal intervention using Bible-smuggling into China as a case in point.[3] This raises an important question: When does it become necessary to go against the law? As a Christian living in a country that is increasingly becoming intolerant, such questions come up naturally. The book's discussion brings out the distinction between illegal and immoral. It sheds light on the fact that when the law becomes discriminatory the right thing to do may be illegal, but it is still the right thing to do. This is in no way a call to do illegal things but a call for being prepared to hold on to the fundamentals of our faith and to do what is right even when the situation gets tough.

Our Commitment

The author also underscores the difficulties that face donors who want to support the right organizations and recommends eight tests as a way of shortlisting reliable ministries to support financially. Such words of caution are worth heeding since some (not all) ministries and organizations that run charities, schools, shelter homes, orphanages, and/or support churches and

---

2. Boyd-MacMillan, *Faith That Endures*, 218.
3. Boyd-MacMillan *Faith That Endures*, 274.

parachurch organizations in Christian minority regions often scam donors. Some of these may be outright lies, while others may have the said operations but siphon off the funds in part or in full for their own interests, and the donors are none the wiser. It is illegal and immoral, as well as contributing to the "rice bag Christians" image that adds to the hatred and discrimination the persecuted church is already facing. This presents a tricky situation for the donors; nonetheless, it is helpful to raise awareness so that donors are more vigilant about where they give their support.

The book's emphasis that the persecuted church must be served in the way it wishes to be served is one that should be taken seriously. On one hand, for those unaware of the difficult situations in which Christians live the book serves as a meaningful and balanced introduction. On the other hand, for those who are familiar with violent persecution this book is a reminder that persecution need not always be violent; acts of silencing, shaming, or pressuring to dilute one's convictions are also persecution. It highlights sufferings but it also underscores God's work among and through the persecuted. Readers come away not with a sense of despair but with a sense of awe at the demonstration of faith, resilience, endurance, and passion that Christians all over the world have – all the varied forms of persecution have not succeeded in snuffing out the light.

Reflection

The poem below was written by Rabindranath Tagore (1861–1941; Nobel laureate 1913) before India's independence. It embodies Tagore's vision of a free and awakened India. Although India is now politically independent, this vision still largely remains to be achieved, and, in my opinion, expresses a prayer that can be said by those facing persecution.

Where the Mind Is Without Fear[4]

Where the mind is without fear and the head is held high,
Where knowledge is free.
Where the world has not been broken up into fragments
By narrow domestic walls.
Where words come out from the depth of truth,

---

4. First published in *Gitanjali* (i.e. "Song Offering"), Tagore's 1910 Bengali language anthology of his poetry, as "Chitto Jetha Bhayshunyo Bhayshunyo" ("Where the Mind Is Without Fear"). Tagore's own English translation of this anthology was published in 1912; Tagore won the 1913 Nobel Prize in Literature for the translation.

Where tireless striving stretches its arms toward perfection.
Where the clear stream of reason has not lost its way
Into the dreary desert sand of dead habit.
Where the mind is led forward by thee
Into ever-widening thought and action.
Into that heaven of freedom, my father,
Let my country awake!

Middle East

Egypt

Martyrdom and Martyrs: A Spiritual Study[1]
Fr. Matta El-Meskeen

Contributed by Riad Ghobrial (Egypt)

Summary

Martyrdom is a tangible reality for Egyptian Christians (also called Copts); the Egyptian church has been known for its past and present experiences of multiple waves of persecution and martyrdom. It is from and to this context that Fr. Matta El-Meskeen (1919–2006) presents a biblical, patristic, historical, and spiritual overview of the concept of martyrdom. He wants to offer a true Christian reflection on what martyrdom is and who martyrs are. He has two aims in this: on one hand, to strengthen the faith of his fellow Christians, and on the other hand, to remind them that the Christian faith in which they stand is delivered with blood. We can summarize the main themes that Fr. Matta speaks about to achieve his goals as follows: the work of the Holy Spirit in martyrdom, love and martyrdom, martyrdom as witnessing, and the remembrance of the martyrs by the church.

Throughout the book, Fr. Matta emphasizes the role of the Holy Spirit in strengthening the believers in the face of death. He affirms that accepting death for Christ's sake cannot happen by human power. He expands this idea by asking, "If no one can say that Jesus is Lord except by the Holy Spirit (cf. 1 Cor 12:3), how much more would it be so for laying down one's life for Christ?" Stories of martyrs do not intend to illustrate the courage that a little child or young woman exhibits in front of death; rather, they reveal the work of the Holy Spirit in these weak vessels, convincing the faithful that death is already defeated in Christ. Fr. Matta builds this concept on the notion that the work of the Holy Spirit is to transmit to us what is Christ's (cf. John 16:14). As Christ did not fear death and did not spare his life for those he loved, the Holy Spirit fills the faithful with the same attitude to lay their life down for the one they

---

1. Third Edition. Scetis, Egypt: The Monastery of St Macarius, 1987. [Arabic]

love without fear. Indeed, through the Holy Spirit, past martyrs overcame the fear of death with perfect love (cf. 1 John 4:18).

It is appropriate here to introduce another line of thought which often appears in Fr. Matta's work – that love *is* the way to martyrdom. Martyrdom is the highest form of partaking in the sufferings of the beloved Christ. At the same time, martyrdom is proof of the victory of life over death. Fr. Matta describes the history of the church, the history of martyrdom, as a history of love. Throughout the centuries, the church has never ceased to show her love to Christ, her bridegroom, in many ways, among which martyrdom stands the greatest. By dying for Christ, the Coptic church survived miraculously till this day: death has led to life. This is the Christian mystery revealed in the resurrection (John 12:24–5). Moreover, in Fr. Matta's understanding, love is not merely sentimental or instantaneous. It entails growing in obedience and humility, in carrying the cross ourselves, until we reach the point of martyrdom. Love is then demonstrated by a continuous process of inner and outer self-emptying, where the inner precedes the outer. When the believer is no longer living but Christ is living in them, they are able to face all kinds of persecutions and sufferings.

Every life reflects and witnesses its archetype; hence the Christian life is supposed to reflect and witness Christ. In this regard, Fr. Matta points out that the liturgical Coptic year begins with the feast of *Nairouz*, that is, the feast of the Martyrs. By doing this, the Coptic Church underlines the aim and the significance of witnessing to Christ through life and death. This is an essential value for believers to follow throughout the year. Witnessing by life is with words and deeds of evangelism; witnessing by death is with suffering and the blood of martyrdom. The first is the duty of every Christian, while the latter, according to Fr. Matta, is a special gift from God given to those who carry greater love to God in their hearts (cf. Phil 1:29). Furthermore, he affirms that the testimonies of martyrs given in the hours or days before their death are considered jewels for the church. They are more than just pastoral sermons or theological treatises – they are words of the Holy Spirit speaking through a person who sees the heavens open and the Son of Man sitting at the right hand of God and who therefore is able to forgive those who persecute them, just as Christ did (cf. Acts 7: 56). We may not have preserved a thorough record of the words thousands of martyrs uttered before their departure but, to the little we have, we must pay attention. Here, Fr. Matta lists words from the letters of St. Ignatius and St. Polycarp, among others. On the other hand, we know from various accounts that many of the pagans who attended the trials, tortures, and executions of the saints, upon seeing the saints' perseverance and hearing their few words calling out the name of Jesus Christ, were converted to Christ and martyred with the saints.

To conclude, we must present an important topic that Fr. Matta addressed in his book: the meaning of remembering and celebrating the martyrs. To reform this concept in today's practices, he goes back to its origin in the Scriptures and the first centuries of Christianity. If Jesus Christ ordered that the actions of the woman who poured the fragrant oil on his feet out of love must be remembered wherever the gospel is preached (cf. Matt 26:13), how much more must the church remember the love of the saints who poured out their lives for Christ? Here comes the importance of recording and reading the biographies of the martyrs. In order not to forget them, or rather not to lose the encouragement and inspiration which their remembrance brings, the church decreed certain days for celebrating their martyrdom. In this regard, Fr. Matta affirms that no celebration can take place without partaking in the Eucharist in which our unity with the martyrs is realized only through our unity as members in the body of Christ. In addition, he tells us that spiritually celebrating the martyrdom of the saints means following their example of love and faithfulness to the end.

Response
On the Summary

In our modern times, Christians are subtly tempted to preach and live a lofty Christianity. Unconsciously, we may be encouraging each other to fall into these temptations. With this book, Fr. Matta El-Meskeen comes to awaken in us the spirit of radical discipleship into which Christ has called us. He challenges our lukewarm spirituality and our relaxation in the wide path by showing the strong Christian zeal of the martyrs. The lives and deaths of the martyrs humble our view of ourselves.

Additionally, Fr. Matta's words do not only rebuke us, but they also show us that the Holy Spirit can still ignite the fire of love that entered our hearts when we first met Christ. They tell us that the Holy Spirit is ready to encourage us once again to walk in the way of the cross without fear. Truly, if the Holy Spirit assisted weak people like us to grow in love to the point of accepting dying for Christ, he can do the same with us today. The Holy Spirit does not want us to imitate the heroic actions of the martyrs of the past, but to live with sincerity, growing in obedience and love, and offering ourselves daily as a living sacrifice so that if death through martyrdom enters our path, we will be able to accept it as a gift from God to crown our lives.

In My Context

In the Egyptian Christian context, martyrdom is not only past history nor is it a distant concept. For us, martyrdom is part of our ongoing story. Of course, currently Christians in Egypt are not under heavy and constant persecution as in the past, but due to several incidents in the last two decades, it is very common to be a relative of a martyr or at least to have met a friend of one. From another perspective, being a Christian in Egypt does not grant any social or financial privileges; you do not become part of the dominant group if you are a Christian. Here is the importance of the work of Fr. Matta El-Meskeen for today's Egyptian context. It urges us to witness Christ in our everyday lives and to comfort our sisters and brothers in their distress as the martyrs did for one another and for generations to follow.

Our Commitment

- We must acknowledge the fear that motivates us to refrain from carrying the cross and confess this fear to God and one another.
- As a church, we need to reconsider the outcome of the lives and faith of the martyrs. We need to look at them as solid evidence and true witnesses to the teachings of the gospel, as reflections of the image of Christ, and as models of Christian love.
- In our prayers, we should ask God to renew the Holy Spirit in us, the spirit of sacrificial love, and the spirit of humility and obedience. Only by God's Spirit can we witness the truth of the gospel without fear of any consequences.

Reflection

Pain ... bleeding ... thirst ...
Finally, the grain of wheat fell with her own will and died!
Now I know the meaning of love.
The meaning of conquering the world.
I offer you, my Lord, my strength in honour
of your bleeding wounds ...
My health and my youth I put under your bloody feet ...
All that I own I put in your two wounded hands ...
I will fast in honour of your thirst.
I will rejoice in my sickness for the sake of your suffering.
I will sacrifice my life for the memory of your death ...
I will do so in secret and, if necessary, in public too.[2]

—Fr. Matta El-Meskeen

---

2. Translated by Riad Ghobrial from Fr. Matta El-Meskeen, *With Christ in His Sufferings until His Crucifixion*, 2nd ed. (Scetis, Egypt: The Monastery of St Macarius, 1965), 26. [Arabic]

Lebanon

Following Jesus in Turbulent Times: Disciple-Making in the Arab World[1]
Hikmat Kashouh

Contributed by Angukali Rotokha (India)

Summary

The author of this book is a pastor of a church in Beirut who has reached out to Muslim refugees from Syria and Iraq and has had a fruitful ministry among them. In this book, he shares the insights gleaned from their years of endeavour to assimilate the new refugee believers and the local believers into one unified body of Christ. The book begins by telling the author's own story of coming to believe in Jesus (chapter 2). He shares his testimony of struggle, conversion, and passionate witnessing which eventually led to him pastoring a church that grew exponentially, with refugees constituting seventy percent of the attendees. The sharing of the author's own story lays the foundation for doing what he and his church do among the Muslim refugees.

The author makes the important observation that when working among displaced people it is crucial to build relationships if you want to be given a space and a hearing. In his context, he found that building such relationships requires one to take the time to visit the refugees in their homes and to engage in a two-way sharing of stories (chapters 3 and 4). This enables the refugees to be the host which can be empowering in Eastern contexts where hospitality is an essential social virtue.

While reaching out to refugees is crucial, the author highlights the importance of a transformed leadership if the church is to embrace people from all ethnic and cultural backgrounds (chapter 5). This is especially key in contexts which have a history of, or are still experiencing, violence and hatred rooted in ethnic prejudices where resistance to such openness is to be expected. The author uses anecdotes and also highlights various aspects

---

1. Carlisle, Cumbria: Langham Global Library, 2018.

when considering what worked for their church to make it more inclusive in embracing the growing and diverse congregation and leadership. He points to instances in the Bible which reflect those aspects. The author is also realistic in warning that the change of willingness in leadership to embrace others will not automatically be accepted by the congregation. Challenges will come and should be expected. However, patience and making room for discussion and for the others to share their experience and faith will lead to trust building and hence acceptance.

The author is not oblivious to the enormous responsibility and challenges facing the church after successfully bringing people to Christ. He knows the seriousness of the need to disciple and is not idealistic about how discipleship happens – it can be messy and disappointing, and often the attitude of one's own church congregation can be something to overcome. The rest of the chapters are a practical guide teaching how to disciple the new believers and the role the church – both the leaders and the congregation – plays in reaching out to others and integrating them into one family. Chapters 6–12 discuss some of the practical steps involved in taking care of and integrating the new believers. The author discusses: the need for mature believers to walk along with the new believers so that they see living examples and are encouraged to emulate them, the importance of teaching the new believers to read the Scriptures reflectively, and the importance of engaging the new believers in ministry to others. The book also looks at the fruit of the Spirit and spiritual gifts in the New Testament. It highlights what these could look like in the context of ministry among Muslim refugees and compares these to similar elements in Islam, explaining the apparent similarities and the fundamental differences. Further, since the author's ministry context is one of war, violence, displacement, and trauma, he stresses the need for a ministry of prayer, healing, and freeing, which in its extreme can take the form of exorcism. Apart from these, the author emphasizes the importance of ensuring that the new believers find their identity in the community. This, he says, can be achieved by explaining to the new believers the history and beliefs of the church, the elements of Christian identity that are non-negotiable and those that are cultural. The steps discussed in these chapters are a helpful reminder and are especially relevant to those working among the Muslims since they are explained from that perspective.

As stated earlier, the author's church saw rapid growth. Thus, in chapter 13, the author provides a guide to how church growth can be supported without breaking the essential unity of the church. The author emphasizes that it is essential to define what the church believes, that is, its core values, and establish a healthy structure and governance. The author's context also means that suffering and the need for resources are a constant challenge (chapters 14–15). As such, he reflects on how they can manage suffering since suffering is part and parcel of discipleship in his region. Sharing real examples of the kinds of persecution the people in his congregation have faced, or are facing, he demonstrates how heavy the cost of following Christ is and emphasizes how leaders in similar contexts should prepare themselves and the believers for that cost. Taking the sudden influx of refugees fleeing war as an instance, the author also highlights the significance of a partnership of the local church with other churches or organizations and what practical considerations need to be agreed upon by partners before collaborating.

Response
On the Summary
Although this book makes for an interesting read and can appeal to a wide audience, it would be most useful to those looking for insights into reaching out to refugees in general, particularly Muslim refugees, and especially to new church leaders or planters who need some practical guidance to navigate the complex and often challenging process of disciple making. For instance, the lesson on church structure and governance could be useful for those who are involved in church planting ministry. The author's explanations of the various permutations of couples from different backgrounds planning to get married demonstrate the challenges of working among a multi-cultural, multi-ethnic community, and how an element like prayer, which is naturally accepted by Christians, needs to be explained to the Muslims who are well acquainted with the concept of prayer, but have a different experience with prayer. The author's approach is practical and his teachings in the book comes from years of experience from what has worked in his context; as such, this book is like a lamp lighting the path for others who are called to a similar ministry.

Since prayer and the element of vengeance is vital in Islam, the book could perhaps have been strengthened by also looking at prayer in the Old Testament since the author primarily looks at prayer from the New Testament perspective (chapter 11). Praying for enemies is emphasized in the Bible, as the author rightly says, but the Old Testament contains instances of curses on the enemies and prayers or cries to God to avenge enemies. If this aspect of prayer in the Bible could be highlighted, and then the author explained how these verses are to be understood in the context of leaving vengeance to God, not exacting it ourselves, but as a prayer for God's justice to prevail, it would provide a more balanced view of what prayer is in the Bible. Otherwise, it gives the impression that there are no prayers for some kind of "victory" over enemies in the Christian Scriptures.

In My Context

Since India is home to one of the largest Muslim populations in the world (it has the third largest number of Muslims),[2] this book is a useful window into the worldview and inner lives of Muslims and how they may be more open than we think they are. While the refugee situation may render the Muslims in the author's context more open as compared to India it still is thought provoking, sensitizing readers to the various aspects of the practices and views common among the Muslims and shedding light on the avenues for and challenges in ministry to them.

The author's discussion on the negotiables and non-negotiables of Christian identity is also illuminating. While the specifics will differ according to one's own ministry contexts, he lists some principles from Romans 14:1–12 that can be helpful for churches with multi-ethnic congregations facing issues with identity and customs to be adopted or rejected. This can be useful in Indian churches where problems with castes, ethnicities, and classes still exists. For instance, the example of how the question of wearing or removing the hijab for a new believer was handled sheds light regarding how one custom may have different answers depending on the underlying reasons and demonstrates Christian maturity that needs to be emulated.

Our Commitment

- Staying put with our church doors open is not enough; we need to go where the people are.
- We need to be more inclusive in leadership.
- We must trust new believers and involve them in ministry, ensuring that they have someone they can shadow initially.

---

2. See: https://worldpopulationreview.com/country-rankings/muslim-population-by-country.

Reflection

St. Ignatius's Prayer

Lord Jesus, teach me to be generous.
Teach me to serve as you deserve,
To give and not to count the cost,
To fight and not to heed the wounds,
To labour and not to seek to rest,
To give of myself and not ask for a reward,
Except the reward of knowing that I am doing your will.

Palestine

The Politics of Persecution: Middle Eastern Christians in an Age of Empires[1]
Mitri Raheb

Contributed by Brent Hamoud (USA/Lebanon)

Summary

Literature on Christian persecution can certainly be contentious. It is, after all, a field of inquiry addressing malicious forms of human oppression, and any serious exploration of this kind is bound to delve into provocative waters. Yet even for such a prickly area of study, Mitri Raheb's 2021 text *The Politics of Persecution: Middle Eastern Christians in an Age of Empires* stands apart as a savage critique upending much about the conventional discourse on Christian persecution in the Middle East. He accomplishes this by tracking two centuries of Middle Eastern history to forge political analysis of persecution within the context of empire. Writing from his homeland and lived experiences in Palestine, Raheb implores via impassioned, forceful, and comprehensive scholarship that aims to move the diagnosis of religious persecution from one pinning blame on Islamic intolerance to one that exposes chronic and calculated Western oppression. The bold thesis is propelled by a thoughtful yet harsh polemic that unravels a political knot and shows that ruthless politics have undermined Middle Eastern Christianity in both pronounced and subtle ways. Raheb comes out swinging from the start; he holds back no punches while compelling readers to rethink the nature of Christian persecution and the ways it has been inflicted, misrepresented, and co-opted within campaigns of empire. It is a powerful treatise for the global church that is bound to provoke strong feelings and acute judgements. Even those who thoroughly disagree with *The Politics of Persecution* will not be able to deny its visceral impact and sharp political commentary.

---

1. Waco, Texas: Baylor University Press, 2021.

Raheb casts his personal orientation towards Christian persecution in the introduction. Here we see the personal, contextual, and intellectual impetus undergirding the book's argument. As a socially engaged Palestinian Lutheran scholar, he is amplifying a decolonial voice into a Western-dominated choir. A revisionist tone comes across strongly when he says, "the days when Western forces claimed a mandate over us . . . are over. Now it is time for us to speak on our own, to tell our story, and to resist all attempts to turn us into objects."[2] It is clear from the start that this book is more than simply an academic study; it is a fervent outcry to a global faith community. What follows is an intense condemnation of imperialism's assault against Middle Eastern Christians as witnessed in the "geopolitical tectonic plates" stretching areas of empire within and outside the region. Its prevailing argument contends that the primary threat to Middle Eastern Christian persecution falls not on Islam and Muslims but rather on the shoulders of a hegemonic Christian West.

The Politics of Persecution is primarily historical in its methodology. Twelve chapters (mostly in chronicle) craft interdisciplinary analysis about the political currents unleashed in the Middle East. Raheb draws generously from fields of church history, international relations, political science, economics, and postcolonial studies. This results in a metanarrative retelling of religious persecution. Raheb constantly shifts his discussion between macro events happening across global levels and micro developments unfolding at the national and local levels. This wide view of history and politics is used to paint the political forces impacting Middle Eastern Christianity. He looks both at structural phenomena (such as the status and treatment of Christians within the Ottoman *millet* system) as well as specific times, peoples, and places (such as the Maronite of Mount Lebanon during the 1860 massacres and the catastrophic events befalling Palestinian Christians around the 1948 declaration of the State of Israel). The book constitutes an extensive study spanning multiple historical eras, but it moves at a brisk, almost unrelenting, pace that refuses to linger at any one stage or location for long. The focus shifts in the later parts from a survey of history to a general commentary of Middle Eastern social issues including topics like the environment, youth, and women. *The Politics of Persecution* is an ambitious undertaking that never shies away from its disruptive yet hopeful intentions.

As indicated in its title, the theme of empire remains at the heart of the book. Raheb traces centuries of events starting with Ottoman Empire rule to interventions by European powers, culminating in French-British colonial rule

---

2. Raheb, *The Politics of Persecution*, 6.

in the aftermath of WWI It continues into eras marked by the establishment of nation-states, the emergence of Zionism, and the State of Israel, movements of Arab nationalism and pan-Islamism, and the age of America's entrenched hegemony. Likewise, discussion about authoritarian Arab regimes uncovers how the essence of empire plays out through national political expressions as well, although this receives much less treatment and is set against the backdrop of foreign imperial engagement. Histories of this kind can be found in a host of books about modern Middle Eastern history, but Raheb distinguishes his unique work by casting it within a framework of Christian persecution. One of its main distinctions is the attention paid to the region's Protestant Christian experiences, which includes questioning how Christian missionary projects took place within wider campaigns of empire. These points of investigation demonstrate how the history of Protestants in the Middle East can be as dynamic and convoluted as the political drama happening around them.

Raheb's rhetoric is fiery throughout the text, and the heat is punctuated in the epilogue when he arrives at a number of biting conclusions. Here the ferocity of his thesis is laid bare, as conveyed in the following:

> Christian persecution is a Western construct that says more about the West than about the Christians of the Middle East. It is a perception rather than an actual description, and the politics that underlie it should not be underestimated. It was the evangelicals in the United States who created the concept of Christian persecution as a central theme in their teaching and promoted it in Congress with some success. Geopolitical changes provided the framework for this development.[3]

Readers would do well to take in the book's concluding points first in order to see plainly where *The Politics of Persecution* lands. Raheb bemoans the ways in which religious liberty advocates play their part in political agendas while remaining selective, narrow, and ultimately subservient to the interests of empires. He goes so far as to claim they are willing to see Middle Eastern Christians "sacrificed on the altar of Western nation interests"; well-known Christian organizations are called out by name and accused of having far from genuine intentions. These hard-hitting assertions come at the end of a book that has no qualms in landing blows on popular assumptions and common conventions permeating the global Christian consciousness.

---

3. Raheb, *The Politics of Persecution*, 185.

Response
On the Summary

The history in *The Politics of Persecution* is thoroughly sweeping and well-informed (though its commentary on contemporary social and political matters is noticeably thin). Raheb provides a critical contribution to Christian persecution studies by insisting that we peer through political lenses, which is something severely remiss in the discourse. His discussion is lofty but widely relevant to anyone concerned about the Middle East and its Christian presence. Those already well read in Middle Eastern history and politics will benefit from an evoking, innovative, and edgy narrative robust with fresh insights, particularly regarding the twists and turns of the region's Protestant tradition. Readers with scant knowledge of the Middle East or only a dim understanding of its intense political complexities will profit from its comprehensive overview covering hundreds of years of history. The book may not be sufficient as a singular resource for Christians seeking to understand Middle Eastern history and politics, but it certainly is a valuable resource that adds spice to the way we think about a host of issues in this part of the world, and beyond.

The information dispensed in *The Politics of Persecution* is hefty and rich, but the book's vibrancy lies more in Raheb's direct confrontation against prevailing assumptions and ideologies regarding Christian persecution in the Middle East. He establishes his authoritative credibility at the forefront as someone speaking from within a particular social location. This must be kept in mind not simply to make the points more palatable (those who find his arguments revolting are in need of honest self-examination) but to see that the potency is not misunderstood as poison. As a Protestant Christian in Palestine, Raheb speaks from a complex identity extending across diverse sets of networks, which effectively position him beyond the mainstream. His background and life experiences under the weight of empire give the treatise a real credence; whether his arguments are agreeable or disagreeable does not dismiss their significance for global Christians (especially those in the West). Even so, *The Politics of Persecution* does warrant critique.

Persecution and empire pose the conceptual pillars of the text, but Raheb puts little into defining or framing the two concepts theoretically. Persecution is given only a general definition at the very start – "the systematic mistreatment of an individual Christian or a Christian community by another individual or group based on their religious belief"[4] – and then hardly disseminated any further. It is evident in the text, however, that Raheb's notion of persecution

---

4. Raheb, *The Politics of Persecution*, 14.

is quite narrow and mainly limited to large genocidal campaigns of religious violence. This is evidenced in his claim that only two cases of Christian persecution by Muslims have occurred in the past two centuries – namely the Armenian genocide by Ottoman forces and the recent assault on Christians by ISIS. His failure to acknowledge the extent to which "micro" persecutions terrorize people of faith at individual levels will likely not be acceptable to those concerned about Christian persecution. Additionally, empire is described extensively but little is offered to present it theoretically despite the abundance of decolonial, imperialism, and critical theory research about the topic. Skirting over the conceptual elements of the discussion and diving straight away into implications ultimately does disservice to the power of the argument and may actually work to disengage readers from the main argument all together. Fleshing out more robust theory would certainly require a larger text, but it is needed.

Raheb dutifully exposes the entanglements of Middle Eastern Christian persecution with Western interests, and it is definitely cutting to consider his suggestion that ulterior motives (and economic incentives) drive the way religious persecution is handled. The assertion that Islam and Islamization by no means equate to persecution is an important nugget for those who are enthusiastic to colour Middle Eastern Christians' plight as a work of Muslims; however, neglecting the Islamic dimensions of persecution is highly problematic. A host of evidence via personal accounts, religious structures, and text-based polemics show that Islam, in many ways, is a serious factor in religious persecution, which is something that also can be said of other religions from Christianity to Judaism to Hinduism. (Political pollution of religion is a profound part of any religion.) Islam's role in playing a harmful role in persecution is seemingly underplayed by Raheb, and a study on Christianity in the Middle East calls for a more critical assessment of Islam's past and present than what is provided here.

Finally, *The Politics of Persecution* is an important reminder of how easily discussions on Christian persecution in the Middle East can succumb to reductionist thinking. Raheb's historical, political, and sociological analysis is a compelling methodological example of the way we should inform our understandings by incorporating broad intellectual considerations. However, it is difficult to read the book and not sense that it too often resorts to reductionist thinking. Examples of this emerge from loaded statements of the epilogue: "Christian persecution is a Western construct," Christian persecution exists as an "Anglo-Saxon discourse," "we can say that evangelical Christians love to see Middle Eastern Christians persecuted and killed by Islamic violence," and "Evangelical Christians and Western political forces want to frame the story of the Middle Eastern Christians as one simply of persecution."[5] Even if mentioned here apart from their textual contexts, the proclamations are extreme. They threaten to weaken the complexity of the discourse by having Raheb come across as pompous, bombastic, and ideological. Even in the face of something as powerful and perverse as empire it is imperative for scholarship to refrain from pitfalls of reductionism. A host of readers will likely read such lines and unfortunately throw out Raheb's baby with the bathwater. (Or is this critique simply evidence of my privileged sensibilities rather than my concern for academic authenticity?)

In My Context

The relevance of *The Politics of Persecution* to the Lebanese context is nearly self-evident. Politics is fundamental to understanding the national religious milieu, and Lebanon with its convoluted colonial past and even more convoluted sectarianism present receives particular focus in the study. Many of the tropes about Christian persecution that Raheb decries are quite present in Lebanon, as are the imperial interventions by governments and organizations. Framing Lebanese history within a wider story of the region works to place the context within regional and global narratives of the past two hundred years. This works to counter any temptation to evaluate its national experience in isolation from events beyond, which some tend to do through sentiments of Lebanese exceptionalism. One major importance of the book is the way it problematizes the nature of Western engagement in the Middle East, and Lebanon's historical and contemporary encounters with the West are thick. This is especially the case for Lebanese Protestants who share a strong link (or is it an umbilical cord?) to Western Christians. By challenging the conventional historical narratives about Middle East Christians being constantly victimized by Islam, Raheb undermines many false narratives inherent within much of the Lebanese national ideas and experiences. That said, some are likely to find his treatment of Lebanon over-generalized and thin. Politics and religion are extremely complex here, and these complexities must be dutifully acknowledged within any type of commentary.

It is necessary to mention here that chapter 7's discussion about the rise of nation-states is vitally important in understanding the political realities of Lebanon and the region today. Despite its enormity in shaping the world and

---

5. Raheb, *The Politics of Persecution*, 202.

the region, scant critical analysis has been given to the nation-state from a Christian perspective. Raheb's chapter is utterly urgent and illuminating since it rightfully frames nation-states as the continuation of empire, and an entire book expanding such a Middle Eastern Christian examination of nation-states would be of great service for understanding Christian persecution as well as a host of other issues related to Lebanon and the Middle East.

Our Commitment

Contentious discourse tends not to be pleasant and, when it comes to topics as evocative and deep-seated as Christian persecution, there is often an impulse to dismiss opposing viewpoints as irrelevant or destructive. This is not an edifying way forward for growing our hearts and minds, and so commitment is needed time and again to nurture postures of listening. This is especially necessary when receiving hard truths delivered by folks with situational insight and hard truths are needed to expose our own blinkers and refine our intellectual and spiritual convictions. As with all discourses, our thinking about Christian persecution must consider voices on the margins not simply for the sake of acquiring empirical data to validate existing theories but to gain disruptive analysis. This may require suspending our own positions at times, but doing so with the intention of hearing what others have to say and then allowing it to shape our thinking and feeling is indeed an act of humility and wisdom. Likewise, issues as complex as Christian persecution can never be distilled to any particular discipline of study. It is prudent to initiate broad critical explorations that are interdisciplinary in scope. Talking about politics may seem like a pointless measure that only leads to strife, but neglecting politics risks terrible consequences, and people of faith must be committed to faithful grappling with politics and its histories.

The Politics of Persecution in all of its critical severity has the potential to sharpen thinking and inspire resolve to work in solidarity with God's people for gospel witness, but this cannot happen without commitments to generous listening and open-mindedness. Raheb's hope in writing such a text is that it will stir commitments from a range of readers by shaking them up into new ways of thinking about persecution, the Middle East, and Christian narratives. All of this is punctuated in the final lines pointing to a new vision of Middle Eastern Christians:

> Evangelical Christians and Western political forces want to frame the story of the Middle Eastern Christians as one simply

of persecution. This study clearly demonstrates that the story is one of struggle, resistance, social involvement, and resilience.⁶

Reflection

Fleeing . . . from the Massacre⁷
Abed Abdi, 1976

---

6. Raheb, *The Politics of Persecution*, 156.
7. Source: https://commons.wikimedia.org/wiki/File:Fleeing..._from_the_Massacre,_Abed_Abdi,_1976.jpg.

Syria

Called for Martyrdom, Called for Victory[1]
Father Samy Hallaq, SJ

Contributed by Riad Kassis (Lebanon)

Summary

In his introduction the author lists three main reasons that motivated him to write this book. First, he has felt that the word "martyr" (*shaheed* in Arabic) has been misunderstood and misused in the Arab world. There is a need to redefine the meaning of the Christian martyr in the midst of the perception that sees anyone killed for a cause whether religious, social or political is considered a martyr. Second, he admits the need of having a martyrdom theology for the present time for many believe that martyrdom is a historical fact only occurred in the first three centuries after Christ. Third, most of the books that deal with this topic have approached it from a historical perspective or, they have focused on certain Christian individual martyrs; however, the author sees the need for more in-depth treatment of this vital topic that ultimately defines the identity and mission of the church as a "church of witnesses and martyrs."

The book is divided into eight chapters. The first chapter focuses on providing definitions of misused terminology in an attempt to understand the exact meaning of Christian martyrdom. The author distinguishes between two kinds of martyrdom – active and passive. The active martyr is the one who incites his death by being proactive to defend the faith and will do that until the hour of death while the passive martyr is the one who does not fight for the faith but will silently accept dying for the sake of the Christian faith. The history of Christian martyrdom reveals that both kinds were common. However, one should not prefer one way over the other as, in both cases, the martyr is exemplifying faithfulness to Christ and willingness to die for the sake of the gospel.

---

1. Theological Studies. Beirut, Lebanon: Dar al-Machreq, 2021. [Arabic]

The second chapter sees the New Testament – and particularly the letter to the Hebrews, the letter of 1 Peter, and Revelation – as "persecution and witness literature" addressed to persecuted faith communities. The Christian as a witness has not yet witnessed by sight the Risen Christ, but nonetheless has experienced the Risen Lord (Acts 1:21; John 20:29). It is this experience that grants courage to face martyrdom. The "persecution literature" introduces us to two realities – one is visible, and the other is invisible. The visible one is the pain and the persecution that the church endures in this world and the invisible one is the power that the Lord grants to his church to be victorious even after much pain and suffering. The author emphasizes the role of the Holy Spirit in sustaining and encouraging the church in times of persecution (John 16:16, 26; 1 Peter 4:13–14). When Jesus speaks about the Holy Spirit, he describes him as the comforter in the midst of suffering (Matthew 10:17–20; Mark 13:9–11; Luke 21:12–19). The author concludes this chapter by saying: "Martyrdom is an integral part of the church call and mission in this world, a call that leads to martyrdom and martyrdom itself will be transformed into a call and mission."[2]

The third chapter defines "persecution" and distinguishes between "general persecution," "religious persecution," and "Christian persecution." "General persecution" is any violent treatment to others that causes physical, psychological, or social pain and suffering, and results in injustice. "Religious persecution," according to the human rights declaration, occurs when one's freedom to believe, to change belief or not to believe, is violated.[3] "Christian persecution" is any unjust act directed towards Christians because they believe in Christ. It could be physical, psychological, or social. Christians in this context should have a proper understanding and practice of discipleship (1 Peter 4:12–14; 2 Timothy 3:12). In discussing the relationship between discipleship and persecution, the author notes that the Christian should not doubt his sincere discipleship to Christ if he is not being persecuted. What is required is that one should be vigilant and ready to face persecution when it occurs, trusting in God's providence.

The fourth chapter is an elaboration of being Christ's disciples by following his example as the suffering servant. It also explains what is meant by "suffering for (or on behalf of) Christ." The author explains the meaning of "suffering for

---

2. Hallaq, *Called for Martyrdom*, 23.

3. See, United Nations, *Universal Declaration of Human Rights*, United Nations, https://www.ohchr.org/sites/default/files/UDHR/Documents/UDHR_Translations/eng.pdf.

Christ/on behalf of Christ" according to the Apostle Paul in 2 Corinthians 4 and 5 as follows.

- The grace of my suffering will spread among many – and they will become aware of Christ.
- The grace of my suffering will glorify God.
- My suffering will bring glory to me in eternity.
- Each believer will be judged.
- This understating seems to be nonsense, but we are committed to it.
- Christ's love to me does leave me any option except this one.
- The cross drives me not to live for my own self but for the sake of Christ.
- I am Christ's ambassador. God speaks and works through me. I am God's co-worker.

The fifth chapter addresses a practical matter on whether Christians should flee persecution or face it with courage. The author argues that martyrdom is not the only criteria for faithful witness; however, true martyrdom must be combined with a genuine inner desire. He goes on to discuss how the church fathers addressed the issue of fleeing or facing persecution and martyrdom. He cites several examples from the Bible for both cases. According to him, most church fathers preferred avoiding martyrdom if at all possible. The author briefly discusses the controversial issue on how to treat the Christians who were weak in the face of persecution and denied their faith to avoid suffering and martyrdom.

Chapter six approaches the topic of martyrdom from a perspective of the meaning of life and death. The author argues that the heart of the matter is whether the persecutor is the source of life or whether God is its source. The author asserts that the Christian church from its early inception has differentiated between two concepts: life and existence. Life for Christians does not entail merely existing and living on this earth and therefore they are always ready to sacrifice "their existence" for the sake of "their lives." The belief that God grants life and has conquered death is the main motivation for the Christian to live, to face persecution, and to die as a martyr.

The author begins chapter seven by emphasizing the fact that the theology of persecution was not formulated at church councils, but in the darkest and violent places where it actually occurred. He presents ideas and suggestions on how to face persecution, even when that persecution could lead to martyrdom. He also addresses the ethical values that Christians should exemplify when they encounter persecution. One of the most noticeable values is courage, but it is not any kind of courage. It is to be accompanied with love, prudence, and wisdom.

The final chapter responds to the question whether martyrdom is to be considered only as a witness or a participation in Christ's sacrifice. Ignatius of Antioch did not use the term "martyrdom" to describe his expected death: he described it as a "sacrifice." The concept of "sacrificial death" was transferred from the Eastern church to the Western church. Therefore, even in the fourth century, martyrdom was viewed as a witness and a sacrifice. It is Saint Augustine (354–430) who downplayed the language of sacrifice to be associated with martyrdom. Since then, the common understanding in the church is to regard the martyr as a witness rather than as a sacrifice.

Response
On the Summary
This is a fascinating book written by a well-known author from Syria. Being a Syrian himself, he has firsthand knowledge of the persecution by fundamentalist terrorists which Christians (and non-Christians) have endured. Therefore, he is not theorizing about persecution and martyrdom; he is writing from a real-life context and addressing the issue with a deep theological understanding and a sensitive pastoral perspective.

The author is able to dive deep into the history of martyrdom as viewed by the church fathers and to connect their perception of it as a witness rather than a sacrifice in formulating a theology of martyrdom for our present time. The author succeeds in bringing clarity to often confused concepts that are commonly used in the Arab word such as "passive vs active persecution," "witness and martyrdom," and "martyrdom and sacrificial death."

In his treatment of the topic on how to face persecution, the author stresses the importance of courage by reminding us that the church has viewed courage as one of the four cardinal virtues. However, he argues that for courage to be identified specifically as a "Christian courage," two virtues are needed to accompany it: love and wisdom.

In addition of his interaction with the church fathers on the topic of persecution and martyrdom, the author interacts well with the biblical text on issues pertaining to his discussion. He sheds a new light on what it means to participate in the suffering of Christ and delineates the relationship between persecution and discipleship.

Our Commitment

Please take time to reflect on the following.

- How is "martyrdom" defined in your own context? What is the distinctiveness of "Christian martyrdom"?
- In your opinion, should Christians avoid or face persecution even if it leads to martyrdom? Why?
- Read 1 Corinthians 4–5 and reflect on how Paul understood what it means to suffer for Christ.
- How should Christians respond to their persecutors? Please read the two statements below and comment on them:
    - Tawadros Yousif is one of the Egyptians workers who was martyred in Libya in February 2015. His mother said about those who killed her son: "I do not wish them evil. I pray for them that God may open their hearts and give them his light."
    - On the same tragic event Bishop Angaelos, general bishop of the Coptic Orthodox Church in the UK, commented: "We don't forgive the act because the act is heinous. But we do forgive the killers from the depths of our hearts. Otherwise, we would become consumed by anger and hatred. It becomes a spiral of violence that has no place in this world."[4]
- Share this book review with one of your friends and spend time in conversing about its importance to your life and context.

---

4. From an interview with the bishop here: https://edition.cnn.com/2015/02/20/living/coptic-bishop-isis/index.html.

Reflection

A Testimony of a Recent Martyr

Mehdi Dibaj

At his trial, Mehdi Dibaj, an Iranian Christian martyr, testified

> They tell me, 'Return!' But from the arms of my God, whom can I return to? Is it right to accept what people are saying instead of obeying the Word of God? It is now 45 years that I am walking with the God of miracles, and His kindness upon me is like a shadow and I owe Him much for His fatherly love and concern. In response to His kindness, He has asked me to deny myself and be His fully surrendered follower, and not fear people, even if they kill my body.[5]

---

5. Mehdi Dibaj, "The Testimony and Defence of Mehdi Dibaj," Banner of Truth, 5 January 2015, https://banneroftruth.org/us/resources/articles/2015/testimony-defence-mehdi-dibaj/.

North America

Canada

Prison Power: How God Uses Imprisonment to Enlarge His Kingdom[1]
Jim Cunningham and Paul Estabrooks

Contributed by Ashkenaz Asif Khan (Pakistan)

Summary

Imprisonment is a difficult topic, a human tragedy, and an ugly expression of fallen human nature. In this book, imprisonment is described as a crucible for refining character, forging resilience, showing love, and, above all, an opportunity for telling others what God has done to save sinners through Jesus Christ – even in the dungeons of rottenness and death. Prisons can become gardens, places of hope and faith. And that is the power of prison!

Drawing on biblical narratives and modern-day heroes of faith, the authors have composed a beautiful tapestry of the kingdom of God in the making! We read the Bible and in it all the incidents where God's people, both men and women, risked their lives and came out resilient. But we miss the principles which play the role of guiding paths when the time comes to suffer for Christ. The faith values and principles, alongside divine help, act together to help a prisoner not only to survive atrocities but also to thrive as a witness for Jesus in the midst of all odds a human being can face. The book is formatted into small sections, each building on the narrative of a Bible character together with other relevant verses to develop a principle that the church needs to understand today. These biblical pericopes are followed by a true story of a modern prisoner. About twelve principles have been formulated in this manner. The authors have used a wide range of Bible passages from both the Old Testament and the New Testament. No early church fathers or apocryphal sources have been used. The references are cited as footnotes and

---

1. Santa Ana, California: Open Doors International, 1999. The authors published a second edition in 2021; it is available for Kindle.

no bibliography is provided. The language in non-technical and easy to read with sufficient flow to keep the reader attentive.

Response
On the Summary

The recurring theme in this article is suffering and imprisonment of people because of their Christian faith. So, the first question is its theological implication. Old Testament examples provide inspiration for believers and the opportunity to learn lessons from someone who has suffered. While principles of life and conduct can be deduced from the experience of Old Testament believers, contemporary readers may not come to the conclusion that they should follow the example of the biblical heroes of faith. Turning to the New Testament, the authors describe three levels of teaching. One is clear teaching from our Lord Jesus Christ, such as the instructions for everyday conduct found in the Sermon on the Mount. This includes instruction on how to face opposition, how to react to the perpetrators of injustice, and what to do as one suffers. Then Acts provides accounts of New Testament heroes of faith. The Epistles provide both practical teaching for the daily conduct and theological foundations for the choices we should make. Precedents may not become binding commands unless supported by the plain teaching of Jesus Christ and his apostles as taught in the Epistles. Using these different categories, the authors have provided a balanced teaching on suffering and its results.

Our Lord experienced injustice including false charges, arrests, court appearances, and unlawful treatment and sentence. Having warned his disciples of what they would face, he himself faced the same trials and tribulations. The disciples themselves faced what they had been warned of. So, the apostles could say that suffering was not a surprise. The believer is warned, "in this world you will have trouble" (John 16:33a). But at the same time, we are not alone. Jesus also tells us to "take heart!" because he has "overcome the world" (John 16:33b) and he will always be with us (Matthew 28:20). This book features many accounts of imprisoned Christians experiencing that they were not alone. The theology of suffering is perhaps a new topic for some quarters of the Western church, but it is a daily life experience in the rest of the world where the church has been facing opposition and believers have gone through immense suffering. Perhaps not much has been written by these believers, but much has been experienced. There is thus a strong case for constructing a comprehensive theology of suffering. This book provides a good summary of the important passages, examples, and principles.

In My Context

Most of the examples in this book are drawn from Africa, Asia, and Latin America; one is from Canada. The political context in these countries is a complex one. The authors have not dealt with those issues and did not qualify suffering accordingly. The regimes in these countries, be they communist, socialist, or Islamic, operate with specific forms of government which differ from those of Western democracy. For various reasons, these governments perceive the West as their rival and thus position themselves against them. They also perceive the West as Christian, as they think about their countries as being Muslim, Buddhist or Hindu. They do not accept that the church and state are separate. Thus, they consider local Christians to have allegiance with the West, with its political and economic and social systems. This brings everything associated with the West into suspicion. As Christians in these countries are in the minority, they tend to be isolated, not interested in politics, and marginalized. Many of the stories have some element of that kind of reaction shown by the rulers and religious elite against the Christian minority. One story in this book clearly mentioned that the person imprisoned was blamed as an agent of the foreign country!

How to overcome this perception is a big challenge; a simple declaration that one is not a foreign agent does not suffice. Political elites and the state perceive a Christian to be guilty unless proven innocent. It is a matter of the narrative and perception which have been built around a specific philosophy. The issue of freedom struggles, revolutions, or guerrilla wars in various countries against their own governments is again a complex political reality. There might not be a simple black and white answer for the ethical issues involved. Christians may with a good conscience be seen on the wrong side of the fence from the perspective of the state's political narrative. One living in the West must use caution when making any judgement about the political situation of a country far away. Another caution may be observed about the level and nature of freedom of religious beliefs and freedom of thought. These rights are taken for granted in the West, but this is not so in many countries. Christians can be caught up in the political debate, which may affect the unity of the church. Thus, a fine balance is always required. Nevertheless, no matter what the context is, the truth is that God is with his people in their suffering.

Our Commitment

The authors have demonstrated by teaching, examples, and principles that no matter how deep the wounds or how bad the perpetrators of injustice, the power of God will prevail, and he is able to do the unthinkable – even showing his power through intervening with miracles as he delivered the Israelites. He is doing this in order to fulfil his purpose to bring people to himself, even the ones languishing in the prisons, their guards, and their executioners. The wonderful and unbelievable stories demonstrate that many came to know Jesus only when a Christian was put in the same prison in which non-Christians were present. But the evangelistic purpose is not the only result nor even the most desired result. God wants his people to be holy and this is the way, though painful, that his people become holy, strong, and mature. Almost all the stories shared testify that Christians who spent months and years in the prison came out stronger.

The book did not cover duties on the part of the church. Prayer support is mentioned but it is a mammoth task to help the families of the imprisoned and at the same time fight legal battles. It can drain both energy and emotions. Thus, imprisonment is a multi-pronged battle with one front in the prison and another outside the prison. Only a great measure of grace will carry the church through this ordeal. Sadly, humanly speaking, there are still countries where the loyalty of Christians is seen with suspicion and they are treated as second-class citizens. The third battle is the mandate to always shine as light in the darkness. This is Jesus's command; a believer must have faith that light will overcome the darkness.

Reflection

Going Deeper
A monthly prayer meeting for the suffering church can be a practice which will soften the hearts of the church members. Is there going to be a change in the Western society? It all depends on the politics and the economic and social systems. These can change anytime. The believer must be ready to face suffering, opposition, injustice, and extreme threats, even in the Western society. This does not mean that we should become fearful. Rather, we should remain brave and ready to share the gospel. We should not worry much if there is opposition – but we should ask what is wrong if there is none. All Scriptures and principles drawn in the book are very helpful for planning a lesson series. May the Lord give greater strength to those who are imprisoned because of their faith in Jesus. May the Lord change the hearts of those who are persecuting that they may know Jesus as their Saviour and Lord.

St. Paul's Prison in Philippi[2]

---

2. According to an ancient Christian tradition, the prison functioned as a place of worship. Photograph by Myrto Theocharous.

The United States of America and the United Kingdom

Creating Shared Resilience: The Role of the Church in a Hopeful Future[1]
David M. Boan and Josh Ayers

Contributed by Loreen Maseno (Kenya)

Summary

In this book, local faith communities (LFC, or churches) are considered as playing a part in the resilience and well-being of the society. The authors are moved to look at how God extends his grace to reconcile people to himself and so should the LFC reconcile people to community.

The authors reflect on resilience: they define it, exhibit various examples and propose a comprehensive model of resilience. It is noted that people can be vulnerable to disaster due to social, political, economic, human and environmental reasons, and that risk is socially and politically constructed. The church therefore has a role to play in disaster risk reduction and resilience; this is what the authors wanted to explore. They were persuaded that, as the LFC serves the community, one of the results of that service can be a community that is more resilient when disaster strikes.

But what is resilience? Resilience is the reciprocal process between the individual and the community to (or preparation for) disaster where the community demonstrates the capacity to withstand shock and stress.[2] The authors emphasize that the "relatively loose meaning of resilience," citing Christoph Béné and his colleagues, "creates communication bridges between disciplines and communities of practice."[3] It is a holistic process – one based on access to resources, quality of relationships, a commitment to justice, and

---

1. Carlisle, UK: Langham Global Library, 2020.
2. Ayers, *Creating Shared Resilience*, 12.
3. Ayers, *Creating Shared Resilience*, 10.

respect for all members of the community. At the same time, resilience has multiple dimensions such as faith, spirituality and community, and an ongoing process of engaging with stressful events of widely varying intensities. In considering the range of models of resilience, it is possible to isolate the role of the LFC.

The explicit models of resilience are:

1. Resilience and the trustworthy community.
2. Resilience and the just community.
3. Resilience and the conservation of resources.
4. Resilience, the ecological model and the LFC.
5. Resilience, social capital and the LFC.
6. Resilience, spiritual integration and the LFC.[4]

It is clear that, through these listed models, the authors seek to demonstrate the dynamism of resilience and its multiple dimensions and practice within ecology, spirituality, resource conservation, and community.

The authors proceed to place the LFC at centre stage to consider the theological models of resilience in line with an ecclesiology of resilience that is anchored in the work of the church, in addition, providing the theological basis for resilience. Christian communities and the LFC are to practice integral mission. They are to engage in and within a community in a way that builds peace and health by demonstrating the values and the power of the kingdom. LFCs are also to engage in advocacy as an expression of the gospel. Here transformational advocacy speaks to power and is a work of the Spirit in the church such that churches become advocates for our communities. The theological model of resilience, urban shalom, and creation care proposes that LFCs are being called to respond to the creation resiliently, where creation care is part of our gospel commitment in a world facing an ecological crisis.

Shared resilience is fostered where emphasis is laid on the community and relational pillars of resilience. Here the authors note that in times of disaster and crisis, shared resilience requires cooperation, understanding, and respect to work toward a shared understanding of a resilient and thriving community and organization. To create shared resilience, there must be low barriers to access and inclusion, sufficient resources, commitment to justice, transparency and restoration following resource loss, timely responses to disaster, engaged

---

4. Ayers, *Creating Shared Resilience*, 18–39.

LFCs, advocacy, and ecological mindfulness. In all, resilience here is shown to emanate not from technical solutions to disaster or climate change, but rather from a strong and shared sense of community.

But how are all these applicable to LFCs? The LFCs' actions can be proactive, passive, or destructive. In order for LFCs in crises to enhance resilience, they need to engage in basic actions such as seeking justice, building social capital, practicing engagements, creating restoration, and setting their own house in order. In this way, the application of these principles to individuals and churches is reflected.

In conclusion, the authors demonstrate the need for constructive interactions between the faith community(ies), individuals, and the broader society. The connection between the LFC and the resilience of individuals is vital to reclaim the church's identity as a window into God's just community.

Response
On the Summary

My first reaction to the authors' thoughts was to the profound statement that people are vulnerable due to social, political, economic, human, and environmental reasons, and that risk is socially and politically constructed, not merely to the disasters that strike. It made me reflect on the essentials of life in community so that there are shared capacities to withstand risk and disasters.

These thoughts, in the midst of suffering and tragedy, are important and resonate in the sphere of things to do – communities to build and to nurture. The thoughts of the authors are emergent for me, but they are not alien or distant.

In My Context

In the Kenyan context, we have suffered post-election violence especially in 2008 following the contested 2007 elections. People have been made vulnerable by these politically constructed risks which continue to show their wicked faces in present day Kenya. Many Kenyans were displaced and labelled internally displaced persons. Such memories are still fresh in the minds of many Kenyans. For a number of internally displaced persons, their communities of origin acted as buffer zones for them and their families.

Our Commitment

In view of what I have learned from this book, my commitment is that LFCs cannot sit easy but must have a mandate for advocacy and enhancing the resilience of the communities in which they exist. I have learned that the strength of a community is its ability both to absorb any shocks that emanate from crisis and to cushion everyone. I have learned that without transparency, sufficient resources, commitment to justice and restoration following resource loss, etc., a community's resilience is compromised. These reflections change my thoughts, prayers and practice, to be part of God's agenda for a better world in the face of disasters and risks and promotes new ways of thinking for me and my practice of faith.

Reflection

A Prayer

Lord, we pray for the vulnerable in our society. We ask that community will be evidenced in and out of season. We ask that, in these spaces, there shall be Dorcas-es and Shunamite women, and men of good will. Let restoration for losses be made and let our communities bounce back in unity, peace, and liberty. Amen.

The United States of America

Finding Hagar: God's Pursuit of a Runaway[1]
Michael Kuhn

Contributed by Loreen Maseno (Kenya)

Summary

Finding Hagar is a book in which Kuhn combines his imagination and skills in biblical exegesis to weave a tapestry of ideas and subthemes worth exploring. Hagar is an Egyptian woman who is subjected to the harsh conditions of slavery. Kuhn demonstrates Hagar's humanity, personhood, and real identity through his association of Hagar with the God of Abraham. This he then links to other women and persons who were not directly in the line of God's chosen people, such as Ruth, Rahab, Jethro, etc., and who found a place in connection with God. According to Kuhn, God pursued Hagar until he found her. This pursuit is, in his words, from "a God whose grace is scandalous, whose love is profligate, and who pursues a fugitive until he finds her."[2]

Kuhn begins his journey with an introduction of how Hagar came to be a slave in Abram's household. He introduces us to Hagar's family and Hagar's age (an act of imagination from his knowledge of the culture and languages of the Middle East). Hagar is an African woman who is given away into slavery as a commodity of exchange and gains the identity of Sarai's maid. In this chapter, Kuhn concludes that God is a God of covenant, hears the cries of his people and delivers them, but at the same time posits the question of whether the Egyptian in Abraham's household would be better treated than the Israelites in Egypt when the reverse happens. But could the slavery and the agony of Hagar in Abraham's household have been a factor which contributed to the period of enslavement the seed of Abraham would have in Egypt? Could God have been demonstrating his justice and vengeance across generations, I ask?

---

1. Carlisle, UK: Langham Global Library, 2019.
2. Kuhn, *Finding Hagar*, xii.

Kuhn places the question of women's infertility at the centre of chapter 2. According to him, God is the one who withholds the fruit of the womb. God is wholly responsible. To him, the delay of thirteen years after the birth of Ishmael before Sarai gives birth to Isaac demonstrates the miraculous nature of conception. The decision to have Hagar bear seed for Abraham was for Sarai's self-interest whose wish was to be built up and to sustain the family name and reputation.[3]

Kuhn unveils the encounter between Abraham and Hagar. His imagination depicts a pseudo-marriage between Hagar and Abraham, which lacks any hint of emotion and makes Hagar a second wife. But was this really the case? Was Hagar a wife or a concubine or a surrogate? What about her own emotions and feelings in all this? Was she ready to be intimate with Abraham, her senior of over sixty years? It is clear that Hagar was fully owned as an object: her energy, time, body, and all.

Kuhn gives Hagar the benefit of the doubt and suggests that she was not outrightly arrogant or hostile to Sarai but that her pregnancy had given her one thing: maternal pride which she could not hide. But how could Sarai know any of this given that she had never conceived? Sarai dealt harshly with Hagar. Hagar's time, body, and energy were already owned by Sarai, her slave-owner. How much more was this the case when the text explicitly names harsh treatment? This was a terrible place to be – to the extent that Hagar had to flee. Kuhn unpacks dealing harshly as physical and psychological abuse from Sarai, noting the very same verb is used of Egyptians oppressing Israelites.

Hagar flees; in this action, she is a lone woman in the desert, a fugitive and easy prey for harm. While she flees, one pursues her, and this one is the God who finds his people in the wilderness. He finds Hagar: God – the God who sees her – finds her and makes promises to her. God/the Angel pronounces that Hagar should go back to Sarai and submit to the harsh treatment. Does God sanction slavery and suffering? Was Hagar not a person in herself, so that she needed be identified with being Sarai's maid? The command to return is but a test of her obedience. Will she obey?

Hagar obeys and returns to Sarai. But she returns with a promise, so she named her son Ishmael, meaning God who hears. It is important to note that Hagar was comforted by knowing that God heard when Sarai treated her harshly and God heard when she was in the wilderness in tears and anguish. Ishmael would be a wild donkey of a man; his hand would be against everybody, and everyone's hand would be against him. To this, Kuhn notes that there is no

---

3. Kuhn, *Finding Hagar*, 12.

curse linked to Ishmael. Rather, this is a covenantal promise meaning that he would be subject to no man but live a life of protected isolation, having cast away the bonds of slavery to live a life free and fiercely independent.

Hagar is sent away a second time. During her sojourn she becomes the only woman within the biblical narratives to designate a name for God: *El Roi* "the God who sees me" and *Lahai Roi*, "the living One who sees me" (Gen 16:13–14). Hagar bestows a name upon divinity, an act of initiative power, action, and ultimate agency. Since God sees, God cares, and God knows all. Consider the impact on Hagar that *this* God followed her all the way to Shur. Kuhn suggests that he and we are Ishmael, insofar as we have experiences of grafting and being adopted into God's house. He insists that Ishmael was never cursed but instead was blessed as the first to be circumcised with Abraham, as a father himself of twelve princes, and as one whom Abraham wanted to live before God.

Sarai got a child; he was named Isaac, literally "he laughs." Kuhn suggests that it was not a coincidence that Ishmael is cast out and expelled because of his laughter. His laughter is met with Sarah's displeasure but not with God's. Hagar is sent away with only one skin of water together with her son. To set Hagar free had the implication that Ishmael would not have any claim to the family property. Hagar weeps in the wilderness, not wanting to see the death of her son. The voice of her son is heard by God who provides water at a nearby well or spring, and he is promised to be made a great nation even while he was away from Abraham. God's pursuit ensures Hagar's destiny and continues to challenge long-held views of Hagar and Ishmael. Ishmael is seen in the company of his brother, Isaac, during the burial of his father. This is not to be glossed over. Ishmael himself dies and is gathered to his ancestors, having partaken of the promises that were attached to him. Kuhn draws parallels between Hagar and Moses and posits that Hagar is a prototype of God's deliverance of the Hebrew people. Kuhn concludes that Hagar speaks to our world, to our generation, and to us as individuals, challenging us to confront self-preservation, to reject exploitation and classism, to die to self by practicing uncomfortable obedience, and to reflect on the global reality of slavery. Kuhn also calls us to reflect, via Hagar, on the sensitivity of cultural elements present in the text for further truthful and willing conversation around Scripture, Ishmael, Abraham, and Hagar.

Response
On the Summary

Kuhn takes up a biblical personality who is often diminished, overlooked, and obscured. Often, Hagar is misrepresented and judged harshly but Kuhn has tried to empathetically re-envision her for the contemporary reader. I resonate, in part, with his thoughts in the following:

- Empathy with Hagar.
- Imaginative tropes used to build a narrative.
- The gaps the author tries to fill.
- The rebuttal that Ishmael was not cursed and that a blessing and a curse cannot exist in the same promise.

Kuhn's thoughts are alien to me on the following fronts:

- An apparent shyness to locate Hagar as an African woman.
- The connection between slavery and race is not explored in depth
- The shock that God could ask someone to continue in harsh slave conditions is not problematized.
- Additional imagination and creativity around Hagar's motherhood would be a plus.
- Elements of attaching Hagar to Sarai tightly continue in the narrative, so that Hagar's independence is glossed over.
- The place of naming in African culture.

In My Context

My context and positioning as an African woman present some relevant thoughts. Kuhn's ideas on taking people's cultures seriously, on confronting exploitation, sexism and classism are relevant to my context. African women theologians and members of the circle of concerned African women theologians, of which I am a member, touch upon the above listed thoughts with an aim of emancipation.

My Commitment

My commitment is to:

- Continue giving African women a voice through my research and writing.

- Mentor young African women to know that God sees them, cares and wants their very best.
- Walk with young, single, pregnant girls and single mothers who are abandoned by the father of their child.
- Explore sexuality in Africa further, and its implications for the church.

On repentance, my commitment will be about:

- Being passive around single mothers and teenage pregnancies.
- Practicing a new way of faith by seeking and pursuing such vulnerable African young women and teenagers so that I can be a channel of love and blessing to them.

Reflection

A Prayer

Lord, make me an instrument of your love to those many vulnerable young women abandoned in their hour of need by their families, the church, and the society. Let your help and healing flow through those who have been sexually defrauded and taken advantage of at the family level, within the church, and in society. Open my eyes to oppressions and exploitations that happen around me and help me do something about these. In Jesus's name, Amen.

The United States of America

What Can We Expect from God Now:
Seven Spiritual Truths for Trusting God in Troubled Times[1]
Timothy C. Geoffrion

Contributed by Loreen Maseno (Kenya)

Summary

Timothy shares his experiences of the Christian life in full view of suffering and troubling times. He gives us a glimpse of some of his own challenges that troubled and almost shipwrecked his faith. To begin with, he shares about a miscarriage his young family suffered in the mid-1980s. Miscarriages are losses that no one would wish to have to go through. The loss of his baby girl was a tragedy that shook Timothy and his bride. At the time, he and his wife were pastors in a small congregation, and this only made the tragedy more difficult to navigate. They were servants of the Lord, ministers of the gospel and resident pastors, and yet they suffered the loss of a baby girl. Emotional outbursts, tears, and pain were the order of the day.

The second pain he experienced was the loss of his former roommate at the age of twenty-eight. This was not easy for him and his wife in ministry. The loss of a roommate or an acquaintance with whom one has shared living space and conversations leaves scars in one's life, and coming to terms with such death is always difficult. Familiarity and memories keep lingering on in the imagination of the living, with trigger points always at hand.

As if this were not enough, Timothy and his wife were working seventy hours a week in an attempt to grow a church into a vibrant congregation. But this was not to be because the church remained small; he attests to "forces much larger than himself" being at play in this. The frustrations that accompanied this were great and he did not know where to turn.

Then, in 1986, Timothy became sick and was diagnosed with a fatal skin disease; the doctors' prognosis suggested that he had at most ten years to live.

---

1. Minneapolis, Minnesota: Self-published–Faith, Hope, and Love Global Ministries, 2020.

The news to him was like a "punch in the stomach" and the dread of leaving behind a widow and a child under ten years of age was too much for him to bear. He wondered what was really going on and why God did not seem to be helping the situation as he had desired.

In another twist of events, his mother got Alzheimer's disease and her health declined so quickly that his father had to retire early to care for her. However, the stresses of caring for his wife ultimately led to his father's death in 1998, before his mother died in 2002.

Do troubled times really end? Timothy thought that if he served the Lord faithfully, the Lord would take care of him. But was God playing his part as he ought? If so, why all this turmoil in his life, even as a minister of God? Timothy notes that, in all this, it was his expectations of God that failed him, and not God. Taking stock of his life, he considers that through the troubled times, he had the expectation that God should deliver him totally from sickness, suffering, and death, yet all these things happened to and around him. The COVID-19 pandemic was another context that shook Timothy.

Timothy shows in his writing that in the times of crisis and distress there are some spiritual truths that can help one weather the storm. These truths are:

1. The ways of God are not the ways of man.
2. Expect God to lead and guide us all the way, even as we surrender all of our will to him.
3. Expect God to strengthen our faith and restore hope even in our suffering.
4. Expect to share in Christ's sufferings.
5. Note that nothing can separate us from the love of God.
6. Expect peace as we put our anxieties in God's hands.
7. Expect to be renewed by accepting our limitations.

In general, Timothy suggests that we need to pray for every need and concern in our lives and trust in God for spirit-led decision-making as we reach out actively to God for wisdom, clarity, and to better perceive what we may not understand at the time. In all, when we devote ourselves to serving Christ and the gospel, we and our families will have to make sacrifices and even suffer, yet God will carry us through the darkest day. A beautiful turn of events and an answered prayer is that Timothy was alive in 2020 to write a book of his experiences, defying the ten years to live that had been given to him by the doctors years before.

Response
On the Summary

As I read, I experienced an immediate identification with the experiences of Timothy's life. He has aptly packaged his thoughts in an easily accessible way. His immersion in cultures other than his own endears him to readers who note his reflexivity on matters and his general sensitivity. The sincerity of the content, how one can be disillusioned and even disappointed with God, yet a minister of the gospel, is quite refreshing His thoughts resonate with me in many way: suffering is not desirable, it is painful, and we must trust in God through this time even when we do not understand everything.

What is alien to me in his thoughts is his assertion that God promises to protect and care for us in general but not in every circumstance. I disagree with this and choose to posit that God still protects and cares for us in each and every trouble we face – not merely in some of them.

In My Context

Here in Kenya where Christianity has been embraced by a majority of the people, there are many pastors and ministers of the gospel who have similarly gone through very difficult experiences of death, loss of health, etc. The test of trusting in God during pandemics and crises is another relevant concurrence that we share.

Our Commitment

My commitment is to be empathetic with pastors when they are passing through crisis, to be there for them, and pray with them. A commitment to prayer is also clear from the summary – to take everything to God in prayer. This could change our thoughts, worship, and practices, when we adopt a lifestyle of deeper, consistent prayer and Spirit-filled decision-making across our congregations.

I choose repentance for expecting a "smooth sailing" pilgrim journey as a Christian and I choose repentance for doubting God when I face challenges, especially when these responses affect my ways of thinking, worshipping, and practicing faith.

Prayer

Heavenly Father, you are the one who watches over us. Our eyes are lifted up to you, the maker of heaven and earth, from whom our help comes. Help us trust your unfailing gaze over us, that you neither slumber nor sleep, and that you will continue to guide us in all areas of life. We pray for ministers of the gospel not to lose heart but be encouraged to keep encouraging others. Amen.

The United States of America

Forgiveness and Justice: A Christian Approach[1]
Bryan Maier

Contributed by Ruth Barron and Joshua Robert Barron (Kenya)

Summary

Bryan Maier has written an excellent study that explores the relationship between lament for wrongs suffered and hope for justice. We cannot over-recommend his *Forgiveness and Justice: A Christian Approach*. At just 160 pages, it's a fairly quick read.

There is nearly a cottage industry of books on forgiveness. Most contemporary teachings on forgiveness follow one of five models (though there are others):

- Therapeutic forgiveness – the victim should forgive for the sake of the victim's well-being; the state of unforgiveness only causes further injury to the victim, and may cause the victim to risk damnation.
- Forensic forgiveness – forgiveness as a transaction – the cancelling of debt, granting clemency from deserved punishment.
- Relational forgiveness – transactional forgiveness plus possible reconciliation of a ruptured relationship.
- Unilateral forgiveness – forgiveness is a one-sided action, all on the side of the victim, and it does not matter whether the perpetrator repents.
- Dispositional forgiveness – having a forgiving or conciliatory spirit.

Each of these has some merit but tends to try to say either too much or too little. Offering an alternative course which is more robustly biblical, Maier lays out three boundaries delimiting forgiveness.

---

[1]. Grand Rapids, Michigan: Kregel Publications, 2017.

Forgiveness Is a Response to a Moral Violation

"Forgiveness, in order to make sense, must presuppose that an offence has been committed; otherwise, there would be nothing to forgive."[2] Forgiveness is only required when there has been a moral violation, an offence that is inherently unrighteous/unjust.

Forgiveness Is Not a Cognitive Reframe

Cognitive behaviourism may have its place, within appropriate limits, to offer a fresh perspective – life has handed me a bunch of lemons? No problem, I'll just make lemonade! Clearly, perception does shape behaviour. Changing our perception can help us not to get stuck in resentment.

But forgiveness is something different. Defining forgiveness in this way can blur the lines of reality, foster gaslighting, and confuse such concepts as condoning, excusing, justifying, and showing mercy. Often cognitive reframing can ultimately call evil, good – see, God can bring good out of that situation, so what happened to you was really good after all! And you should praise God for this abuse!

Sadly, we have each heard this type of teaching many times over the years and know that this is a common experience for many people. As a result, this type of focus ultimately makes victims more vulnerable to future acts of injustice and harm.

Forgiveness Is More Than Empathy

Maier notes that "many forgiveness authors suggest some kind of empathy with the perpetrator as a means of ameliorating the resentment" which a victim feels as a result of the moral violation he or she suffered.[3] Of course, we know that "all have sinned and fall short of the glory of God" (Rom 3:23). But we must also recognize

> that if the victim's sin cancels out the sin of the perpetrator, then the whole basis for justice collapses. If we are always guilty in some kind of morally equivalent way, then we can never charge our offenders. If a victim must be totally free of any sinful behaviours or thoughts before the offender can be addressed, justice would

---

2. Maier, *Forgiveness and Justice*, 33.
3. Maier, *Forgiveness and Justice*, 39.

never occur. In the classic passage on confronting a brother (Matt 18:15–20), the victim's sin (which we know is present from the rest of Scripture) is never mentioned.[4]

Maier then outlines "four contours of a Christian approach to forgiveness," asking a series of questions that we must answer to reach a biblical definition of forgiveness on the foundation of the three boundaries listed above. The questions are:[5]

1. How does God forgive?
2. How does healing relate to forgiveness?
3. Is forgiveness primarily self-centred or other-centred?
4. Is forgiveness active or passive?

After examining the relationship between resentment and repentance (chapter 3), he explores each of those four questions. Reminiscent of Bonhoeffer's discussion of "cheap grace" in *The Cost of Discipleship*, Maier explains the hidden costs of the "cheap forgiveness" that many in the church insist upon. With cheap forgiveness, because the offender has neither confessed nor repented, "there is no agreement that what was done was wrong" and the victim remains unsafe, and true reconciliation is impossible.[6] It is appropriate to address ongoing resentment harboured by a victim once the offender has confessed and demonstrated signs of repentance, including where necessary some type of restitution to restore justice. And so, because "trust is the basis of true unilateral healing for victims," if such "resentment poses a barrier to genuine forgiveness," this should be dealt with. But often "resentment is merely an appropriate emotional reaction to sin yet to be addressed." In such circumstances, "healing can only come by means of some assurance that one day justice will be complete and final."[7] This is not a desire for revenge and vengeance borne out of bitterness and rancorous resentment, but a godly and natural desire for justice and righteousness.

Maier has chapters on authentic repentance, trusting God for justice, results of forgiveness, and forgiveness and justice in counselling. Here is his exposition of what the simple statement, "I forgive you," should mean.

---

4. Maier, *Forgiveness and Justice*, 39.
5. Maier, *Forgiveness and Justice*, 41–44.
6. Maier, *Forgiveness and Justice*, 75.
7. Maier, *Forgiveness and Justice*, 77.

Because of your repentance and the facts that the price for your sin has been paid (by God), the effects of your sin against me have been substantially healed, and your repentance has stopped the previously hostile messages to me, your sin can no longer damage me. Since you are taking responsibility for your sin, I no longer have to make up distorted reasons why it happened, and that is good for both of us. Finally, our relationship is now different and I agree to treat you in light of this new relationship.[8]

Response
On the Summary

Forgiveness and justice are incompatible, right? Forgiving someone means *foregoing* justice, doesn't it? Isn't it just cognitively impossible to think of pursuing justice and forgiving at the same time? That's how the popular thinking goes . . . but that's not biblical thinking at all.

Lamentation (and even anger) at injustice, the seeking of justice, and the practice of forgiveness are all closely intertwined. W. E. B. Du Bois (1868–1963) included in his book *Souls of Black Folk* a chapter entitled "Songs of Sorrow." He astutely notes that such songs of sorrow (e.g. the "Negro Spirituals") offer hope, "a faith in the ultimate justice of things."

Maier emphasizes that a desire for justice and righteousness is both natural and godly. Readers who have studied the biblical languages will recall that both the Old Testament Hebrew root *tz-d-q* and the New Testament Greek root *-dik-* are inclusive of our English ideas of "righteousness" and "justice." There is no justice in unrighteousness and no righteousness in injustice.

We should note that it was after Israel named their daughters "Miriam" and "Mary," or themselves "Mara" – names that mean "bitter" or "bitterness" – that God sent saviour-redeemers (Moses, Boaz, and ultimately Jesus). God in God's wisdom acted salvifically after God's people recognized that their bitter lot was, in fact, bitter.[9]

---

8. Maier, *Forgiveness and Justice*, 115.
9. See Ruth Barron, "Bitter Roots and Bitter Herbs," *Mutuality*, 30 August 2023, https://www.cbeinternational.org/resource/bitter-roots-and-bitter-herbs/.

In My Context (by Ruth Barron)

As a victim of severe abuse, I noticed a deeply harmful pattern. When I spoke about my abuse and asked for help from pastors and other church leaders, the first question they asked was always, "Have you forgiven?" Not "Are you safe?" Not "What support do you need?" Their only concern was that I "get over" the abuse by "letting go of offence." When I continued to show signs of trauma and pain, those leaders would begin to reprimand me: it was clear that my "unforgiving" heart was the true problem, not the abuse and the continuing harm it was causing in my life. When I insisted that I needed them to call out the abuse both for my own healing and for the safety of other vulnerable children and adults, they condemned me instead. There was no justice.

Their responses added to my trauma rather than alleviating it. By condemning me, they showed they were willing to call out sin. When contrasted with their refusal to call out my abusers, this conveyed a clear message that, in the eyes of the church, I was the greater sinner for being wounded by the abuse than my abusers were for deeply harming me. I found myself struggling with a deep sense of unsafety. No matter how I tried to just "trust God," the reality that I could be abused at any time in full view of the church, and no one would lift a finger to protect me made it impossible for my heart and mind and body to experience the safety necessary for trauma healing. A ministry friend asked me, "You seem more upset at those who saw and did nothing than at the abusers themselves. Why is that?" At that time, I, myself, didn't understand why I felt so hurt by the failed responses of the church to my abuse. When I tried to explain, I didn't have the words to express how the refusal to offer justice was (and still is) harming me.

Our Commitment (by Ruth Barron and Joshua Robert Barron)

I, Ruth, turned to Google and typed "forgiveness" and "justice." That search led me to this book. The section "Cascading Levels of Damage as a Result of Interpersonal Sin" in chapter 3 described my own struggle exactly. I finally felt heard. Maier described how the church's failure to deal justly with abuse leaves victims with two harmful choices.

1. They can accept the lie that the abuse is their fault, thus imbuing them with the false hope that they can end the abuse if they just keep trying harder.
2. They can conclude that there is no possibility of justice whatsoever, leading to despair.

As Proverbs 13:12 says, "Hope deferred makes the heart sick, but a longing fulfilled is like a tree of life." Maier's book told me there was nothing wrong with me for how betrayed and abandoned I felt in the face of the church's failure to protect me. He notes that this struggle is common among those who have suffered abuse. His advice to meditate on the imprecatory psalms and to allow the biblical lament passages to give voice to my pain was very important to my continued healing.

We recommend this book to everyone who has suffered abuse or who knows an abuse victim. It should be required reading for anyone who recommends forgiveness as the solution to trauma and abuse. We recommend this gospel-oriented book to any pastor, preacher, counsellor, or missionary in any context. It is practical, theologically robust, accessibly written in everyday language, and firmly grounded in Scripture.

Reflections

The Church is Inaccessible to Me
by Beth Barrett[10]

Stained-glass beauty glimmered in your walls,
The life of Jesus told in coloured light.[11]
Yet you were inaccessible to those
Whose wheelchairs could not climb the stairs inside.
They lifted up their voices in protest
"Should those who cannot walk be kept from Church?
Must we depend on others to come in?
We will not enter through the roof today.
We'll take up our own wheeled chairs or leave."
Then echoed voices joined in full assent.
I watched you change the church which was my home.
You heard the voice of those you'd kept without.
You did not tell them they were wrong to speak.
You did not say "We are not here for you.
We preach to the majority who walk."
The Church is now accessible to more.

---

10. Shared with permission from the author. Previously posted on the author's Facebook page, https://www.facebook.com/profile.php?id=100068052053365, on 11 October 2021.

11. Many church buildings in the West and Global North are adorned with colorful stained-glass depictions of scenes from biblical narratives.

Yet even now I cry to them unheard
As I lie bruised and bleeding on the way.
For as I wept at stained-glass Jesus's feet.
Their watchman of the stained-glass windowed halls,
Their pastor, found and beat me for my voice:
"How dare you ask for help with your abuse."
No echoed voice took up the cause with me.
They drove me from their halls with stones of blame:
"You ask too much of us. This problem's yours."
That very Church that heard the voiced protest
Of those who longed to come with all themselves,
Whose wheelchairs are a part of who they are
Has thrown me out for pleading for their help:
"We are not here to help with your abuse.
We're here for the majority, the safe."
The Church is inaccessible to me.

Our trauma great, we sobbed outside your walls.
Our very pain convinced you of our shame.
Your blessings great, you sang within your halls.
Your blessings gave you reason for your joy.
You saw yourselves like David before God
You worshipped God with all your might and scorned
The grieving Michal sobbing while you danced.
Yet you were fully clothed in royal robes
While Michal lay there naked at your gates.
Bathsheba, Tamar, concubines unnamed,
Are taken on the walls while you rejoice.
You give your voice to God in songs of praise,
No echoed voice for victims of abuse,
You ask, "For what has joy to do with grief?
We're here for the majority, the glad."
The Church is inaccessible to us.

I came to you in victims of abuse.
I came to you in bruised and bleeding form.
I lay beside you on the way to church.
I wept beside you as you sang to me.
I came to you with everything I am.
The Church refused me entry as I AM.
The Church is inaccessible to ME!

A Vision of Justice[12]
By Hannahgail Barron

In this image, there are both predators and prey listening to life-giving words spoken by the released captive. The golden thread stitches up wounds and then bursts into life.

---

12. Used by permission of the artist. Hannahgail is the daughter of Ruth and Joshua Barron. She created this art piece as a prayer/present for her mother.

Langham Literature and its imprints are a ministry of Langham Partnership.

Langham Partnership is a global fellowship working in pursuit of the vision God entrusted to its founder John Stott –

> *to facilitate the growth of the church in maturity and Christ-likeness through raising the standards of biblical preaching and teaching.*

Our vision is to see churches in the Majority World equipped for mission and growing to maturity in Christ through the ministry of pastors and leaders who believe, teach and live by the word of God.

Our mission is to strengthen the ministry of the word of God through:
- nurturing national movements for biblical preaching
- fostering the creation and distribution of evangelical literature
- enhancing evangelical theological education

especially in countries where churches are under-resourced.

Our ministry

Langham Preaching partners with national leaders to nurture indigenous biblical preaching movements for pastors and lay preachers all around the world. With the support of a team of trainers from many countries, a multi-level programme of seminars provides practical training, and is followed by a programme for training local facilitators. Local preachers' groups and national and regional networks ensure continuity and ongoing development, seeking to build vigorous movements committed to Bible exposition.

Langham Literature provides Majority World preachers, scholars and seminary libraries with evangelical books and electronic resources through publishing and distribution, grants and discounts. The programme also fosters the creation of indigenous evangelical books in many languages, through writer's grants, strengthening local evangelical publishing houses, and investment in major regional literature projects, such as one volume Bible commentaries like *The Africa Bible Commentary* and *The South Asia Bible Commentary*.

Langham Scholars provides financial support for evangelical doctoral students from the Majority World so that, when they return home, they may train pastors and other Christian leaders with sound, biblical and theological teaching. This programme equips those who equip others. Langham Scholars also works in partnership with Majority World seminaries in strengthening evangelical theological education. A growing number of Langham Scholars study in high quality doctoral programmes in the Majority World itself. As well as teaching the next generation of pastors, graduated Langham Scholars exercise significant influence through their writing and leadership.

To learn more about Langham Partnership and the work we do visit **langham.org**

www.ingramcontent.com/pod-product-compliance
Lightning Source LLC
Chambersburg PA
CBHW060557230426
43670CB00011B/1867